Introduction to Statistics

Online Edition

Primary author and editor:
David M. Lane[1]

Other authors:
David Scott[1], Mikki Hebl[1], Rudy Guerra[1], Dan Osherson[1], and Heidi Zimmer[2]

[1]Rice University; [2]University of Houston, Downtown Campus

Section authors specified on each section.

1. Introduction

This chapter begins by discussing what statistics are and why the study of statistics is important. Subsequent sections cover a variety of topics all basic to the study of statistics. The only theme common to all of these sections is that they cover concepts and ideas important for other chapters in the book.

What Are Statistics

by Mikki Hebl

Learning Objectives
1. Describe the range of applications of statistics
2. Identify situations in which statistics can be misleading
3. Define "Statistics"

Statistics include numerical facts and figures. For instance:

• The largest earthquake measured 9.2 on the Richter scale.

• Men are at least 10 times more likely than women to commit murder.

• One in every 8 South Africans is HIV positive.

• By the year 2020, there will be 15 people aged 65 and over for every new baby born.

The study of statistics involves math and relies upon calculations of numbers. But it also relies heavily on how the numbers are chosen and how the statistics are interpreted. For example, consider the following three scenarios and the interpretations based upon the presented statistics. You will find that the numbers may be right, but the interpretation may be wrong. Try to identify a major flaw with each interpretation before we describe it.

1) A new advertisement for Ben and Jerry's ice cream introduced in late May of last year resulted in a 30% increase in ice cream sales for the following three months. Thus, the advertisement was effective.

A major flaw is that ice cream consumption generally increases in the months of June, July, and August regardless of advertisements. This effect is called a history effect and leads people to interpret outcomes as the result of one variable when another variable (in this case, one having to do with the passage of time) is actually responsible.

2) The more churches in a city, the more crime there is. Thus, churches lead to crime.

A major flaw is that both increased churches and increased crime rates can be explained by larger populations. In bigger cities, there are both more churches and more crime. This problem, which we will discuss in more detail in Chapter 6, refers to the third-variable problem. Namely, a third variable can cause both situations; however, people erroneously believe that there is a causal relationship between the two primary variables rather than recognize that a third variable can cause both.

3) 75% more interracial marriages are occurring this year than 25 years ago. Thus, our society accepts interracial marriages.

A major flaw is that we don't have the information that we need. What is the rate at which marriages are occurring? Suppose only 1% of marriages 25 years ago were interracial and so now 1.75% of marriages are interracial (1.75 is 75% higher than 1). But this latter number is hardly evidence suggesting the acceptability of interracial marriages. In addition, the statistic provided does not rule out the possibility that the number of interracial marriages has seen dramatic fluctuations over the years and this year is not the highest. Again, there is simply not enough information to understand fully the impact of the statistics.

As a whole, these examples show that statistics are *not only facts and figures*; they are something more than that. In the broadest sense, "statistics" refers to a range of techniques and procedures for analyzing, interpreting, displaying, and making decisions based on data.

Importance of Statistics

by Mikki Hebl

Learning Objectives
1. Give examples of statistics encountered in everyday life
2. Give examples of how statistics can lend credibility to an argument

Like most people, you probably feel that it is important to "take control of your life." But what does this mean? Partly, it means being able to properly evaluate the data and claims that bombard you every day. If you cannot distinguish good from faulty reasoning, then you are vulnerable to manipulation and to decisions that are not in your best interest. Statistics provides tools that you need in order to react intelligently to information you hear or read. In this sense, statistics is one of the most important things that you can study.

To be more specific, here are some claims that we have heard on several occasions. (We are not saying that each one of these claims is true!)

• 4 out of 5 dentists recommend Dentine.
• Almost 85% of lung cancers in men and 45% in women are tobacco-related.
• Condoms are effective 94% of the time.
• Native Americans are significantly more likely to be hit crossing the street than are people of other ethnicities.
• People tend to be more persuasive when they look others directly in the eye and speak loudly and quickly.
• Women make 75 cents to every dollar a man makes when they work the same job.
• A surprising new study shows that eating egg whites can increase one's life span.
• People predict that it is very unlikely there will ever be another baseball player with a batting average over 400.
• There is an 80% chance that in a room full of 30 people that at least two people will share the same birthday.
• 79.48% of all statistics are made up on the spot.

All of these claims are statistical in character. We suspect that some of them sound familiar; if not, we bet that you have heard other claims like them. Notice how diverse the examples are. They come from psychology, health, law, sports, business, etc. Indeed, data and data interpretation show up in discourse from virtually every facet of contemporary life.

Statistics are often presented in an effort to add credibility to an argument or advice. You can see this by paying attention to television advertisements. Many of the numbers thrown about in this way do not represent careful statistical analysis. They can be misleading and push you into decisions that you might find cause to regret. For these reasons, learning about statistics is a long step towards taking control of your life. (It is not, of course, the only step needed for this purpose.) The present electronic textbook is designed to help you learn statistical essentials. **It will make you into an intelligent consumer of statistical claims**.

You can take the first step right away. To be an intelligent consumer of statistics, your first reflex must be to **question** the statistics that you encounter. The British Prime Minister Benjamin Disraeli is quoted by Mark Twain as having said, "There are three kinds of lies -- lies, damned lies, and statistics." This quote reminds us why it is so important to understand statistics. So let us invite you to reform your statistical habits from now on. No longer will you blindly accept numbers or findings. Instead, you will begin to think about the numbers, their sources, and most importantly, the procedures used to generate them.

We have put the emphasis on defending ourselves against fraudulent claims wrapped up as statistics. We close this section on a more positive note. Just as important as detecting the deceptive use of statistics is the appreciation of the proper use of statistics. You must also learn to recognize statistical evidence that supports a stated conclusion. Statistics are all around you, sometimes used well, sometimes not. We must learn how to distinguish the two cases.

Now let us get to work!

Descriptive Statistics

by Mikki Hebl

Prerequisites
* none

Learning Objectives
1. Define "descriptive statistics"
2. Distinguish between descriptive statistics and inferential statistics

Descriptive statistics are numbers that are used to summarize and describe data. The word "data" refers to the information that has been collected from an experiment, a survey, an historical record, etc. (By the way, "data" is plural. One piece of information is called a "datum.") If we are analyzing birth certificates, for example, a descriptive statistic might be the percentage of certificates issued in New York State, or the average age of the mother. Any other number we choose to compute also counts as a descriptive statistic for the data from which the statistic is computed. Several descriptive statistics are often used at one time to give a full picture of the data.

Descriptive statistics are just descriptive. They do not involve **generalizing** beyond the data at hand. Generalizing from our data to another set of cases is the business of inferential statistics, which you'll be studying in another section. Here we focus on (mere) descriptive statistics.

Some descriptive statistics are shown in Table 1. The table shows the average salaries for various occupations in the United States in 1999.

Table 1. Average salaries for various occupations in 1999.

$112,760	pediatricians
$106,130	dentists
$100,090	podiatrists
$76,140	physicists
$53,410	architects,
$49,720	school, clinical, and counseling psychologists
$47,910	flight attendants
$39,560	elementary school teachers
$38,710	police officers
$18,980	floral designers

Descriptive statistics like these offer insight into American society. It is interesting to note, for example, that we pay the people who educate our children and who protect our citizens a great deal less than we pay people who take care of our feet or our teeth.

For more descriptive statistics, consider Table 2. It shows the number of unmarried men per 100 unmarried women in U.S. Metro Areas in 1990. From this table we see that men outnumber women most in Jacksonville, NC, and women outnumber men most in Sarasota, FL. You can see that descriptive statistics can be useful if we are looking for an opposite-sex partner! (These data come from the Information Please Almanac.)

Table 2. Number of unmarried men per 100 unmarried women in U.S. Metro Areas in 1990.

Cities with mostly men	Men per 100 Women	Cities with mostly women	Men per 100 Women
1. Jacksonville, NC	224	1. Sarasota, FL	66
2. Killeen-Temple, TX	123	2. Bradenton, FL	68
3. Fayetteville, NC	118	3. Altoona, PA	69

4. Brazoria, TX	117	4. Springfield, IL	70
5. Lawton, OK	116	5. Jacksonville, TN	70
6. State College, PA	113	6. Gadsden, AL	70
7. Clarksville-Hopkinsville, TN-KY	113	7. Wheeling, WV	70
8. Anchorage, Alaska	112	8. Charleston, WV	71
9. Salinas-Seaside-Monterey, CA	112	9. St. Joseph, MO	71
10. Bryan-College Station, TX	111	10. Lynchburg, VA	71

NOTE: Unmarried includes never-married, widowed, and divorced persons, 15 years or older.

These descriptive statistics may make us ponder why the numbers are so disparate in these cities. One potential explanation, for instance, as to why there are more women in Florida than men may involve the fact that elderly individuals tend to move down to the Sarasota region and that women tend to outlive men. Thus, more women might live in Sarasota than men. However, in the absence of proper data, this is only speculation.

You probably know that descriptive statistics are central to the world of sports. Every sporting event produces numerous statistics such as the shooting percentage of players on a basketball team. For the Olympic marathon (a foot race of 26.2 miles), we possess data that cover more than a century of competition. (The first modern Olympics took place in 1896.) The following table shows the winning times for both men and women (the latter have only been allowed to compete since 1984).

Table 3. Winning Olympic marathon times.

Women			
Year	Winner	Country	Time
1984	Joan Benoit	USA	2:24:52
1988	Rosa Mota	POR	2:25:40

1992	Valentina Yegorova	UT	2:32:41
1996	Fatuma Roba	ETH	2:26:05
2000	Naoko Takahashi	JPN	2:23:14
2004	Mizuki Noguchi	JPN	2:26:20
Men			
Year	**Winner**	**Country**	**Time**
1896	Spiridon Louis	GRE	2:58:50
1900	Michel Theato	FRA	2:59:45
1904	Thomas Hicks	USA	3:28:53
1906	Billy Sherring	CAN	2:51:23
1908	Johnny Hayes	USA	2:55:18
1912	Kenneth McArthur	S. Afr.	2:36:54
1920	Hannes Kolehmainen	FIN	2:32:35
1924	Albin Stenroos	FIN	2:41:22
1928	Boughra El Ouafi	FRA	2:32:57
1932	Juan Carlos Zabala	ARG	2:31:36
1936	Sohn Kee-Chung	JPN	2:29:19
1948	Delfo Cabrera	ARG	2:34:51
1952	Emil Ztopek	CZE	2:23:03
1956	Alain Mimoun	FRA	2:25:00
1960	Abebe Bikila	ETH	2:15:16
1964	Abebe Bikila	ETH	2:12:11
1968	Mamo Wolde	ETH	2:20:26
1972	Frank Shorter	USA	2:12:19
1976	Waldemar Cierpinski	E.Ger	2:09:55
1980	Waldemar Cierpinski	E.Ger	2:11:03
1984	Carlos Lopes	POR	2:09:21
1988	Gelindo Bordin	ITA	2:10:32

1992	Hwang Young-Cho	S. Kor	2:13:23
1996	Josia Thugwane	S. Afr.	2:12:36
2000	Gezahenge Abera	ETH	2:10.10
2004	Stefano Baldini	ITA	2:10:55

There are many descriptive statistics that we can compute from the data in the table. To gain insight into the improvement in speed over the years, let us divide the men's times into two pieces, namely, the first 13 races (up to 1952) and the second 13 (starting from 1956). The mean winning time for the first 13 races is 2 hours, 44 minutes, and 22 seconds (written 2:44:22). The mean winning time for the second 13 races is 2:13:18. This is quite a difference (over half an hour). Does this prove that the fastest men are running faster? Or is the difference just due to chance, no more than what often emerges from chance differences in performance from year to year? We can't answer this question with descriptive statistics alone. All we can affirm is that the two means are "suggestive."

Examining Table 3 leads to many other questions. We note that Takahashi (the lead female runner in 2000) would have beaten the male runner in 1956 and all male runners in the first 12 marathons. This fact leads us to ask whether the gender gap will close or remain constant. When we look at the times within each gender, we also wonder how far they will decrease (if at all) in the next century of the Olympics. Might we one day witness a sub-2 hour marathon? The study of statistics can help you make reasonable guesses about the answers to these questions.

Inferential Statistics

by Mikki Hebl

Prerequisites
• Chapter 1: Descriptive Statistics

Learning Objectives
1. Distinguish between a sample and a population
2. Define inferential statistics
3. Identify biased samples
4. Distinguish between simple random sampling and stratified sampling
5. Distinguish between random sampling and random assignment

Populations and samples

In statistics, we often rely on a sample --- that is, a small subset of a larger set of data --- to draw inferences about the larger set. The larger set is known as the population from which the sample is drawn.

> Example #1: You have been hired by the National Election Commission to examine how the American people feel about the fairness of the voting procedures in the U.S. Who will you ask?

It is not practical to ask every single American how he or she feels about the fairness of the voting procedures. Instead, we query a relatively small number of Americans, and draw inferences about the entire country from their responses. The Americans actually queried constitute our sample of the larger population of all Americans. The mathematical procedures whereby we convert information about the sample into intelligent guesses about the population fall under the rubric of inferential statistics.

A sample is typically a small subset of the population. In the case of voting attitudes, we would sample a few thousand Americans drawn from the hundreds of millions that make up the country. In choosing a sample, it is therefore crucial that it not over-represent one kind of citizen at the expense of others. For example, something would be wrong with our sample if it happened to be made up entirely of Florida residents. If the sample held only Floridians, it could not be used to infer the attitudes of other Americans. The same problem would arise if the sample were comprised only of Republicans. Inferential statistics are based on the assumption that sampling is random. We trust a random sample to represent different segments of society in close to the appropriate proportions (provided the sample is large enough; see below).

Example #2: We are interested in examining how many math classes have been taken on average by current graduating seniors at American colleges and universities during their four years in school. Whereas our population in the last example included all US citizens, now it involves just the graduating seniors throughout the country. This is still a large set since there are thousands of colleges and universities, each enrolling many students. (New York University, for example, enrolls 48,000 students.) It would be prohibitively costly to examine the transcript of every college senior. We therefore take a sample of college seniors and then make inferences to the entire population based on what we find. To make the sample, we might first choose some public and private colleges and universities across the United States. Then we might sample 50 students from each of these institutions. Suppose that the average number of math classes taken by the people in our sample were 3.2. Then we might speculate that 3.2 approximates the number we would find if we had the resources to examine every senior in the entire population. But we must be careful about the possibility that our sample is non-representative of the population. Perhaps we chose an overabundance of math majors, or chose too many technical institutions that have heavy math requirements. Such bad sampling makes our sample unrepresentative of the population of all seniors.

To solidify your understanding of sampling bias, consider the following example. Try to identify the population and the sample, and then reflect on whether the sample is likely to yield the information desired.

Example #3: A substitute teacher wants to know how students in the class did on their last test. The teacher asks the 10 students sitting in the front row to state their latest test score. He concludes from their report that the class did extremely well. What is the sample? What is the population? Can you identify any problems with choosing the sample in the way that the teacher did?

In Example #3, the population consists of all students in the class. The sample is made up of just the 10 students sitting in the front row. The sample is not likely to be representative of the population. Those who sit in the front row tend to be more interested in the class and tend to perform higher on tests. Hence, the sample may perform at a higher level than the population.

Example #4: A coach is interested in how many cartwheels the average college freshmen at his university can do. Eight volunteers from the freshman class step forward. After observing their performance, the coach concludes that college freshmen can do an average of 16 cartwheels in a row without stopping.

In Example #4, the population is the class of all freshmen at the coach's university. The sample is composed of the 8 volunteers. The sample is poorly chosen because volunteers are more likely to be able to do cartwheels than the average freshman; people who can't do cartwheels probably did not volunteer! In the example, we are also not told of the gender of the volunteers. Were they all women, for example? That might affect the outcome, contributing to the non-representative nature of the sample (if the school is co-ed).

Simple Random Sampling

Researchers adopt a variety of sampling strategies. The most straightforward is simple random sampling. Such sampling requires every member of the population to have an equal chance of being selected into the sample. In addition, the selection of one member must be independent of the selection of every other member. That is, picking one member from the population must not increase or decrease the probability of picking any other member (relative to the others). In this sense, we can say that simple random sampling chooses a sample by pure chance. To check your understanding of simple random sampling, consider the following example. What is the population? What is the sample? Was the sample picked by simple random sampling? Is it biased?

> Example #5: A research scientist is interested in studying the experiences of twins raised together versus those raised apart. She obtains a list of twins from the **National Twin Registry**, and selects two subsets of individuals for her study. First, she chooses all those in the registry whose last name begins with Z. Then she turns to all those whose last name begins with B. Because there are so many names that start with B, however, our researcher decides to incorporate only every other name into her sample. Finally, she mails out a survey and compares characteristics of twins raised apart versus together.

In Example #5, the population consists of all twins recorded in the National Twin Registry. It is important that the researcher only make statistical generalizations to the twins on this list, not to all twins in the nation or world. That is, the National Twin Registry may not be representative of all twins. Even if inferences are limited to the Registry, a number of problems affect the sampling procedure we described. For instance, choosing only twins whose last names begin with Z does not give every individual an equal chance of being selected into the sample. Moreover, such a procedure risks over-representing ethnic groups with many surnames that begin with Z. There are other reasons why choosing just the Z's may bias the sample. Perhaps such people are more patient than average because they often find themselves at the end of the line! The same problem occurs with choosing twins whose last name begins with B. An additional problem for the B's is that the "every-other-one" procedure disallowed adjacent names on the B part of the list from being both selected. Just this defect alone means the sample was not formed through simple random sampling.

Sample size matters

Recall that the definition of a random sample is a sample in which every member of the population has an equal chance of being selected. This means that the **sampling procedure** rather than the **results** of the procedure define what it means for a sample to be random. Random samples, especially if the sample size is small, are not necessarily representative of the entire population. For example, if a random sample of 20 subjects were taken from a population with an equal number of males and females, there would be a nontrivial probability (0.06) that 70% or more of the sample would be female. (To see how to obtain this probability, see the section on the binomial distribution in Chapter 5.) Such a sample would not be representative, although it would be drawn randomly. Only a large sample size makes it likely that our sample is close to representative of the population. For this reason, inferential statistics take into account the sample size when generalizing results from samples to populations. In later chapters, you'll see what kinds of mathematical techniques ensure this sensitivity to sample size.

More complex sampling

Sometimes it is not feasible to build a sample using simple random sampling. To see the problem, consider the fact that both Dallas and Houston are competing to be hosts of the 2012 Olympics. Imagine that you are hired to assess whether most Texans prefer Houston to Dallas as the host, or the reverse. Given the impracticality of obtaining the opinion of every single Texan, you must construct a sample of the Texas population. But now notice how difficult it would be to proceed by simple random sampling. For example, how will you contact those individuals who don't vote and don't have a phone? Even among people you find in the telephone book, how can you identify those who have just relocated to California (and had no reason to inform you of their move)? What do you do about the fact that since the beginning of the study, an additional 4,212 people took up residence in the state of Texas? As you can see, it is sometimes very difficult to develop a truly random procedure. For this reason, other kinds of sampling techniques have been devised. We now discuss two of them.

Random assignment

In experimental research, populations are often hypothetical. For example, in an experiment comparing the effectiveness of a new anti-depressant drug with a placebo, there is no actual population of individuals taking the drug. In this case, a specified population of people with some degree of depression is defined and a random sample is taken from this population. The sample is then randomly divided into two groups; one group is assigned to the treatment condition (drug) and the other group is assigned to the control condition (placebo). This random division of the sample into two groups is called **random assignment**. Random assignment is critical for the validity of an experiment. For example, consider the bias that could be introduced if the first 20 subjects to show up at the experiment were assigned to the experimental group and the second 20 subjects were assigned to the control group. It is possible that subjects who show up late tend to be more depressed than those who show up early, thus making the experimental group less depressed than the control group even before the treatment was administered.

In experimental research of this kind, failure to assign subjects randomly to groups is generally more serious than having a non-random sample. Failure to randomize (the former error) invalidates the experimental findings. A non-random sample (the latter error) simply restricts the generalizability of the results.

Stratified Sampling

Since simple random sampling often does not ensure a representative sample, a sampling method called stratified random sampling is sometimes used to make the sample more representative of the population. This method can be used if the population has a number of distinct "strata" or groups. In stratified sampling, you first identify members of your sample who belong to each group. Then you randomly sample from each of those subgroups in such a way that the sizes of the subgroups in the sample are proportional to their sizes in the population.

Let's take an example: Suppose you were interested in views of capital punishment at an urban university. You have the time and resources to interview 200 students. The student body is diverse with respect to age; many older people work during the day and enroll in night courses (average age is 39), while younger students generally enroll in day classes (average age of 19). It is possible that night students have different views about capital punishment than day students. If 70% of the students were day students, it makes sense to ensure that 70% of the sample consisted of day students. Thus, your sample of 200 students would consist of 140 day students and 60 night students. The proportion of day students in the sample and in the population (the entire university) would be the same. Inferences to the entire population of students at the university would therefore be more secure.

Variables

by Heidi Ziemer

Prerequisites
- none

Learning Objectives

1. Define and distinguish between independent and dependent variables

2. Define and distinguish between discrete and continuous variables

3. Define and distinguish between qualitative and quantitative variables

Independent and dependent variables

Variables are properties or characteristics of some event, object, or person that can take on different values or amounts (as opposed to constants such as π that do not vary). When conducting research, experimenters often manipulate variables. For example, an experimenter might compare the effectiveness of four types of antidepressants. In this case, the variable is "type of antidepressant." When a variable is manipulated by an experimenter, it is called an independent variable. The experiment seeks to determine the effect of the independent variable on relief from depression. In this example, relief from depression is called a dependent variable. In general, the independent variable is manipulated by the experimenter and its effects on the dependent variable are measured.

Example #1: Can blueberries slow down aging? A study indicates that antioxidants found in blueberries may slow down the process of aging. In this study, 19-month-old rats (equivalent to 60-year-old humans) were fed either their standard diet or a diet supplemented by either blueberry, strawberry, or spinach powder. After eight weeks, the rats were given memory and motor skills tests. Although all supplemented rats showed improvement, those supplemented with blueberry powder showed the most notable improvement.

1. What is the independent variable? (dietary supplement: none, blueberry, strawberry, and spinach)

2. What are the dependent variables? (memory test and motor skills test)

Example #2: Does beta-carotene protect against cancer? Beta-carotene supplements have been thought to protect against cancer. However, a study published in the Journal of the National Cancer Institute suggests this is false. The study was conducted with 39,000 women aged 45 and up. These women were randomly assigned to receive a beta-carotene supplement or a placebo, and their health was studied over their lifetime. Cancer rates for women taking the beta-carotene supplement did not differ systematically from the cancer rates of those women taking the placebo.

1. What is the independent variable? (supplements: beta-carotene or placebo)

2. What is the dependent variable? (occurrence of cancer)

Example #3: How bright is right? An automobile manufacturer wants to know how bright brake lights should be in order to minimize the time required for the driver of a following car to realize that the car in front is stopping and to hit the brakes.

1. What is the independent variable? (brightness of brake lights)

2. What is the dependent variable? (time to hit brakes)

Levels of an Independent Variable

If an experiment compares an experimental treatment with a control treatment, then the independent variable (type of treatment) has two levels: experimental and control. If an experiment were comparing five types of diets, then the independent variable (type of diet) would have 5 levels. In general, the number of levels of an independent variable is the number of experimental conditions.

Qualitative and Quantitative Variables

An important distinction between variables is between qualitative variables and quantitative variables. Qualitative variables are those that express a qualitative attribute such as hair color, eye color, religion, favorite movie, gender, and so on. The values of a qualitative variable do not imply a numerical ordering. Values of the variable "religion" differ qualitatively; no ordering of religions is implied. Qualitative variables are sometimes referred to as categorical variables. Quantitative variables are those variables that are measured in terms of numbers. Some examples of quantitative variables are height, weight, and shoe size.

In the study on the effect of diet discussed previously, the independent variable was type of supplement: none, strawberry, blueberry, and spinach. The variable "type of supplement" is a qualitative variable; there is nothing quantitative about it. In contrast, the dependent variable "memory test" is a quantitative variable since memory performance was measured on a quantitative scale (number correct).

Discrete and Continuous Variables

Variables such as number of children in a household are called discrete variables since the possible scores are discrete points on the scale. For example, a household could have three children or six children, but not 4.53 children. Other variables such as "time to respond to a question" are continuous variables since the scale is continuous and not made up of discrete steps. The response time could be 1.64 seconds, or it could be 1.64237123922121 seconds. Of course, the practicalities of measurement preclude most measured variables from being truly continuous.

Percentiles

by David Lane

Prerequisites
- none

Learning Objectives
1. Define percentiles
2. Use three formulas for computing percentiles

A test score in and of itself is usually difficult to interpret. For example, if you learned that your score on a measure of shyness was 35 out of a possible 50, you would have little idea how shy you are compared to other people. More relevant is the percentage of people with lower shyness scores than yours. This percentage is called a percentile. If 65% of the scores were below yours, then your score would be the 65th percentile.

Two Simple Definitions of Percentile

There is no universally accepted definition of a percentile. Using the 65th percentile as an example, the 65th percentile can be defined as the lowest score that is greater than 65% of the scores. This is the way we defined it above and we will call this "Definition 1." The 65th percentile can also be defined as the smallest score that is greater than or equal to 65% of the scores. This we will call "Definition 2." Unfortunately, these two definitions can lead to dramatically different results, especially when there is relatively little data. Moreover, neither of these definitions is explicit about how to handle rounding. For instance, what rank is required to be higher than 65% of the scores when the total number of scores is 50? This is tricky because 65% of 50 is 32.5. How do we find the lowest number that is higher than 32.5% of the scores? A third way to compute percentiles (presented below) is a weighted average of the percentiles computed according to the first two definitions. This third definition handles rounding more gracefully than the other two and has the advantage that it allows the median to be defined conveniently as the 50th percentile.

A Third Definition

Unless otherwise specified, when we refer to "percentile," we will be referring to this third definition of percentiles. Let's begin with an example. Consider the 25th percentile for the 8 numbers in Table 1. Notice the numbers are given ranks ranging from 1 for the lowest number to 8 for the highest number.

Table 1. Test Scores.

Number	Rank
3	1
5	2
7	3
8	4
9	5
11	6
13	7
15	8

The first step is to compute the rank (R) of the 25th percentile. This is done using the following formula:

$$R = \frac{P}{100} \times (N + 1)$$

where P is the desired percentile (25 in this case) and N is the number of numbers (8 in this case). Therefore,

$$R = \frac{25}{100} \times (8 + 1) = \frac{9}{4} = 2.25$$

If R is an integer, the Pth percentile is be the number with rank R. When R is not an integer, we compute the Pth percentile by interpolation as follows:

1. Define IR as the integer portion of R (the number to the left of the decimal point). For this example, IR = 2.

2. Define FR as the fractional portion of R. For this example, FR = 0.25.

3. Find the scores with Rank I_R and with Rank $I_R + 1$. For this example, this means the score with Rank 2 and the score with Rank 3. The scores are 5 and 7.

4. Interpolate by multiplying the difference between the scores by F_R and add the result to the lower score. For these data, this is $(0.25)(7 - 5) + 5 = 5.5$.

Therefore, the 25th percentile is 5.5. If we had used the first definition (the smallest score greater than 25% of the scores), the 25th percentile would have been 7. If we had used the second definition (the smallest score greater than or equal to 25% of the scores), the 25th percentile would have been 5.

For a second example, consider the 20 quiz scores shown in Table 2.

Table 2. 20 Quiz Scores.

Score	Rank
4	1
4	2
5	3
5	4
5	5
5	6
6	7
6	8
6	9
7	10
7	11
7	12
8	13
8	14
9	15
9	16
9	17
10	18
10	19
10	20

We will compute the 25th and the 85th percentiles. For the 25th,

$$R = \frac{25}{100} \times (20 + 1) = \frac{21}{4} = 5.25$$

IR = 5 and FR = 0.25.

Since the score with a rank of IR (which is 5) and the score with a rank of IR + 1 (which is 6) are both equal to 5, the 25th percentile is 5. In terms of the formula:

25th percentile = (.25) x (5 - 5) + 5 = 5.

For the 85th percentile,

$$R = \frac{85}{100} \times (20 + 1) = 17.85$$

IR = 17 and FR = 0.85

Caution: FR does not generally equal the percentile to be computed as it does here.

The score with a rank of 17 is 9 and the score with a rank of 18 is 10. Therefore, the 85th percentile is:

(0.85)(10 - 9) + 9 = 9.85

Consider the 50th percentile of the numbers 2, 3, 5, 9.

$$R = \frac{50}{100} \times (4 + 1) = 2.5$$

IR = 2 and FR = 0.5.

The score with a rank of IR is 3 and the score with a rank of IR + 1 is 5. Therefore, the 50th percentile is:

(0.5)(5 - 3) + 3 = 4.

Finally, consider the 50th percentile of the numbers 2, 3, 5, 9, 11.

$$R = \frac{50}{100} \times (5 + 1) = 3$$

IR = 3 and FR = 0.

Whenever FR = 0, you simply find the number with rank IR. In this case, the third number is equal to 5, so the 50th percentile is 5. You will also get the right answer if you apply the general formula:

50th percentile = (0.00) (9 - 5) + 5 = 5.

Levels of Measurement

by Dan Osherson and David M. Lane

Prerequisites
- Chapter 1: Variables

Learning Objectives
1. Define and distinguish among nominal, ordinal, interval, and ratio scales
2. Identify a scale type
3. Discuss the type of scale used in psychological measurement
4. Give examples of errors that can be made by failing to understand the proper use of measurement scales

Types of Scales

Before we can conduct a statistical analysis, we need to measure our dependent variable. Exactly how the measurement is carried out depends on the type of variable involved in the analysis. Different types are measured differently. To measure the time taken to respond to a stimulus, you might use a stop watch. Stop watches are of no use, of course, when it comes to measuring someone's attitude towards a political candidate. A rating scale is more appropriate in this case (with labels like "very favorable," "somewhat favorable," etc.). For a dependent variable such as "favorite color," you can simply note the color-word (like "red") that the subject offers.

Although procedures for measurement differ in many ways, they can be classified using a few fundamental categories. In a given category, all of the procedures share some properties that are important for you to know about. The categories are called "scale types," or just "scales," and are described in this section.

Nominal scales

When measuring using a nominal scale, one simply names or categorizes responses. Gender, handedness, favorite color, and religion are examples of variables measured on a nominal scale. The essential point about nominal scales is that they do not imply any ordering among the responses. For example, when classifying people according to their favorite color, there is no sense in which green is placed "ahead of" blue. Responses are merely categorized. Nominal scales embody the lowest level of measurement.

Ordinal scales

A researcher wishing to measure consumers' satisfaction with their microwave ovens might ask them to specify their feelings as either "very dissatisfied," "somewhat dissatisfied," "somewhat satisfied," or "very satisfied." The items in this scale are ordered, ranging from least to most satisfied. This is what distinguishes ordinal from nominal scales. Unlike nominal scales, ordinal scales allow comparisons of the degree to which two subjects possess the dependent variable. For example, our satisfaction ordering makes it meaningful to assert that one person is more satisfied than another with their microwave ovens. Such an assertion reflects the first person's use of a verbal label that comes later in the list than the label chosen by the second person.

On the other hand, ordinal scales fail to capture important information that will be present in the other scales we examine. In particular, the difference between two levels of an ordinal scale cannot be assumed to be the same as the difference between two other levels. In our satisfaction scale, for example, the difference between the responses "very dissatisfied" and "somewhat dissatisfied" is probably not equivalent to the difference between "somewhat dissatisfied" and "somewhat satisfied." Nothing in our measurement procedure allows us to determine whether the two differences reflect the same difference in psychological satisfaction. Statisticians express this point by saying that the differences between adjacent scale values do not necessarily represent equal intervals on the underlying scale giving rise to the measurements. (In our case, the underlying scale is the true feeling of satisfaction, which we are trying to measure.)

What if the researcher had measured satisfaction by asking consumers to indicate their level of satisfaction by choosing a number from one to four? Would the difference between the responses of one and two necessarily reflect the same difference in satisfaction as the difference between the responses two and three? The answer is No. Changing the response format to numbers does not change the meaning of the scale. We still are in no position to assert that the mental step from 1 to 2 (for example) is the same as the mental step from 3 to 4.

Interval scales

Interval scales are numerical scales in which intervals have the same interpretation throughout. As an example, consider the Fahrenheit scale of temperature. The difference between 30 degrees and 40 degrees represents the same temperature difference as the difference between 80 degrees and 90 degrees. This is because each 10-degree interval has the same physical meaning (in terms of the kinetic energy of molecules).

Interval scales are not perfect, however. In particular, they do not have a true zero point even if one of the scaled values happens to carry the name "zero." The Fahrenheit scale illustrates the issue. Zero degrees Fahrenheit does not represent the complete absence of temperature (the absence of any molecular kinetic energy). In reality, the label "zero" is applied to its temperature for quite accidental reasons connected to the history of temperature measurement. Since an interval scale has no true zero point, it does not make sense to compute ratios of temperatures. For example, there is no sense in which the ratio of 40 to 20 degrees Fahrenheit is the same as the ratio of 100 to 50 degrees; no interesting physical property is preserved across the two ratios. After all, if the "zero" label were applied at the temperature that Fahrenheit happens to label as 10 degrees, the two ratios would instead be 30 to 10 and 90 to 40, no longer the same! For this reason, it does not make sense to say that 80 degrees is "twice as hot" as 40 degrees. Such a claim would depend on an arbitrary decision about where to "start" the temperature scale, namely, what temperature to call zero (whereas the claim is intended to make a more fundamental assertion about the underlying physical reality).

Ratio scales

The ratio scale of measurement is the most informative scale. It is an interval scale with the additional property that its zero position indicates the absence of the quantity being measured. You can think of a ratio scale as the three earlier scales rolled up in one. Like a nominal scale, it provides a name or category for each object (the numbers serve as labels). Like an ordinal scale, the objects are ordered (in terms of the ordering of the numbers). Like an interval scale, the same difference at two places on the scale has the same meaning. And in addition, the same ratio at two places on the scale also carries the same meaning.

The Fahrenheit scale for temperature has an arbitrary zero point and is therefore not a ratio scale. However, zero on the Kelvin scale is absolute zero. This makes the Kelvin scale a ratio scale. For example, if one temperature is twice as high as another as measured on the Kelvin scale, then it has twice the kinetic energy of the other temperature.

Another example of a ratio scale is the amount of money you have in your pocket right now (25 cents, 55 cents, etc.). Money is measured on a ratio scale because, in addition to having the properties of an interval scale, it has a true zero point: if you have zero money, this implies the absence of money. Since money has a true zero point, it makes sense to say that someone with 50 cents has twice as much money as someone with 25 cents (or that Bill Gates has a million times more money than you do).

What level of measurement is used for psychological variables?

Rating scales are used frequently in psychological research. For example, experimental subjects may be asked to rate their level of pain, how much they like a consumer product, their attitudes about capital punishment, their confidence in an answer to a test question. Typically these ratings are made on a 5-point or a 7-point scale. These scales are ordinal scales since there is no assurance that a given difference represents the same thing across the range of the scale. For example, there is no way to be sure that a treatment that reduces pain from a rated pain level of 3 to a rated pain level of 2 represents the same level of relief as a treatment that reduces pain from a rated pain level of 7 to a rated pain level of 6.

In memory experiments, the dependent variable is often the number of items correctly recalled. What scale of measurement is this? You could reasonably argue that it is a ratio scale. First, there is a true zero point; some subjects may get no items correct at all. Moreover, a difference of one represents a difference of one item recalled across the entire scale. It is certainly valid to say that someone who recalled 12 items recalled twice as many items as someone who recalled only 6 items.

But number-of-items recalled is a more complicated case than it appears at first. Consider the following example in which subjects are asked to remember as many items as possible from a list of 10. Assume that (a) there are 5 easy items and 5 difficult items, (b) half of the subjects are able to recall all the easy items and different numbers of difficult items, while (c) the other half of the subjects are unable to recall any of the difficult items but they do remember different numbers of easy items. Some sample data are shown below.

Subject	Easy Items					Difficult Items					Score
A	0	0	1	1	0	0	0	0	0	0	2
B	1	0	1	1	0	0	0	0	0	0	3
C	1	1	1	1	1	1	1	0	0	0	7
D	1	1	1	1	1	0	1	1	0	1	8

Let's compare (i) the difference between Subject A's score of 2 and Subject B's score of 3 and (ii) the difference between Subject C's score of 7 and Subject D's score of 8. The former difference is a difference of one easy item; the latter difference is a difference of one difficult item. Do these two differences necessarily signify the same difference in memory? We are inclined to respond "No" to this question since only a little more memory may be needed to retain the additional easy item whereas a lot more memory may be needed to retain the additional hard item. The general point is that it is often inappropriate to consider psychological measurement scales as either interval or ratio.

Consequences of level of measurement

Why are we so interested in the type of scale that measures a dependent variable? The crux of the matter is the relationship between the variable's level of measurement and the statistics that can be meaningfully computed with that variable. For example, consider a hypothetical study in which 5 children are asked to choose their favorite color from blue, red, yellow, green, and purple. The researcher codes the results as follows:

Color	Code
Blue	1
Red	2
Yellow	3
Green	4
Purple	5

This means that if a child said her favorite color was "Red," then the choice was coded as "2," if the child said her favorite color was "Purple," then the response was coded as 5, and so forth. Consider the following hypothetical data:

Subject	Color	Code
1	Blue	1
2	Blue	1
3	Green	4
4	Green	4
5	Purple	5

Each code is a number, so nothing prevents us from computing the average code assigned to the children. The average happens to be 3, but you can see that it would be senseless to conclude that the average favorite color is yellow (the color with a code of 3). Such nonsense arises because favorite color is a nominal scale, and taking the average of its numerical labels is like counting the number of letters in the name of a snake to see how long the beast is.

Does it make sense to compute the mean of numbers measured on an ordinal scale? This is a difficult question, one that statisticians have debated for decades. The prevailing (but by no means unanimous) opinion of statisticians is that for almost all practical situations, the mean of an ordinally-measured variable is a meaningful statistic. However, there are extreme situations in which computing the mean of an ordinally-measured variable can be very misleading.

Distributions

by David M. Lane and Heidi Ziemer

Prerequisites
• Chapter 1: Variables

Learning Objectives
1. Define "distribution"
2. Interpret a frequency distribution
3. Distinguish between a frequency distribution and a probability distribution
4. Construct a grouped frequency distribution for a continuous variable
5. Identify the skew of a distribution
6. Identify bimodal, leptokurtic, and platykurtic distributions

Distributions of Discrete Variables

I recently purchased a bag of Plain M&M's. The M&M's were in six different colors. A quick count showed that there were 55 M&M's: 17 brown, 18 red, 7 yellow, 7 green, 2 blue, and 4 orange. These counts are shown below in Table 1.

Table 1. Frequencies in the Bag of M&M's

Color	Frequency
Brown	17
Red	18
Yellow	7
Green	7
Blue	2
Orange	4

This table is called a frequency table and it describes the distribution of M&M color frequencies. Not surprisingly, this kind of distribution is called a frequency distribution. Often a frequency distribution is shown graphically as in Figure 1.

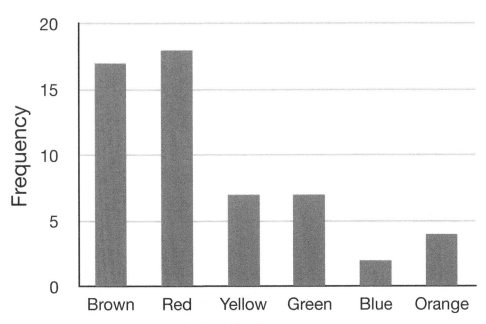

Figure 1. Distribution of 55 M&M's.

The distribution shown in Figure 1 concerns just my one bag of M&M's. You might be wondering about the distribution of colors for all M&M's. The manufacturer of M&M's provides some information about this matter, but they do not tell us exactly how many M&M's of each color they have ever produced. Instead, they report proportions rather than frequencies. Figure 2 shows these proportions. Since every M&M is one of the six familiar colors, the six proportions shown in the figure add to one. We call Figure 2 a probability distribution because if you choose an M&M at random, the probability of getting, say, a brown M&M is equal to the proportion of M&M's that are brown (0.30).

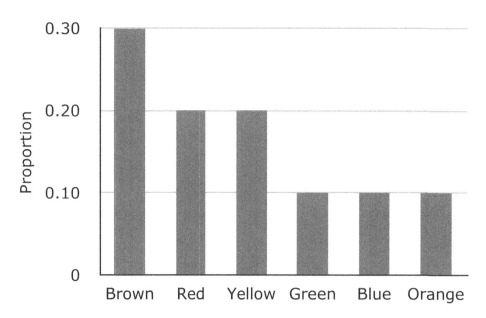

Figure 2. Distribution of all M&M's.

Notice that the distributions in Figures 1 and 2 are not identical. Figure 1 portrays the distribution in a sample of 55 M&M's. Figure 2 shows the proportions for all M&M's. Chance factors involving the machines used by the manufacturer introduce random variation into the different bags produced. Some bags will have a distribution of colors that is close to Figure 2; others will be further away.

Continuous Variables

The variable "color of M&M" used in this example is a discrete variable, and its distribution is also called discrete. Let us now extend the concept of a distribution to continuous variables.

The data shown in Table 2 are the times it took one of us (DL) to move the cursor over a small target in a series of 20 trials. The times are sorted from shortest to longest. The variable "time to respond" is a continuous variable. With time measured accurately (to many decimal places), no two response times would be expected to be the same. Measuring time in milliseconds (thousandths of a second) is often precise enough to approximate a continuous variable in psychology. As you can see in Table 2, measuring DL's responses this way produced times no two of which were the same. As a result, a frequency distribution would be uninformative: it would consist of the 20 times in the experiment, each with a frequency of 1.

Table 2. Response Times

568	720
577	728
581	729
640	777
641	808
645	824
657	825
673	865
696	875
703	1007

The solution to this problem is to create a grouped frequency distribution. In a grouped frequency distribution, scores falling within various ranges are tabulated. Table 3 shows a grouped frequency distribution for these 20 times.

Table 3. Grouped frequency distribution

Range	Frequency
500-600	3
600-700	6
700-800	5
800-900	5
900-1000	0
1000-1100	1

Grouped frequency distributions can be portrayed graphically. Figure 3 shows a graphical representation of the frequency distribution in Table 3. This kind of graph is called a histogram. Chapter 2 contains an entire section devoted to histograms.

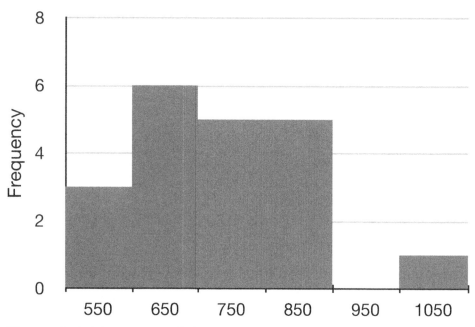

Figure 3. A histogram of the grouped frequency distribution shown in Table 3. The labels on the X-axis are the middle values of the range they represent.

Probability Densities

The histogram in Figure 3 portrays just DL's 20 times in the one experiment he performed. To represent the probability associated with an arbitrary movement (which can take any positive amount of time), we must represent all these potential times at once. For this purpose, we plot the distribution for the continuous variable of time. Distributions for continuous variables are called continuous distributions. They also carry the fancier name probability density. Some probability densities have particular importance in statistics. A very important one is shaped like a bell, and called the normal distribution. Many naturally-occurring phenomena can be approximated surprisingly well by this distribution. It will serve to illustrate some features of all continuous distributions.

An example of a normal distribution is shown in Figure 4. Do you see the "bell"? The normal distribution doesn't represent a real bell, however, since the left and right tips extend indefinitely (we can't draw them any further so they look like they've stopped in our diagram). The Y-axis in the normal distribution represents the "density of probability." Intuitively, it shows the chance of obtaining values near corresponding points on the X-axis. In Figure 4, for example, the probability of an observation with value near 40 is about half of the probability of an observation with value near 50. (For more information, see Chapter 7.)

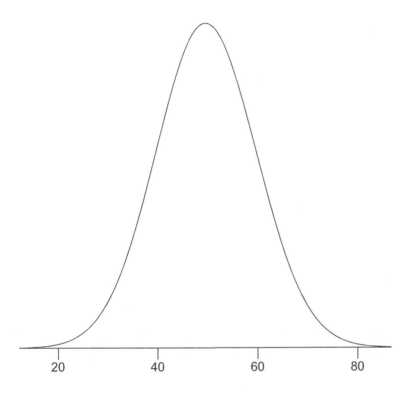

Figure 4. A normal distribution.

Although this text does not discuss the concept of probability density in detail, you should keep the following ideas in mind about the curve that describes a continuous distribution (like the normal distribution). First, the area under the curve equals 1. Second, the probability of any exact value of X is 0. Finally, the area under the curve and bounded between two given points on the X-axis is the probability that a number chosen at random will fall between the two points. Let us illustrate with DL's hand movements. First, the probability that his movement takes some amount of time is one! (We exclude the possibility of him never finishing his gesture.) Second, the probability that his movement takes exactly 598.956432342346576 milliseconds is essentially zero. (We can make the probability as close as we like to zero by making the time measurement more and more precise.) Finally, suppose that the probability of DL's movement taking between 600 and 700 milliseconds is one tenth. Then the continuous distribution for DL's possible times would have a shape that places 10% of the area below the curve in the region bounded by 600 and 700 on the X-axis.

Shapes of Distributions

Distributions have different shapes; they don't all look like the normal distribution in Figure 4. For example, the normal probability density is higher in the middle compared to its two tails. Other distributions need not have this feature. There is even variation among the distributions that we call "normal." For example, some normal distributions are more spread out than the one shown in Figure 4 (their tails begin to hit the X-axis further from the middle of the curve --for example, at 10 and 90 if drawn in place of Figure 4). Others are less spread out (their tails might approach the X-axis at 30 and 70). More information on the normal distribution can be found in a later chapter completely devoted to them.

The distribution shown in Figure 4 is symmetric; if you folded it in the middle, the two sides would match perfectly. Figure 5 shows the discrete distribution of scores on a psychology test. This distribution is not symmetric: the tail in the positive direction extends further than the tail in the negative direction. A distribution with the longer tail extending in the positive direction is said to have a positive skew. It is also described as "skewed to the right."

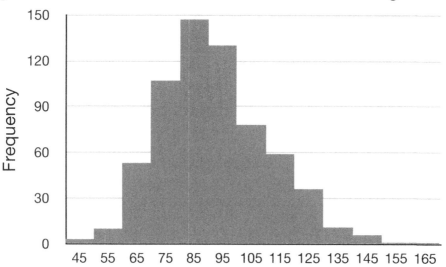

Figure 5. A distribution with a positive skew.

Figure 6 shows the salaries of major league baseball players in 1974 (in thousands of dollars). This distribution has an extreme positive skew.

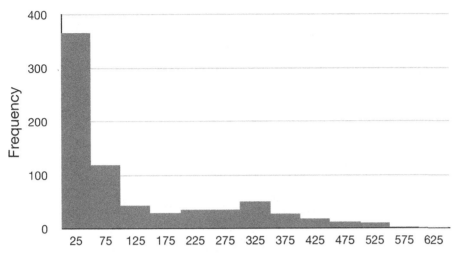
Figure 6. A distribution with a very large positive skew.

A continuous distribution with a positive skew is shown in Figure 7.

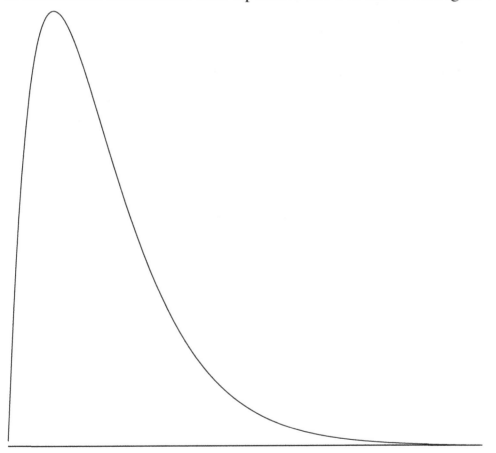
Figure 7. A continuous distribution with a positive skew.

Although less common, some distributions have a negative skew. Figure 8 shows the scores on a 20-point problem on a statistics exam. Since the tail of the distribution extends to the left, this distribution is skewed to the left.

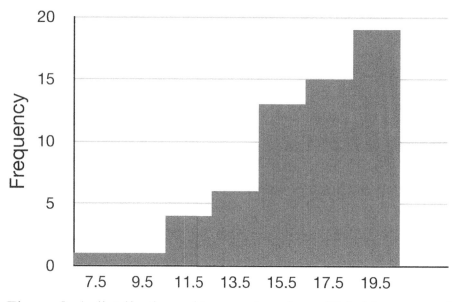

Figure 8. A distribution with negative skew. This histogram shows the frequencies of various scores on a 20-point question on a statistics test.

A continuous distribution with a negative skew is shown in Figure 9.

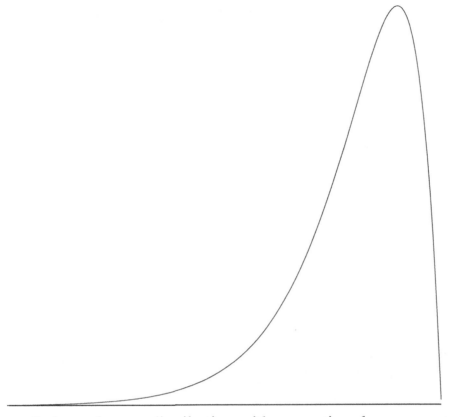

Figure 9. A continuous distribution with a negative skew.

The distributions shown so far all have one distinct high point or peak. The distribution in Figure 10 has two distinct peaks. A distribution with two peaks is called a bimodal distribution.

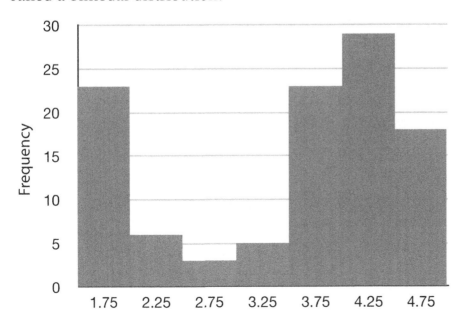

Figure 10. Frequencies of times between eruptions of the Old Faithful
geyser. Notice the two distinct peaks: one at 1.75 and the other at
4.25.

Distributions also differ from each other in terms of how large or "fat" their tails
are. Figure 11 shows two distributions that differ in this respect. The upper
distribution has relatively more scores in its tails; its shape is called leptokurtic.
The lower distribution has relatively fewer scores in its tails; its shape is called
platykurtic.

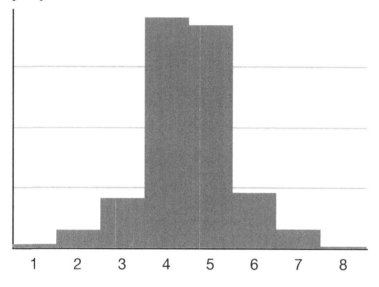

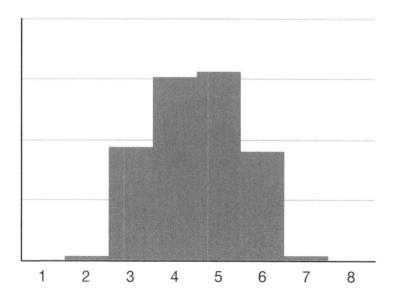

Figure 11. Distributions differing in kurtosis. The top distribution has long tails. It is called "leptokurtic." The bottom distribution has short tails. It is called "platykurtic."

Summation Notation

by David M. Lane

Prerequisites
• None

Learning Objectives
1. Use summation notation to express the sum of all numbers
2. Use summation notation to express the sum of a subset of numbers
3. Use summation notation to express the sum of squares

Many statistical formulas involve summing numbers. Fortunately there is a convenient notation for expressing summation. This section covers the basics of this summation notation.

Let's say we have a variable X that represents the weights (in grams) of 4 grapes. The data are shown in Table 1.

Table 1. Weights of 4 grapes.

Grape	X
1	4.6
2	5.1
3	4.9
4	4.4

We label Grape 1's weight X_1, Grape 2's weight X_2, etc. The following formula means to sum up the weights of the four grapes:

$$\sum_{i=1}^{4} X_i$$

The Greek letter Σ indicates summation. The "i = 1" at the bottom indicates that the summation is to start with X_1 and the 4 at the top indicates that the summation will end with X_4. The "X_i" indicates that X is the variable to be summed as i goes from 1 to 4. Therefore,

$$\sum_{i=1}^{4} X_i = X_1 + X_2 + X_3 + X_4 = 4.6 + 5.1 + 4.9 + 4.4 = 19$$

The symbol

$$\sum_{i=1}^{3} X_i$$

indicates that only the first 3 scores are to be summed. The index variable i goes from 1 to 3.

When all the scores of a variable (such as X) are to be summed, it is often convenient to use the following abbreviated notation:

$$\sum X$$

Thus, when no values of i are shown, it means to sum all the values of X.

Many formulas involve squaring numbers before they are summed. This is indicated as

$$\sum X^2 = 4.6^2 + 5.1^2 + 4.9^2 + 4.4^2$$

$$= 21.16 + 26.01 + 24.01 + 19.36 = 90.54.$$

Notice that:

$$\left(\sum X\right)^2 \neq \sum X^2$$

because the expression on the left means to sum up all the values of X and then square the sum ($19^2 = 361$), whereas the expression on the right means to square the numbers and then sum the squares (90.54, as shown).

Some formulas involve the sum of cross products. Table 2 shows the data for variables X and Y. The cross products (XY) are shown in the third column. The sum of the cross products is $3 + 4 + 21 = 28$.

Table 2. Cross Products.

X	Y	XY
1	3	3
2	2	4
3	7	21

In summation notation, this is written as:

$$\sum XY = 28$$

Linear Transformations

by David M. Lane

Prerequisites
• None

Learning Objectives
1. Give the formula for a linear transformation
2. Determine whether a transformation is linear
3. Describe what is linear about a linear transformation

Often it is necessary to transform data from one measurement scale to another. For example, you might want to convert height measured in feet to height measured in inches. Table 1 shows the heights of four people measured in both feet and inches. To transform feet to inches, you simply multiply by 12. Similarly, to transform inches to feet, you divide by 12.

Table 1. Converting between feet and inches.

Feet	Inches
5.00	60
6.25	75
5.50	66
5.75	69

Some conversions require that you multiply by a number and then add a second number. A good example of this is the transformation between degrees Centigrade and degrees Fahrenheit. Table 2 shows the temperatures of 5 US cities in the early afternoon of November 16, 2002.

Table 2. Temperatures in 5 cities on 11/16/2002.

City	Degrees Fahrenheit	Degrees Centigrade
Houston	54	12.22
Chicago	37	2.78
Minneapolis	31	-0.56
Miami	78	25.56
Phoenix	70	21.11

The formula to transform Centigrade to Fahrenheit is:

$$F = 1.8C + 32$$

The formula for converting from Fahrenheit to Centigrade is

$$C = 0.5556F - 17.778$$

The transformation consists of multiplying by a constant and then adding a second constant. For the conversion from Centigrade to Fahrenheit, the first constant is 1.8 and the second is 32.

Figure 1 shows a plot of degrees Centigrade as a function of degrees Fahrenheit. Notice that the points form a straight line. This will always be the case if the transformation from one scale to another consists of multiplying by one constant and then adding a second constant. Such transformations are therefore called linear transformations.

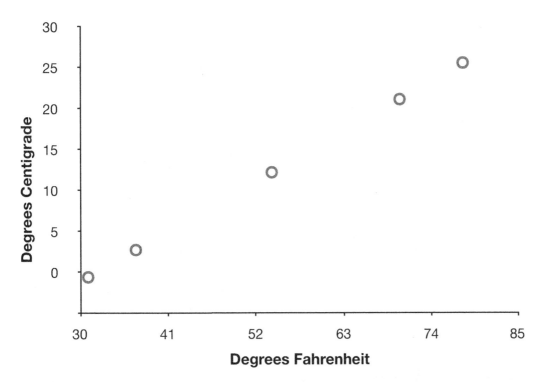

Figure 1. Degrees Centigrade as a function of degrees Fahrenheit

Logarithms

by David M. Lane

Prerequisites
• Chapter 1: Distributions

Learning Objectives
1. Compute logs using different bases
2. Convert between bases
3. State the relationship between logs and proportional change

The log transformation reduces positive skew. This can be valuable both for making the data more interpretable and for helping to meet the assumptions of inferential statistics.

Basics of Logarithms (Logs)

Logs are, in a sense, the opposite of exponents. Consider the following simple expression:

$10^2 = 100$

Here we can say the base of 10 is raised to the second power. Here is an example of a log:

$Log_{10}(100) = 2$

This can be read as: The log base ten of 100 equals 2. The result is the power that the base of 10 has to be raised to in order to equal the value (100). Similarly,

$Log_{10}(1000) = 3$

since 10 has to be raised to the third power in order to equal 1,000.

These examples all used base 10, but any base could have been used. There is a base which results in "natural logarithms" and that is called e and equals approximately 2.718. It is beyond the scope of this book to explain what is "natural" about it. Natural logarithms can be indicated either as: $Ln(x)$ or $log_e(x)$

Changing the base of the log changes the result by a multiplicative constant. To convert from Log_{10} to natural logs, you multiply by 2.303. Analogously, to convert in the other direction, you divide by 2.303.

Taking the antilog of a number undoes the operation of taking the log. Therefore, since $Log_{10}(1000) = 3$, the antilog$_{10}$ of 3 is 1,000. Taking the antilog of a number simply raises the base of the logarithm in question to that number.

Logs and Proportional Change

A series of numbers that increases proportionally will increase in equal amounts when converted to logs. For example, the numbers in the first column of Table 1 increase by a factor of 1.5 so that each row is 1.5 times as high as the preceding row. The Log_{10} transformed numbers increase in equal steps of 0.176.

Table 1. Proportional raw changes are equal in log units.

Raw	Log
4.0	0.602
6.0	0.778
9.0	0.954
13.5	1.130

As another example, if one student increased their score from 100 to 200 while a second student increased their's from 150 to 300, the percentage change (100%) is the same for both students. The log difference is also the same, as shown below.

```
Log10 (100)  =  2.000
Log10 (200)  =  2.301
Difference:  0.301

Log10 (150)  =  2.176
Log10 (300)  =  2.477
Difference:  0.301
```

Arithmetic Operations

Rules for logs of products and quotients are shown below.

```
Log (AB)  =  Log (A)  +  Log (B)
Log (A/B)  =  Log (A)  -  Log (B)
```

For example,

```
Log10 (10 x 100)  =  Log10 (10)  +  Log10 (100)  =  1 + 2 = 3.
```

Similarly,

$$\text{Log}_{10}(100/10) = \text{Log}_{10}(100) - \text{Log}_{10}(10) = 2 - 1 = 1.$$

Statistical Literacy

by Denise Harvey and David M. Lane

Prerequisites
- Chapter 1: Levels of Measurement

The Board of Trustees at a university commissioned a top management-consulting firm to address the admission processes for academic and athletic programs. The consulting firm wrote a report discussing the trade-off between maintaining academic and athletic excellence. One of their key findings was:

> The standard for an athlete's admission, as reflected in SAT scores alone, is lower than the standard for non-athletes by as much as 20 percent, with the weight of this difference being carried by the so-called "revenue sports" of football and basketball. Athletes are also admitted through a different process than the one used to admit non-athlete students.

What do you think?

Based on what you have learned in this chapter about measurement scales, does it make sense to compare SAT scores using percentages? Why or why not?

Think about this before continuing:

> As you may know, the SAT has an arbitrarily-determined lower limit on test scores of 200. Therefore, SAT is measured on either an ordinal scale or, at most, an interval scale. However, it is clearly not measured on a ratio scale. Therefore, it is not meaningful to report SAT score differences in terms of percentages. For example, consider the effect of subtracting 200 from every student's score so that the lowest possible score is 0. How would that affect the difference as expressed in percentages?

Exercises

Prerequisites
• All material presented in Chapter: "Introduction"

1. A teacher wishes to know whether the males in his/her class have more conservative attitudes than the females. A questionnaire is distributed assessing attitudes and the males and the females are compared. Is this an example of descriptive or inferential statistics?

2. A cognitive psychologist is interested in comparing two ways of presenting stimuli on sub- sequent memory. Twelve subjects are presented with each method and a memory test is given. What would be the roles of descriptive and inferential statistics in the analysis of these data?

3. If you are told only that you scored in the 80th percentile, do you know from that description exactly how it was calculated? Explain.

4. A study is conducted to determine whether people learn better with spaced or massed practice. Subjects volunteer from an introductory psychology class. At the beginning of the semester 12 subjects volunteer and are assigned to the massed-practice condition. At the end of the semester 12 subjects volunteer and are assigned to the spaced-practice condition. This experiment involves two kinds of non-random sampling: (1) Subjects are not randomly sampled from some specified population and (2) subjects are not randomly assigned to conditions. Which of the problems relates to the generality of the results? Which of the problems relates to the validity of the results? Which problem is more serious?

5. Give an example of an independent and a dependent variable.

6. Categorize the following variables as being qualitative or quantitative:
   Rating of the quality of a movie on a 7-point scale
   Age
   Country you were born in
   Favorite Color
   Time to respond to a question

7. Specify the level of measurement used for the items in Question 6.

8. Which of the following are linear transformations?
   Converting from meters to kilometers
   Squaring each side to find the area
   Converting from ounces to pounds
   Taking the square root of each person's height.
   Multiplying all numbers by 2 and then adding 5
   Converting temperature from Fahrenheit to Centigrade

9. The formula for finding each student's test grade (g) from his or her raw score (s) on a test is as follows: $g = 16 + 3s$

Is this a linear transformation?

If a student got a raw score of 20, what is his test grade?

10. For the numbers $1, 2, 4, 16$, compute the following:
   ΣX
   ΣX^2
   $(\Sigma X)^2$

11. Which of the frequency polygons has a large positive skew? Which has a large negative skew?

A.

B.

C.

12. What is more likely to have a skewed distribution: time to solve an anagram problem (where the letters of a word or phrase are rearranged into another

word or phrase like "dear" and "read" or "funeral" and "real fun") or scores on a vocabulary test?

Questions from Case Studies

Angry Moods (AM) case study

13. (AM) Which variables are the participant variables? (They act as independent variables in this study.)

14. (AM) What are the dependent variables?

15. (AM) Is Anger-Out a quantitative or qualitative variable?

Teacher Ratings (TR) case study

16. (TR) What is the independent variable in this study?

ADHD Treatment (AT) case study

17. (AT) What is the independent variable of this experiment? How many levels does it have?

18. (AT) What is the dependent variable? On what scale (nominal, ordinal, interval, ratio) was it measured?

2. Graphing Distributions

Graphing data is the first and often most important step in data analysis. In this day of computers, researchers all too often see only the results of complex computer analyses without ever taking a close look at the data themselves. This is all the more unfortunate because computers can create many types of graphs quickly and easily.

This chapter covers some classic types of graphs such bar charts that were invented by William Playfair in the 18th century as well as graphs such as box plots invented by John Tukey in the 20th century.

Graphing Qualitative Variables

by David M. Lane

Prerequisites
• Chapter 1: Variables

Learning Objectives
1. Create a frequency table
2. Determine when pie charts are valuable and when they are not
3. Create and interpret bar charts
4. Identify common graphical mistakes

When Apple Computer introduced the iMac computer in August 1998, the company wanted to learn whether the iMac was expanding Apple's market share. Was the iMac just attracting previous Macintosh owners? Or was it purchased by newcomers to the computer market and by previous Windows users who were switching over? To find out, 500 iMac customers were interviewed. Each customer was categorized as a previous Macintosh owner, a previous Windows owner, or a new computer purchaser.

This section examines graphical methods for displaying the results of the interviews. We'll learn some general lessons about how to graph data that fall into a small number of categories. A later section will consider how to graph numerical data in which each observation is represented by a number in some range. The key point about the qualitative data that occupy us in the present section is that they do not come with a pre-established ordering (the way numbers are ordered). For example, there is no natural sense in which the category of previous Windows users comes before or after the category of previous Macintosh users. This situation may be contrasted with quantitative data, such as a person's weight. People of one weight are naturally ordered with respect to people of a different weight.

Frequency Tables

All of the graphical methods shown in this section are derived from frequency tables. Table 1 shows a frequency table for the results of the iMac study; it shows the frequencies of the various response categories. It also shows the relative frequencies, which are the proportion of responses in each category. For example, the relative frequency for "none" of 0.17 = 85/500.

Table 1. Frequency Table for the iMac Data.

Previous Ownership	Frequency	Relative Frequency
None	85	0.17
Windows	60	0.12
Macintosh	355	0.71
Total	500	1

Pie Charts

The pie chart in Figure 1 shows the results of the iMac study. In a pie chart, each category is represented by a slice of the pie. The area of the slice is proportional to the percentage of responses in the category. This is simply the relative frequency multiplied by 100. Although most iMac purchasers were Macintosh owners, Apple was encouraged by the 12% of purchasers who were former Windows users, and by the 17% of purchasers who were buying a computer for the first time.

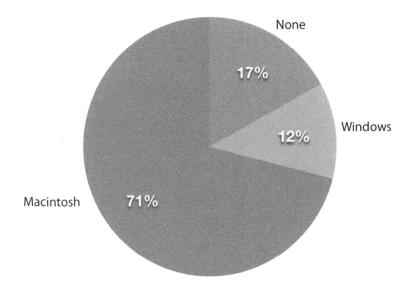

Figure 1. Pie chart of iMac purchases illustrating frequencies of previous computer ownership.

Pie charts are effective for displaying the relative frequencies of a small number of categories. They are not recommended, however, when you have a large number of categories. Pie charts can also be confusing when they are used to compare the outcomes of two different surveys or experiments. In an influential book on the use of graphs, Edward Tufte asserted "The only worse design than a pie chart is several of them."

Here is another important point about pie charts. If they are based on a small number of observations, it can be misleading to label the pie slices with percentages. For example, if just 5 people had been interviewed by Apple Computers, and 3 were former Windows users, it would be misleading to display a pie chart with the Windows slice showing 60%. With so few people interviewed, such a large percentage of Windows users might easily have occurred since chance can cause large errors with small samples. In this case, it is better to alert the user of the pie chart to the actual numbers involved. The slices should therefore be labeled with the actual frequencies observed (e.g., 3) instead of with percentages.

Bar charts

Bar charts can also be used to represent frequencies of different categories. A bar chart of the iMac purchases is shown in Figure 2. Frequencies are shown on the Y-axis and the type of computer previously owned is shown on the X-axis. Typically, the Y-axis shows the number of observations in each category rather than the percentage of observations in each category as is typical in pie charts.

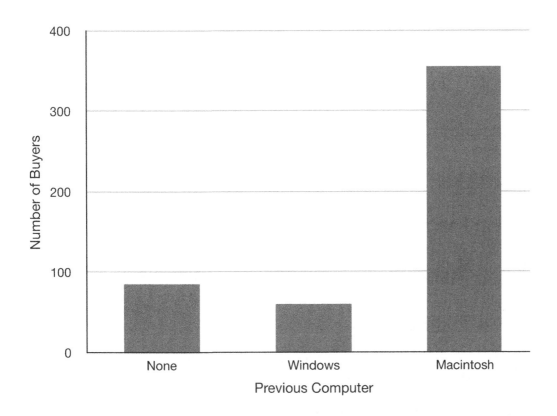

Figure 2. Bar chart of iMac purchases as a function of previous computer ownership.

Comparing Distributions

Often we need to compare the results of different surveys, or of different conditions within the same overall survey. In this case, we are comparing the "distributions" of responses between the surveys or conditions. Bar charts are often excellent for illustrating differences between two distributions. Figure 3 shows the number of people playing card games at the Yahoo web site on a Sunday and on a Wednesday in the spring of 2001. We see that there were more players overall on Wednesday compared to Sunday. The number of people playing Pinochle was nonetheless the same on these two days. In contrast, there were about twice as many people playing hearts on Wednesday as on Sunday. Facts like these emerge clearly from a well-designed bar chart.

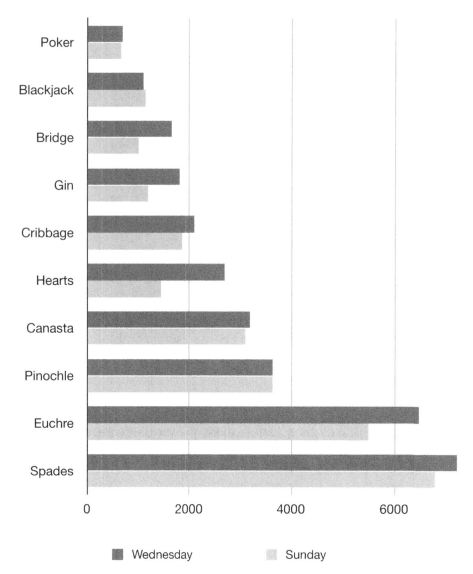

Figure 3. A bar chart of the number of people playing different card games on Sunday and Wednesday.

The bars in Figure 3 are oriented horizontally rather than vertically. The horizontal format is useful when you have many categories because there is more room for the category labels. We'll have more to say about bar charts when we consider numerical quantities later in this chapter.

Some graphical mistakes to avoid

Don't get fancy! People sometimes add features to graphs that don't help to convey their information. For example, 3-dimensional bar charts such as the one shown in Figure 4 are usually not as effective as their two-dimensional counterparts.

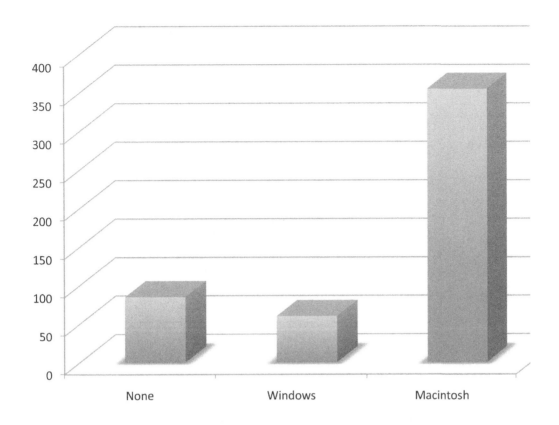

Figure 4. A three-dimensional version of Figure 2.

Here is another way that fanciness can lead to trouble. Instead of plain bars, it is tempting to substitute meaningful images. For example, Figure 5 presents the iMac data using pictures of computers. The heights of the pictures accurately represent the number of buyers, yet Figure 5 is misleading because the viewer's attention will be captured by areas. The areas can exaggerate the size differences between the groups. In terms of percentages, the ratio of previous Macintosh owners to previous Windows owners is about 6 to 1. But the ratio of the two areas in Figure 5 is about 35 to 1. A biased person wishing to hide the fact that many Windows owners purchased iMacs would be tempted to use Figure 5 instead of Figure 2! Edward Tufte coined the term "lie factor" to refer to the ratio of the size of the effect shown in a graph to the size of the effect shown in the data. He suggests that lie factors greater than 1.05 or less than 0.95 produce unacceptable distortion.

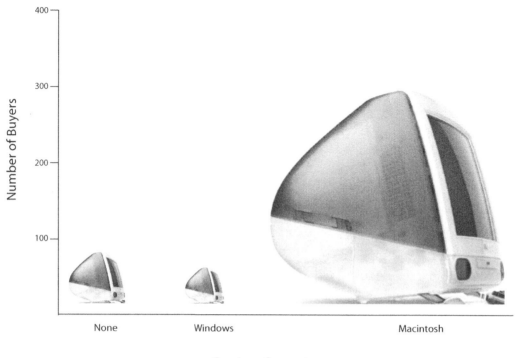

Figure 5. A redrawing of Figure 2 with a lie factor greater than 8.

Another distortion in bar charts results from setting the baseline to a value other than zero. The baseline is the bottom of the Y-axis, representing the least number of cases that could have occurred in a category. Normally, but not always, this number should be zero. Figure 6 shows the iMac data with a baseline of 50. Once again, the differences in areas suggests a different story than the true differences in percentages. The number of Windows-switchers seems minuscule compared to its true value of 12%.

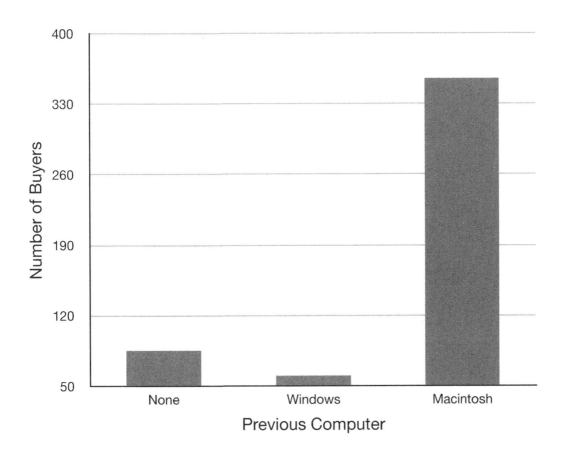

Figure 6. A redrawing of Figure 2 with a baseline of 50.

Finally, we note that it is a serious mistake to use a line graph when the X-axis contains merely qualitative variables. A line graph is essentially a bar graph with the tops of the bars represented by points joined by lines (the rest of the bar is suppressed). Figure 7 inappropriately shows a line graph of the card game data from Yahoo. The drawback to Figure 7 is that it gives the false impression that the games are naturally ordered in a numerical way when, in fact, they are ordered alphabetically.

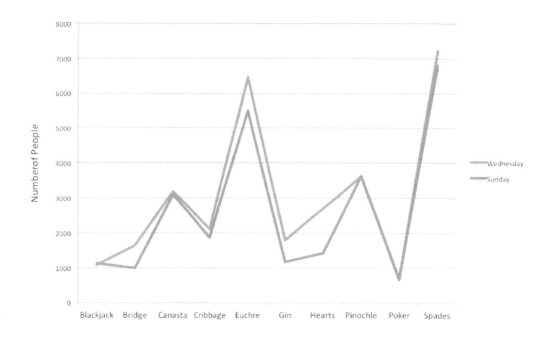

Figure 7. A line graph used inappropriately to depict the number of people playing different card games on Sunday and Wednesday.

Summary

Pie charts and bar charts can both be effective methods of portraying qualitative data. Bar charts are better when there are more than just a few categories and for comparing two or more distributions. Be careful to avoid creating misleading graphs.

Graphing Quantitative Variables

1. Stem and Leaf Displays
2. Histograms
3. Frequency Polygons
4. Box Plots
5. Bar Charts
6. Line Graphs
7. Dot Plots

As discussed in the section on variables in Chapter 1, quantitative variables are variables measured on a numeric scale. Height, weight, response time, subjective rating of pain, temperature, and score on an exam are all examples of quantitative variables. Quantitative variables are distinguished from categorical (sometimes called qualitative) variables such as favorite color, religion, city of birth, favorite sport in which there is no ordering or measuring involved.

There are many types of graphs that can be used to portray distributions of quantitative variables. The upcoming sections cover the following types of graphs: (1) stem and leaf displays, (2) histograms, (3) frequency polygons, (4) box plots, (5) bar charts, (6) line graphs, (7) dot plots, and (8) scatter plots (discussed in a different chapter). Some graph types such as stem and leaf displays are best-suited for small to moderate amounts of data, whereas others such as histograms are best-suited for large amounts of data. Graph types such as box plots are good at depicting differences between distributions. Scatter plots are used to show the relationship between two variables.

Stem and Leaf Displays

by David M. Lane

Prerequisites
• Chapter 1: Distributions

Learning Objectives
1. Create and interpret basic stem and leaf displays
2. Create and interpret back-to-back stem and leaf displays
3. Judge whether a stem and leaf display is appropriate for a given data set

A stem and leaf display is a graphical method of displaying data. It is particularly useful when your data are not too numerous. In this section, we will explain how to construct and interpret this kind of graph.

As usual, we will start with an example. Consider Table 1 that shows the number of touchdown passes (TD passes) thrown by each of the 31 teams in the National Football League in the 2000 season.

Table 1. Number of touchdown passes.

37, 33, 33, 32, 29, 28,
28, 23, 22, 22, 22, 21,
21, 21, 20, 20, 19, 19,
18, 18, 18, 18, 16, 15,
14, 14, 14, 12, 12, 9, 6

A stem and leaf display of the data is shown in Figure 1. The left portion of Figure 1 contains the stems. They are the numbers 3, 2, 1, and 0, arranged as a column to the left of the bars. Think of these numbers as 10's digits. A stem of 3, for example, can be used to represent the 10's digit in any of the numbers from 30 to 39. The numbers to the right of the bar are leaves, and they represent the 1's digits. Every leaf in the graph therefore stands for the result of adding the leaf to 10 times its stem.

```
3|2337
2|001112223889
1|2244456888899
0|69
```

Figure 1. Stem and leaf display of the number of touchdown passes.

To make this clear, let us examine Figure 1 more closely. In the top row, the four leaves to the right of stem 3 are 2, 3, 3, and 7. Combined with the stem, these leaves represent the numbers 32, 33, 33, and 37, which are the numbers of TD passes for the first four teams in Table 1. The next row has a stem of 2 and 12 leaves. Together, they represent 12 data points, namely, two occurrences of 20 TD passes, three occurrences of 21 TD passes, three occurrences of 22 TD passes, one occurrence of 23 TD passes, two occurrences of 28 TD passes, and one occurrence of 29 TD passes. We leave it to you to figure out what the third row represents. The fourth row has a stem of 0 and two leaves. It stands for the last two entries in Table 1, namely 9 TD passes and 6 TD passes. (The latter two numbers may be thought of as 09 and 06.)

One purpose of a stem and leaf display is to clarify the shape of the distribution. You can see many facts about TD passes more easily in Figure 1 than in Table 1. For example, by looking at the stems and the shape of the plot, you can tell that most of the teams had between 10 and 29 passing TD's, with a few having more and a few having less. The precise numbers of TD passes can be determined by examining the leaves.

We can make our figure even more revealing by splitting each stem into two parts. Figure 2 shows how to do this. The top row is reserved for numbers from 35 to 39 and holds only the 37 TD passes made by the first team in Table 1. The second row is reserved for the numbers from 30 to 34 and holds the 32, 33, and 33 TD passes made by the next three teams in the table. You can see for yourself what the other rows represent.

```
3|7
3|233
2|889
2|001112223
1|56888899
1|22444
0|69
```

Figure 2. Stem and leaf display with the stems split in two.

Figure 2 is more revealing than Figure 1 because the latter figure lumps too many values into a single row. Whether you should split stems in a display depends on the exact form of your data. If rows get too long with single stems, you might try splitting them into two or more parts.

There is a variation of stem and leaf displays that is useful for comparing distributions. The two distributions are placed back to back along a common column of stems. The result is a "back-to-back stem and leaf display." Figure 3 shows such a graph. It compares the numbers of TD passes in the 1998 and 2000 seasons. The stems are in the middle, the leaves to the left are for the 1998 data, and the leaves to the right are for the 2000 data. For example, the second-to-last row shows that in 1998 there were teams with 11, 12, and 13 TD passes, and in 2000 there were two teams with 12 and three teams with 14 TD passes.

```
        11 | 4 |
           | 3 | 7
       332 | 3 | 233
      8865 | 2 | 889
  44331110 | 2 | 001112223
 987776665 | 1 | 56888899
       321 | 1 | 22444
         7 | 0 | 69
```

Figure 3. Back-to-back stem and leaf display. The left side shows the 1998
     TD data and the right side shows the 2000 TD data.

Figure 3 helps us see that the two seasons were similar, but that only in 1998 did any teams throw more than 40 TD passes.

There are two things about the football data that make them easy to graph with stems and leaves. First, the data are limited to whole numbers that can be represented with a one-digit stem and a one-digit leaf. Second, all the numbers are positive. If the data include numbers with three or more digits, or contain decimals, they can be rounded to two-digit accuracy. Negative values are also easily handled. Let us look at another example.

Table 2 shows data from the case study Weapons and Aggression. Each value is the mean difference over a series of trials between the times it took an experimental subject to name aggressive words (like "punch") under two conditions. In one condition, the words were preceded by a non-weapon word such as "bug." In the second condition, the same words were preceded by a weapon word such as "gun" or "knife." The issue addressed by the experiment was whether a preceding weapon word would speed up (or prime) pronunciation of the aggressive word compared to a non-weapon priming word. A positive difference implies greater priming of the aggressive word by the weapon word. Negative differences imply that the priming by the weapon word was less than for a neutral word.

Table 2. The effects of priming (thousandths of a second).

```
43.2, 42.9, 35.6, 25.6, 25.4, 23.6, 20.5, 19.9, 14.4, 12.7, 11.3,
10.2, 10.0, 9.1, 7.5, 5.4, 4.7, 3.8, 2.1, 1.2, -0.2, -6.3, -6.7,
-8.8, -10.4, -10.5, -14.9, -14.9, -15.0, -18.5, -27.4
```

You see that the numbers range from 43.2 to -27.4. The first value indicates that one subject was 43.2 milliseconds faster pronouncing aggressive words when they were preceded by weapon words than when preceded by neutral words. The value -27.4 indicates that another subject was 27.4 milliseconds slower pronouncing aggressive words when they were preceded by weapon words.

The data are displayed with stems and leaves in Figure 4. Since stem and leaf displays can only portray two whole digits (one for the stem and one for the leaf) the numbers are first rounded. Thus, the value 43.2 is rounded to 43 and represented with a stem of 4 and a leaf of 3. Similarly, 42.9 is rounded to 43. To represent negative numbers, we simply use negative stems. For example, the bottom row of the figure represents the number –27. The second-to-last row represents the numbers -10, -10, -15, etc. Once again, we have rounded the original values from Table 2.

```
 4 | 33
 3 | 6
 2 | 00456
 1 | 00134
 0 | 1245589
-0 | 0679
-1 | 005559
-2 | 7
```

Figure 4. Stem and leaf display with negative numbers and rounding.

Observe that the figure contains a row headed by "0" and another headed by "-0."
The stem of 0 is for numbers between 0 and 9, whereas the stem of -0 is for
numbers between 0 and -9. For example, the fifth row of the table holds the
numbers 1, 2, 4, 5, 5, 8, 9 and the sixth row holds 0, -6, -7, and -9. Values that are
exactly 0 before rounding should be split as evenly as possible between the "0" and
"-0" rows. In Table 2, none of the values are 0 before rounding. The "0" that
appears in the "-0" row comes from the original value of -0.2 in the table.

Although stem and leaf displays are unwieldy for large data sets, they are
often useful for data sets with up to 200 observations. Figure 5 portrays the
distribution of populations of 185 US cities in 1998. To be included, a city had to
have between 100,000 and 500,000 residents.

```
4|899
4|6
4|4455
4|333
4|01
3|99
3|677777
3|55
3|223
3|111
2|8899
2|666667
2|444455
2|22333
2|000000
1|888888888888899999999999
1|666666777777
1|44444444444455555555555
1|2222222222222222222333333333
1|000000000000000111111111111111111111111111
```

Figure 5. Stem and leaf display of populations of 185 US cities with
populations between 100,000 and 500,000 in 1988.

Since a stem and leaf plot shows only two-place accuracy, we had to round the
numbers to the nearest 10,000. For example the largest number (493,559) was

rounded to 490,000 and then plotted with a stem of 4 and a leaf of 9. The fourth highest number (463,201) was rounded to 460,000 and plotted with a stem of 4 and a leaf of 6. Thus, the stems represent units of 100,000 and the leaves represent units of 10,000. Notice that each stem value is split into five parts: 0-1, 2-3, 4-5, 6-7, and 8-9.

Whether your data can be suitably represented by a stem and leaf display depends on whether they can be rounded without loss of important information. Also, their extreme values must fit into two successive digits, as the data in Figure 5 fit into the 10,000 and 100,000 places (for leaves and stems, respectively). Deciding what kind of graph is best suited to displaying your data thus requires good judgment. Statistics is not just recipes!

Histograms

by David M. Lane

Prerequisites

• Chapter 1: Distributions

• Chapter 2: Graphing Qualitative Data

Learning Objectives

1. Create a grouped frequency distribution
2. Create a histogram based on a grouped frequency distribution
3. Determine an appropriate bin width

A histogram is a graphical method for displaying the shape of a distribution. It is particularly useful when there are a large number of observations. We begin with an example consisting of the scores of 642 students on a psychology test. The test consists of 197 items each graded as "correct" or "incorrect." The students' scores ranged from 46 to 167.

The first step is to create a frequency table. Unfortunately, a simple frequency table would be too big, containing over 100 rows. To simplify the table, we group scores together as shown in Table 1.

Table 1. Grouped Frequency Distribution of Psychology Test Scores

Interval's Lower Limit	Interval's Upper Limit	Class Frequency
39.5	49.5	3
49.5	59.5	10
59.5	69.5	53
69.5	79.5	107
79.5	89.5	147
89.5	99.5	130
99.5	109.5	78
109.5	119.5	59
119.5	129.5	36

129.5	139.5	11
139.5	149.5	6
149.5	159.5	1
159.5	169.5	1

To create this table, the range of scores was broken into intervals, called class intervals. The first interval is from 39.5 to 49.5, the second from 49.5 to 59.5, etc. Next, the number of scores falling into each interval was counted to obtain the class frequencies. There are three scores in the first interval, 10 in the second, etc.

Class intervals of width 10 provide enough detail about the distribution to be revealing without making the graph too "choppy." More information on choosing the widths of class intervals is presented later in this section. Placing the limits of the class intervals midway between two numbers (e.g., 49.5) ensures that every score will fall in an interval rather than on the boundary between intervals.

In a histogram, the class frequencies are represented by bars. The height of each bar corresponds to its class frequency. A histogram of these data is shown in Figure 1.

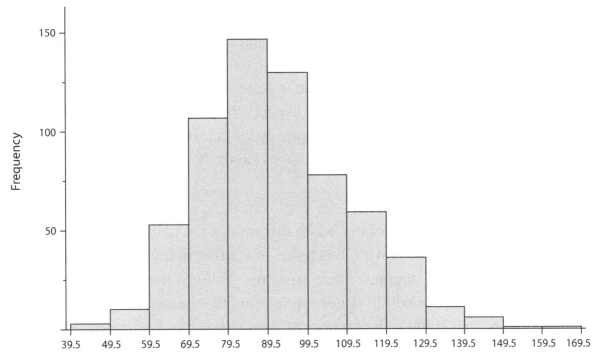

Figure 1. Histogram of scores on a psychology test.

The histogram makes it plain that most of the scores are in the middle of the distribution, with fewer scores in the extremes. You can also see that the distribution is not symmetric: the scores extend to the right farther than they do to the left. The distribution is therefore said to be skewed. (We'll have more to say about shapes of distributions in Chapter 3.)

In our example, the observations are whole numbers. Histograms can also be used when the scores are measured on a more continuous scale such as the length of time (in milliseconds) required to perform a task. In this case, there is no need to worry about fence sitters since they are improbable. (It would be quite a coincidence for a task to require exactly 7 seconds, measured to the nearest thousandth of a second.) We are therefore free to choose whole numbers as boundaries for our class intervals, for example, 4000, 5000, etc. The class frequency is then the number of observations that are greater than or equal to the lower bound, and strictly less than the upper bound. For example, one interval might hold times from 4000 to 4999 milliseconds. Using whole numbers as boundaries avoids a cluttered appearance, and is the practice of many computer programs that create histograms. Note also that some computer programs label the middle of each interval rather than the end points.

Histograms can be based on relative frequencies instead of actual frequencies. Histograms based on relative frequencies show the proportion of scores in each interval rather than the number of scores. In this case, the Y-axis runs from 0 to 1 (or somewhere in between if there are no extreme proportions). You can change a histogram based on frequencies to one based on relative frequencies by (a) dividing each class frequency by the total number of observations, and then (b) plotting the quotients on the Y-axis (labeled as proportion).

There is more to be said about the widths of the class intervals, sometimes called bin widths. Your choice of bin width determines the number of class intervals. This decision, along with the choice of starting point for the first interval, affects the shape of the histogram. There are some "rules of thumb" that can help you choose an appropriate width. (But keep in mind that none of the rules is perfect.) Sturges' rule is to set the number of intervals as close as possible to $1 + Log_2(N)$, where $Log_2(N)$ is the base 2 log of the number of observations. The formula can also be written as $1 + 3.3 Log_{10}(N)$ where $Log_{10}(N)$ is the log base 10 of the number of observations. According to Sturges' rule, 1000 observations would be graphed with 11 class intervals since 10 is the closest integer to $Log_2(1000)$. We prefer the Rice rule, which is to set the number of intervals to twice the cube root of the number of observations. In the case of 1000 observations, the Rice rule yields 20 intervals instead of the 11 recommended by Sturges' rule. For the psychology test example used above, Sturges' rule recommends 10 intervals while the Rice rule recommends 17. In the end, we compromised and chose 13 intervals for Figure 1 to create a histogram that seemed clearest. The best advice is to experiment with different choices of width, and to choose a histogram according to how well it communicates the shape of the distribution.

To provide experience in constructing histograms, we have developed an interactive demonstration (external link; Java required). The demonstration reveals the consequences of different choices of bin width and of lower boundary for the first interval.

Frequency Polygons

by David M. Lane

Prerequisites
• Chapter 2: Histograms

Learning Objectives
1. Create and interpret frequency polygons
2. Create and interpret cumulative frequency polygons
3. Create and interpret overlaid frequency polygons

Frequency polygons are a graphical device for understanding the shapes of distributions. They serve the same purpose as histograms, but are especially helpful for comparing sets of data. Frequency polygons are also a good choice for displaying cumulative frequency distributions.

To create a frequency polygon, start just as for histograms, by choosing a class interval. Then draw an X-axis representing the values of the scores in your data. Mark the middle of each class interval with a tick mark, and label it with the middle value represented by the class. Draw the Y-axis to indicate the frequency of each class. Place a point in the middle of each class interval at the height corresponding to its frequency. Finally, connect the points. You should include one class interval below the lowest value in your data and one above the highest value. The graph will then touch the X-axis on both sides.

A frequency polygon for 642 psychology test scores shown in Figure 1 was constructed from the frequency table shown in Table 1.

Table 1. Frequency Distribution of Psychology Test Scores

Lower Limit	Upper Limit	Count	Cumulative Count
29.5	39.5	0	0
39.5	49.5	3	3
49.5	59.5	10	13
59.5	69.5	53	66
69.5	79.5	107	173

79.5	89.5	147	320
89.5	99.5	130	450
99.5	109.5	78	528
109.5	119.5	59	587
119.5	129.5	36	623
129.5	139.5	11	634
139.5	149.5	6	640
149.5	159.5	1	641
159.5	169.5	1	642
169.5	170.5	0	642

The first label on the X-axis is 35. This represents an interval extending from 29.5 to 39.5. Since the lowest test score is 46, this interval has a frequency of 0. The point labeled 45 represents the interval from 39.5 to 49.5. There are three scores in this interval. There are 147 scores in the interval that surrounds 85.

You can easily discern the shape of the distribution from Figure 1. Most of the scores are between 65 and 115. It is clear that the distribution is not symmetric inasmuch as good scores (to the right) trail off more gradually than poor scores (to the left). In the terminology of Chapter 3 (where we will study shapes of distributions more systematically), the distribution is skewed.

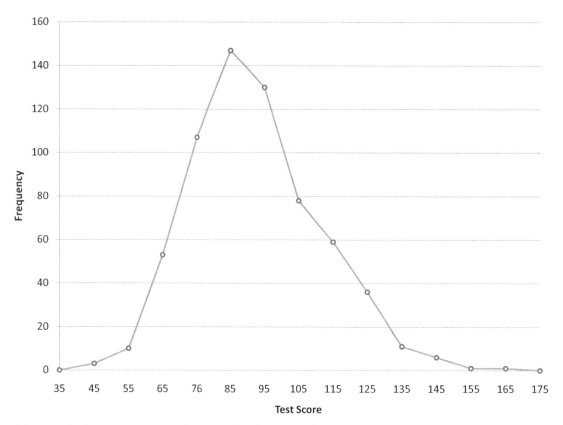

Figure 1. Frequency polygon for the psychology test scores.

A cumulative frequency polygon for the same test scores is shown in Figure 2. The graph is the same as before except that the Y value for each point is the number of students in the corresponding class interval plus all numbers in lower intervals. For example, there are no scores in the interval labeled "35," three in the interval "45," and 10 in the interval "55." Therefore, the Y value corresponding to "55" is 13. Since 642 students took the test, the cumulative frequency for the last interval is 642.

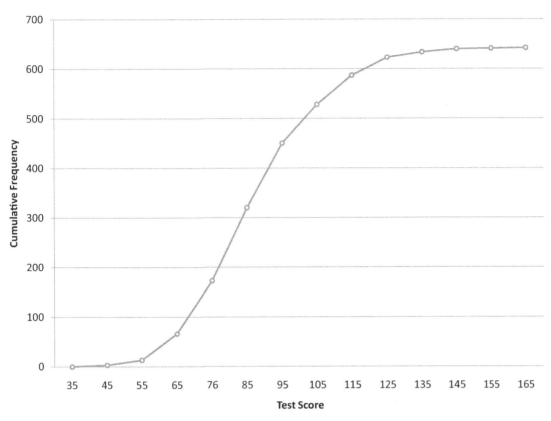

Figure 2. Cumulative frequency polygon for the psychology test scores.

Frequency polygons are useful for comparing distributions. This is achieved by overlaying the frequency polygons drawn for different data sets. Figure 3 provides an example. The data come from a task in which the goal is to move a computer cursor to a target on the screen as fast as possible. On 20 of the trials, the target was a small rectangle; on the other 20, the target was a large rectangle. Time to reach the target was recorded on each trial. The two distributions (one for each target) are plotted together in Figure 3. The figure shows that, although there is some overlap in times, it generally took longer to move the cursor to the small target than to the large one.

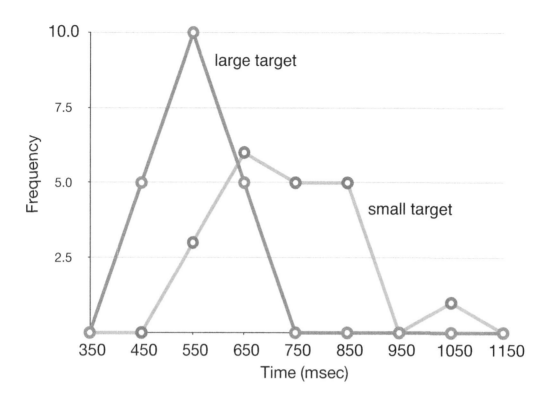

Figure 3. Overlaid frequency polygons.

It is also possible to plot two cumulative frequency distributions in the same graph. This is illustrated in Figure 4 using the same data from the cursor task. The difference in distributions for the two targets is again evident.

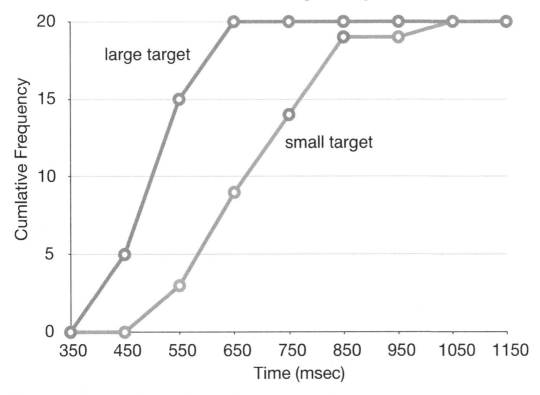

Figure 4. Overlaid cumulative frequency polygons.

Box Plots

by David M. Lane

Prerequisites
• Chapter 1: Percentiles
• Chapter 2: Histograms
• Chapter 2: Frequency Polygons

Learning Objectives
1. Define basic terms including hinges, H-spread, step, adjacent value, outside value, and far out value
2. Create a box plot
3. Create parallel box plots
4. Determine whether a box plot is appropriate for a given data set

We have already discussed techniques for visually representing data (see histograms and frequency polygons). In this section we present another important graph, called a box plot. Box plots are useful for identifying outliers and for comparing distributions. We will explain box plots with the help of data from an in-class experiment. Students in Introductory Statistics were presented with a page containing 30 colored rectangles. Their task was to name the colors as quickly as possible. Their times (in seconds) were recorded. We'll compare the scores for the 16 men and 31 women who participated in the experiment by making separate box plots for each gender. Such a display is said to involve parallel box plots.

There are several steps in constructing a box plot. The first relies on the 25th, 50th, and 75th percentiles in the distribution of scores. Figure 1 shows how these three statistics are used. For each gender we draw a box extending from the 25th percentile to the 75th percentile. The 50th percentile is drawn inside the box. Therefore, the bottom of each box is the 25th percentile, the top is the 75th percentile, and the line in the middle is the 50th percentile.

The data for the women in our sample are shown in Table 1.

Table 1. Women's times.

14	17	18	19	20	21	29
15	17	18	19	20	22	
16	17	18	19	20	23	
16	17	18	20	20	24	
17	18	18	20	21	24	

For these data, the 25th percentile is 17, the 50th percentile is 19, and the 75th percentile is 20. For the men (whose data are not shown), the 25th percentile is 19, the 50th percentile is 22.5, and the 75th percentile is 25.5.

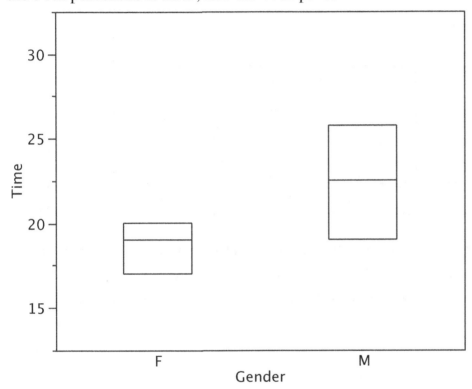

Figure 1. The first step in creating box plots.

Before proceeding, the terminology in Table 2 is helpful.

Table 2. Box plot terms and values for women's times.

Name	Formula	Value
Upper Hinge	75th Percentile	20
Lower Hinge	25th Percentile	17

H-Spread	Upper Hinge - Lower Hinge	3
Step	1.5 x H-Spread	4.5
Upper Inner Fence	Upper Hinge + 1 Step	24.5
Lower Inner Fence	Lower Hinge - 1 Step	12.5
Upper Outer Fence	Upper Hinge + 2 Steps	29
Lower Outer Fence	Lower Hinge - 2 Steps	8
Upper Adjacent	Largest value below Upper Inner Fence	24
Lower Adjacent	Smallest value above Lower Inner Fence	14
Outside Value	A value beyond an Inner Fence but not beyond an Outer Fence	29
Far Out Value	A value beyond an Outer Fence	None

Continuing with the box plots, we put "whiskers" above and below each box to give additional information about the spread of data. Whiskers are vertical lines that end in a horizontal stroke. Whiskers are drawn from the upper and lower hinges to the upper and lower adjacent values (24 and 14 for the women's data).

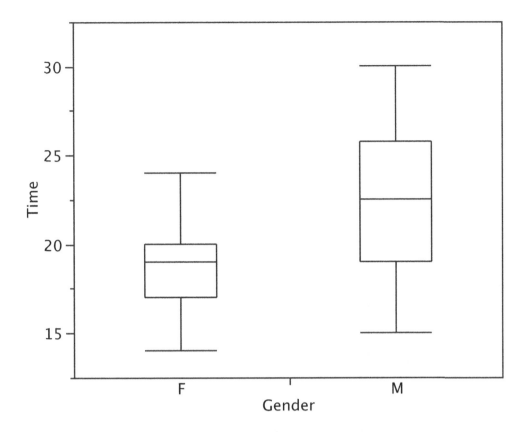

Figure 2. The box plots with the whiskers drawn.

Although we don't draw whiskers all the way to outside or far out values, we still wish to represent them in our box plots. This is achieved by adding additional marks beyond the whiskers. Specifically, outside values are indicated by small "o's" and far out values are indicated by asterisks (*). In our data, there are no far-out values and just one outside value. This outside value of 29 is for the women and is shown in Figure 3.

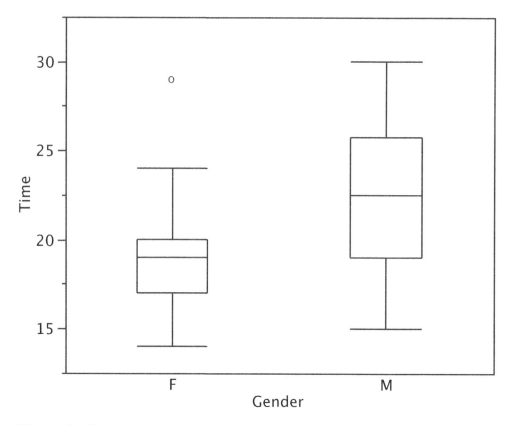

Figure 3. The box plots with the outside value shown.

There is one more mark to include in box plots (although sometimes it is omitted). We indicate the mean score for a group by inserting a plus sign. Figure 4 shows the result of adding means to our box plots.

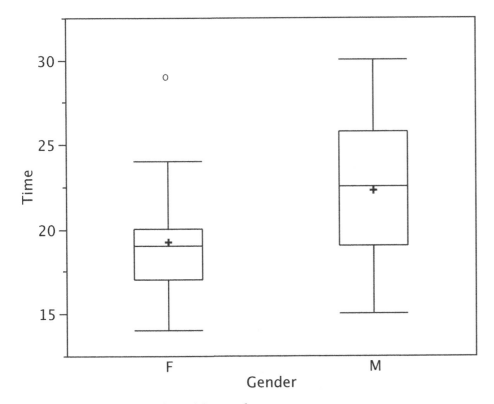

Figure 4. The completed box plots.

Figure 4 provides a revealing summary of the data. Since half the scores in a distribution are between the hinges (recall that the hinges are the 25th and 75th percentiles), we see that half the women's times are between 17 and 20 seconds whereas half the men's times are between 19 and 25.5 seconds. We also see that women generally named the colors faster than the men did, although one woman was slower than almost all of the men. Figure 5 shows the box plot for the women's data with detailed labels.

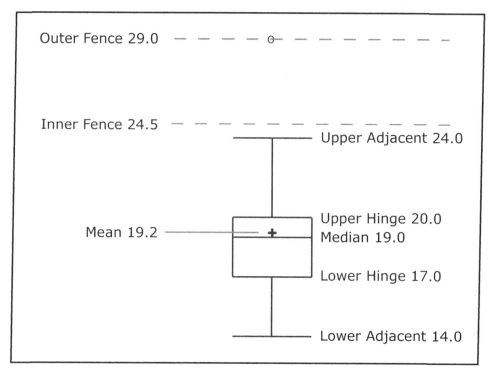

Figure 5. The box plots for the women's data with detailed labels.

Box plots provide basic information about a distribution. For example, a distribution with a positive skew would have a longer whisker in the positive direction than in the negative direction. A larger mean than median would also indicate a positive skew. Box plots are good at portraying extreme values and are especially good at showing differences between distributions. However, many of the details of a distribution are not revealed in a box plot and to examine these details one should use create a histogram and/or a stem and leaf display.

Variations on box plots

Statistical analysis programs may offer options on how box plots are created. For example, the box plots in Figure 6 are constructed from our data but differ from the previous box plots in several ways.
1. It does not mark outliers.
2. The means are indicated by green lines rather than plus signs.
3. The mean of all scores is indicated by a gray line.
4. Individual scores are represented by dots. Since the scores have been rounded to the nearest second, any given dot might represent more than one score.

5. The box for the women is wider than the box for the men because the widths of the boxes are proportional to the number of subjects of each gender (31 women and 16 men).

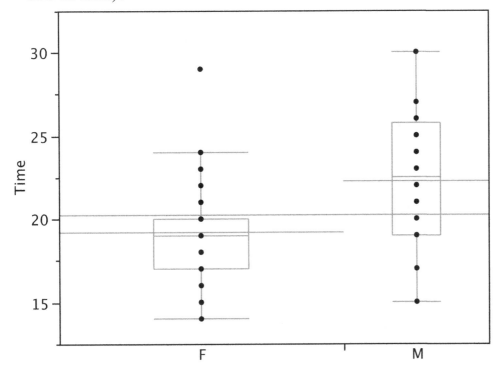

Figure 6. Box plots showing the individual scores and the means.

Each dot in Figure 6 represents a group of subjects with the same score (rounded to the nearest second). An alternative graphing technique is to jitter the points. This means spreading out different dots at the same horizontal position, one dot for each subject. The exact horizontal position of a dot is determined randomly (under the constraint that different dots don't overlap exactly). Spreading out the dots helps you to see multiple occurrences of a given score. However, depending on the dot size and the screen resolution, some points may be obscured even if the points are jittered. Figure 7 shows what jittering looks like.

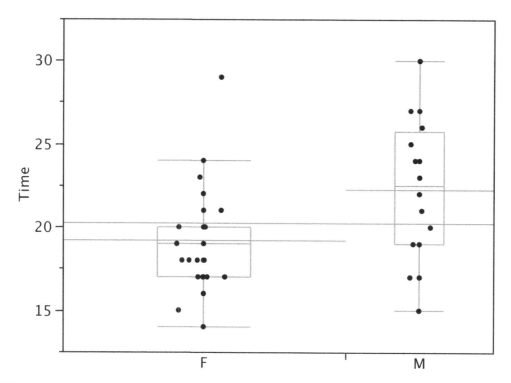

Figure 7. Box plots with the individual scores jittered.

Different styles of box plots are best for different situations, and there are no firm rules for which to use. When exploring your data, you should try several ways of visualizing them. Which graphs you include in your report should depend on how well different graphs reveal the aspects of the data you consider most important.

Bar Charts

by David M. Lane

Prerequisites
• Chapter 2: Graphing Qualitative Variables

Learning Objectives
1. Create and interpret bar charts
2. Judge whether a bar chart or another graph such as a box plot would be more appropriate

In the section on qualitative variables, we saw how bar charts could be used to illustrate the frequencies of different categories. For example, the bar chart shown in Figure 1 shows how many purchasers of iMac computers were previous Macintosh users, previous Windows users, and new computer purchasers.

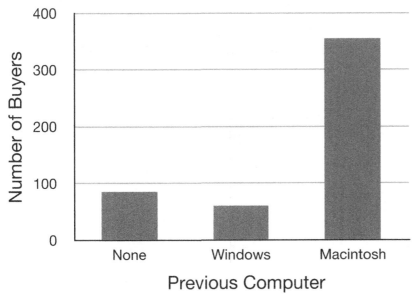

Figure 1. iMac buyers as a function of previous computer ownership.

In this section we show how bar charts can be used to present other kinds of quantitative information, not just frequency counts. The bar chart in Figure 2 shows the percent increases in the Dow Jones, Standard and Poor 500 (S & P), and Nasdaq stock indexes from May 24th 2000 to May 24th 2001. Notice that both the S & P and the Nasdaq had "negative increases" which means that they decreased in value. In this bar chart, the Y-axis is not frequency but rather the signed quantity *percentage increase*.

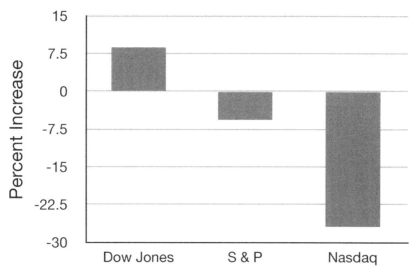

Figure 2. Percent increase in three stock indexes from May 24th 2000 to
May 24th 2001.

Bar charts are particularly effective for showing change over time. Figure 3, for
example, shows the percent increase in the Consumer Price Index (CPI) over four
three-month periods. The fluctuation in inflation is apparent in the graph.

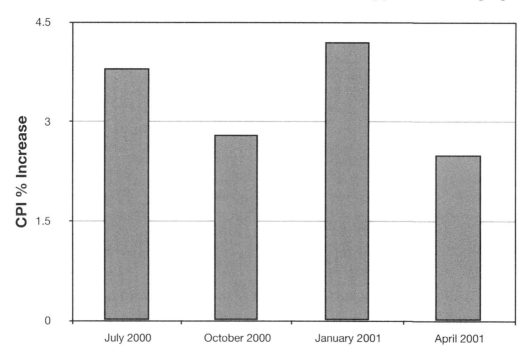

Figure 3. Percent change in the CPI over time. Each bar represents percent increase for the three months ending at the date indicated.

Bar charts are often used to compare the means of different experimental conditions. Figure 4 shows the mean time it took one of us (DL) to move the cursor to either a small target or a large target. On average, more time was required for small targets than for large ones.

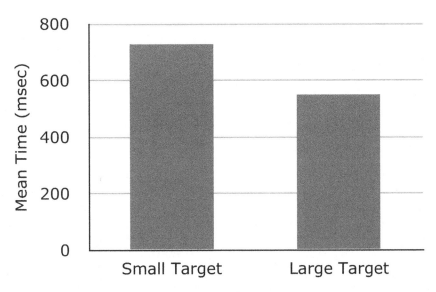

Figure 4. Bar chart showing the means for the two conditions.

Although bar charts can display means, we do not recommend them for this purpose. Box plots should be used instead since they provide more information than bar charts without taking up more space. For example, a box plot of the cursor-movement data is shown in Figure 5. You can see that Figure 5 reveals more about the distribution of movement times than does Figure 4.

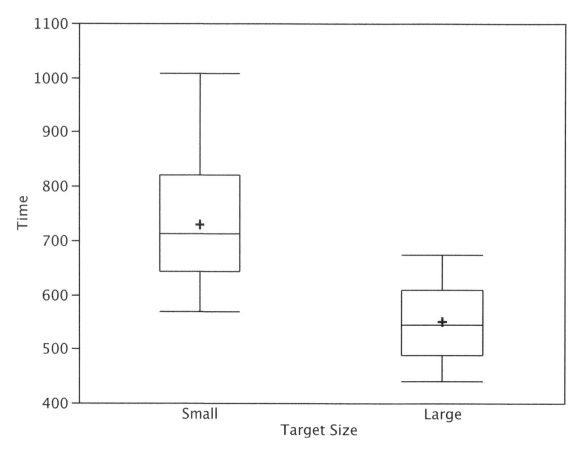

Figure 5. Box plots of times to move the cursor to the small and large
        targets.

The section on qualitative variables presented earlier in this chapter discussed the use of bar charts for comparing distributions. Some common graphical mistakes were also noted. The earlier discussion applies equally well to the use of bar charts to display quantitative variables.

Line Graphs

by David M. Lane

Prerequisites
• Chapter 2: Bar Charts

Learning Objectives
1. Create and interpret line graphs
2. Judge whether a line graph would be appropriate for a given data set

A line graph is a bar graph with the tops of the bars represented by points joined by lines (the rest of the bar is suppressed). For example, Figure 1 was presented in the section on bar charts and shows changes in the Consumer Price Index (CPI) over time.

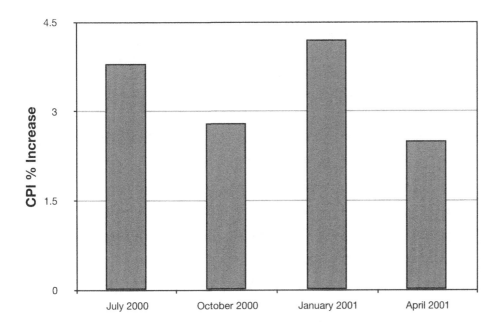

Figure 1. A bar chart of the percent change in the CPI over time. Each bar represents percent increase for the three months ending at the date indicated.

A line graph of these same data is shown in Figure 2. Although the figures are similar, the line graph emphasizes the change from period to period.

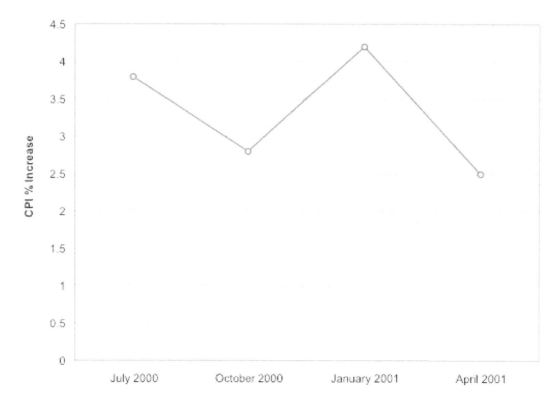

Figure 2. A line graph of the percent change in the CPI over time. Each point represents percent increase for the three months ending at the date indicated.

Line graphs are appropriate only when both the X- and Y-axes display ordered (rather than qualitative) variables. Although bar charts can also be used in this situation, line graphs are generally better at comparing changes over time. Figure 3, for example, shows percent increases and decreases in five components of the CPI. The figure makes it easy to see that medical costs had a steadier progression than the other components. Although you could create an analogous bar chart, its interpretation would not be as easy.

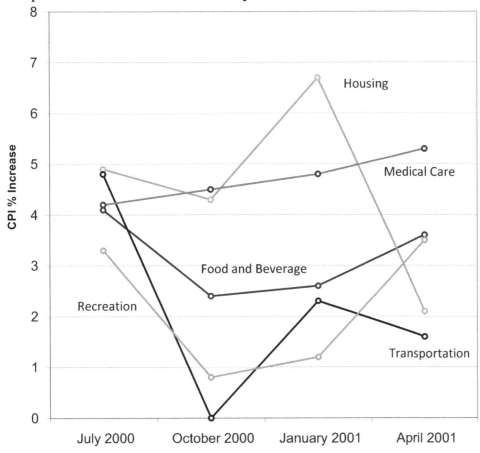

Figure 3. A line graph of the percent change in five components of the CPI over time.

Let us stress that it is misleading to use a line graph when the X-axis contains merely qualitative variables. Figure 4 inappropriately shows a line graph of the card game data from Yahoo, discussed in the section on qualitative variables. The defect in Figure 4 is that it gives the false impression that the games are naturally ordered in a numerical way.

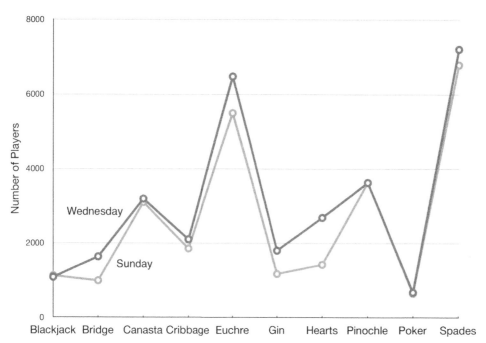

Figure 4. A line graph, inappropriately used, depicting the number of people playing different card games on Wednesday and Sunday.

Dot Plots

by David M. Lane

Prerequisites
• Chapter 2: Bar Charts

Learning Objectives
1. Create and interpret dot plots
2. Judge whether a dot plot would be appropriate for a given data set

Dot plots can be used to display various types of information. Figure 1 uses a dot plot to display the number of M & M's of each color found in a bag of M & M's. Each dot represents a single M & M. From the figure, you can see that there were 3 blue M & M's, 19 brown M & M's, etc.

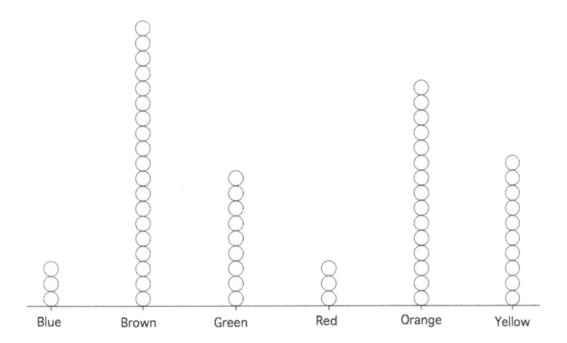

Figure 1. A dot plot showing the number of M & M's of various colors in a bag of
    M & M's.

The dot plot in Figure 2 shows the number of people playing various card
games on the Yahoo website on a Wednesday. Unlike Figure 1, the location rather
than the number of dots represents the frequency.

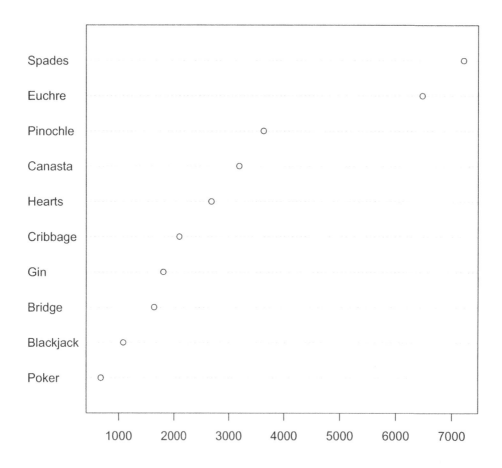

Figure 2. A dot plot showing the number of people playing various card games on a
Wednesday.

The dot plot in Figure 3 shows the number of people playing on a Sunday
and on a Wednesday. This graph makes it easy to compare the popularity of the
games separately for the two days, but does not make it easy to compare the
popularity of a given game on the two days.

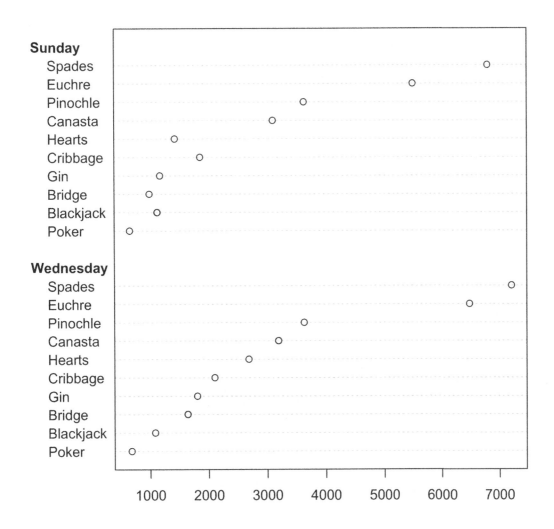

Figure 3. A dot plot showing the number of people playing various card games on a Sunday and on a Wednesday.

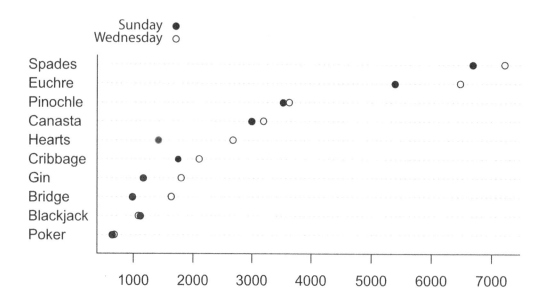

Figure 4. An alternate way of showing the number of people playing various card games on a Sunday and on a Wednesday.

The dot plot in Figure 4 makes it easy to compare the days of the week for specific games while still portraying differences among games.

Statistical Literacy

by Seyd Ercan and David Lane

Prerequisites
* Chapter 2: Graphing Distributions

Fox News aired the line graph below showing the number unemployed during four quarters between 2007 and 2010.

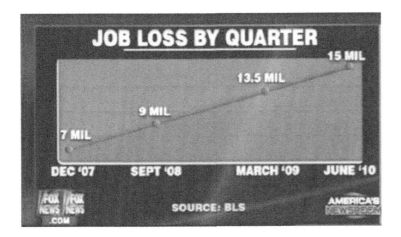

What do you think?
Does Fox News' line graph provide misleading information? Why or Why not?

Think about this before continuing:

> There are major flaws with the Fox News graph. First, the title of the graph is misleading. Although the data show the number unemployed, Fox News' graph is titled "Job Loss by Quarter." Second, the intervals on the X-axis are misleading. Although there are 6 months between September 2008 and March 2009 and 15 months between March 2009 and June 2010, the intervals are represented in the graph by very similar lengths. This gives the false impression that unemployment increased steadily.

> The graph presented below is corrected so that distances on the X-axis are proportional to the number of days between the

dates. This graph shows clearly that the rate of increase in the number unemployed is greater between September 2008 and March 2009 than it is between March 2009 and June 2010.

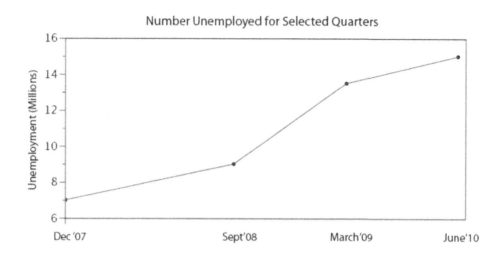

References

Tufte, E. R. (2001). *The Visual Display of Quantitative Information* (2nd ed.) (p. 178). Cheshire, CT: Graphics Press.

Exercises

Prerequisites
• All material presented in the Graphing Distributions chapter

1. Name some ways to graph quantitative variables and some ways to graph qualitative variables.

2. Based on the frequency polygon displayed below, the most common test grade was around what score? Explain.

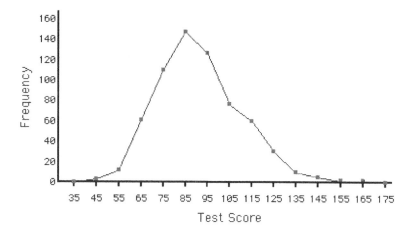

3. An experiment compared the ability of three groups of participants to remember briefly-presented chess positions. The data are shown below. The numbers represent the number of pieces correctly remembered from three chess positions. Create side-by-side box plots for these three groups. What can you say about the differences between these groups from the box plots?

Non-players	Beginners	Tournament players
22.1	32.5	40.1
22.3	37.1	45.6
26.2	39.1	51.2
29.6	40.5	56.4
31.7	45.5	58.1
33.5	51.3	71.1
38.9	52.6	74.9
39.7	55.7	75.9
43.2	55.9	80.3
43.2	57.7	85.3

4. You have to decide between displaying your data with a histogram or with a stem and leaf display. What factor(s) would affect your choice?

5. In a box plot, what percent of the scores are between the lower and upper hinges?

6. A student has decided to display the results of his project on the number of hours people in various countries slept per night. He compared the sleeping patterns of people from the US, Brazil, France, Turkey, China, Egypt, Canada, Norway, and Spain. He was planning on using a line graph to display this data. Is a line graph appropriate? What might be a better choice for a graph?

7. For the data from the 1977 Stat. and Biom. 200 class for eye color, construct:

   a. pie graph

   b. horizontal bar graph

   c. vertical bar graph

   d. a frequency table with the relative frequency of each eye color

Eye Color	Number of students
Brown	11
Blue	10
Green	4
Gray	1

(Question submitted by J. Warren, UNH)

8. A graph appears below showing the number of adults and children who prefer each type of soda. There were 130 adults and kids surveyed. Discuss some ways in which the graph below could be improved.

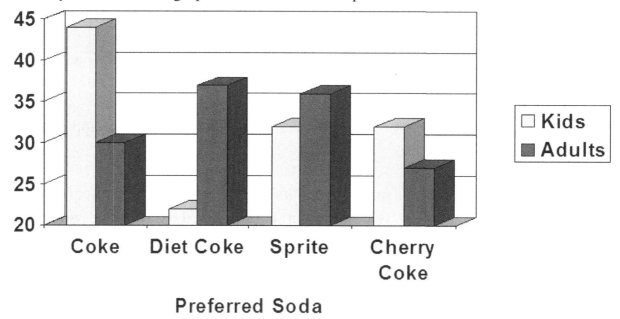

9. Which of the box plots on the graph has a large positive skew? Which has a large negative skew?

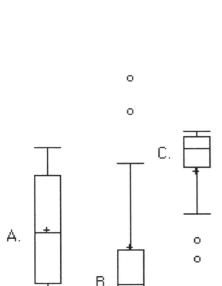

Question from Case Studies

Angry Moods (AM) case study

10. (AM) Is there a difference in how much males and females use aggressive behavior to improve an angry mood? For the "Anger-Out" scores:

    a. Create parallel box plots.

    b. Create a back to back stem and leaf displays (You may have trouble finding a computer to do this so you may have to do it by hand. Use a fixed-width font such as Courier.)

11. (AM) Create parallel box plots for the Anger-In scores by sports participation.

12. (AM) Plot a histogram of the distribution of the Control-Out scores.

13. (AM) Create a bar graph comparing the mean Control-In score for the athletes and the non- athletes. What would be a better way to display this data?

14. (AM) Plot parallel box plots of the Anger Expression Index by sports participation. Does it look like there are any outliers? Which group reported expressing more anger?

Flatulence (F) case study

15. (F) Plot a histogram of the variable "per day."

16. (F) Create parallel box plots of "how long" as a function gender. Why is the 25th percentile not showing? What can you say about the results?

17. (F) Create a stem and leaf plot of the variable "how long." What can you say about the shape of the distribution?

Physicians' Reactions (PR) case study

18. (PR) Create box plots comparing the time expected to be spent with the average-weight and overweight patients.

19. (PR) Plot histograms of the time spent with the average-weight and overweight patients.

20. (PR) To which group does the patient with the highest expected time belong?

Smiles and Leniency (SL) case study

21. (SL) Create parallel box plots for the four conditions.

22. (SL) Create back to back stem and leaf displays for the false smile and neutral conditions. (It may be hard to find a computer program to do this for you, so be prepared to do it by hand).

ADHD Treatment (AT) case study

23. (AT) Create a line graph of the data. Do certain dosages appear to be more effective than others?

24. (AT) Create a stem and leaf plot of the number of correct responses of the participants after taking the placebo (d0 variable). What can you say about the shape of the distribution?

25. (AT) Create box plots for the four conditions. You may have to rearrange the data to get a computer program to create the box plots.

SAT and College GPA (SG) case study

26. (SG)Create histograms and stem and leaf displays of both high-school grade point average and university grade point average. In what way(s) do the distributions differ?

27. The April 10th issue of the Journal of the American Medical Association reports a study on the effects of anti-depressants. The study involved 340 subjects who were being treated for major depression. The subjects were randomly assigned to receive one of three treatments: St. John's wort (an herb), Zoloft (Pfizer's cousin of Lilly's Prozac) or placebo for an 8-week period. The following are the mean scores (approximately) for the three groups of subjects over the eight-week experiment. The first column is the baseline. Lower scores mean less depression. Create a graph to display these means.

Placebo	22.5	19.1	17.9	17.1	16.2	15.1	12.1	12.3
Wort	23.0	20.2	18.2	18.0	16.5	16.1	14.2	13.0
Zoloft	22.4	19.2	16.6	15.5	14.2	13.1	11.8	10.5

28. For the graph below, of heights of singers in a large chorus. What word starting with the letter "B" best describes the distribution?

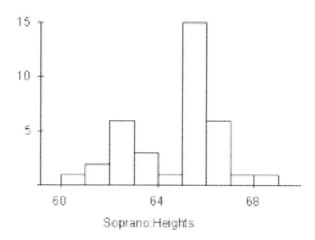

Soprano:Heights

29. Pretend you are constructing a histogram for describing the distribution of salaries for individuals who are 40 years or older, but are not yet retired. (a) What is on the Y-axis? Explain. (b) What is on the X-axis? Explain. (c) What would be the probable shape of the salary distribution? Explain why.

3. Summarizing Distributions

A. Central Tendency

   1. What is Central Tendency

   2. Measures of Central Tendency

   3. Median and Mean

   4. Additional Measures

   5. Comparing measures

B. Variability

   1. Measures of Variability

C. Shape

   1. Effects of Transformations

   2. Variance Sum Law I

D. Exercises

Descriptive statistics often involves using a few numbers to summarize a distribution. One important aspect of a distribution is where its center is located. Measures of central tendency are discussed first. A second aspect of a distribution is how spread out it is. In other words, how much the numbers in the distribution vary from one another. The second section describes measures of variability. Distributions can differ in shape. Some distributions are symmetric whereas others have long tails in just one direction. The third section describes measures of the shape of distributions. The final two sections concern (1) how transformations affect measures summarizing distributions and (2) the variance sum law, an important relationship involving a measure of variability.

What is Central Tendency?

by David M. Lane and Heidi Ziemer

Prerequisites
- Chapter 1: Distributions
- Chapter 2: Stem and Leaf Displays

Learning Objectives
1. Identify situations in which knowing the center of a distribution would be valuable
2. Give three different ways the center of a distribution can be defined
3. Describe how the balance is different for symmetric distributions than it is for asymmetric distributions.

What is "central tendency," and why do we want to know the central tendency of a group of scores? Let us first try to answer these questions intuitively. Then we will proceed to a more formal discussion.

Imagine this situation: You are in a class with just four other students, and the five of you took a 5-point pop quiz. Today your instructor is walking around the room, handing back the quizzes. She stops at your desk and hands you your paper. Written in bold black ink on the front is "3/5." How do you react? Are you happy with your score of 3 or disappointed? How do you decide? You might calculate your percentage correct, realize it is 60%, and be appalled. But it is more likely that when deciding how to react to your performance, you will want additional information. What additional information would you like?

If you are like most students, you will immediately ask your neighbors, "Whad'ja get?" and then ask the instructor, "How did the class do?" In other words, the additional information you want is how your quiz score compares to other students' scores. You therefore understand the importance of comparing your score to the class distribution of scores. Should your score of 3 turn out to be among the higher scores, then you'll be pleased after all. On the other hand, if 3 is among the lower scores in the class, you won't be quite so happy.

This idea of comparing individual scores to a distribution of scores is fundamental to statistics. So let's explore it further, using the same example (the pop quiz you took with your four classmates). Three possible outcomes are shown in Table 1. They are labeled "Dataset A," "Dataset B," and "Dataset C." Which of the three datasets would make you happiest? In other words, in comparing your score with your fellow students' scores, in which dataset would your score of 3 be the most impressive?

In Dataset A, everyone's score is 3. This puts your score at the exact center of the distribution. You can draw satisfaction from the fact that you did as well as everyone else. But of course it cuts both ways: everyone else did just as well as you.

Table 1. Three possible datasets for the 5-point make-up quiz.

Student	Dataset A	Dataset B	Dataset C
You	3	3	3
John's	3	4	2
Maria's	3	4	2
Shareecia's	3	4	2
Luther's	3	5	1

Now consider the possibility that the scores are described as in Dataset B. This is a depressing outcome even though your score is no different than the one in Dataset A. The problem is that the other four students had higher grades, putting yours below the **center of the distribution**.

Finally, let's look at Dataset C. This is more like it! All of your classmates score lower than you so your score is above the center of the distribution.

Now let's change the example in order to develop more insight into the center of a distribution. Figure 1 shows the results of an experiment on memory for chess positions. Subjects were shown a chess position and then asked to reconstruct it on an empty chess board. The number of pieces correctly placed was recorded. This was repeated for two more chess positions. The scores represent the total number of chess pieces correctly placed for the three chess positions. The maximum possible score was 89.

```
        8  05
        7  156

        6  233

        5  168

   330  4  06

  9420  3

   622  2
```

Figure 1. Back-to-back stem and leaf display. The left side shows the
memory scores of the non-players. The right side shows the scores of
the tournament players.

Two groups are compared. On the left are people who don't play chess. On the
right are people who play a great deal (tournament players). It is clear that the
location of the center of the distribution for the non-players is much lower than the
center of the distribution for the tournament players.

We're sure you get the idea now about the center of a distribution. It is time
to move beyond intuition. We need a formal definition of the center of a
distribution. In fact, we'll offer you three definitions! This is not just generosity on
our part. There turn out to be (at least) three different ways of thinking about the
center of a distribution, all of them useful in various contexts. In the remainder of
this section we attempt to communicate the idea behind each concept. In the
succeeding sections we will give statistical measures for these concepts of central
tendency.

Definitions of Center

Now we explain the three different ways of defining the center of a distribution. All
three are called measures of central tendency.

Balance Scale

One definition of central tendency is the point at which the distribution is in
balance. Figure 2 shows the distribution of the five numbers 2, 3, 4, 9, 16 placed
upon a balance scale. If each number weighs one pound, and is placed at its

position along the number line, then it would be possible to balance them by placing a fulcrum at 6.8.

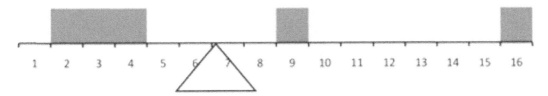

Figure 2. A balance scale.

For another example, consider the distribution shown in Figure 3. It is balanced by placing the fulcrum in the geometric middle.

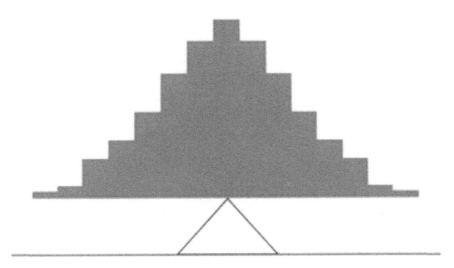

Figure 3. A distribution balanced on the tip of a triangle.

Figure 4 illustrates that the same distribution can't be balanced by placing the fulcrum to the left of center.

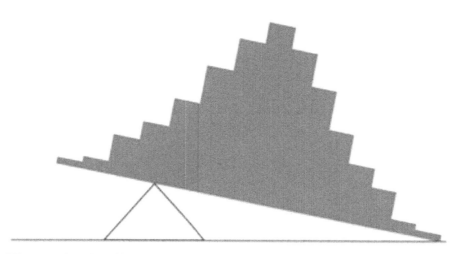

Figure 4. The distribution is not balanced.

Figure 5 shows an asymmetric distribution. To balance it, we cannot put the fulcrum halfway between the lowest and highest values (as we did in Figure 3). Placing the fulcrum at the "half way" point would cause it to tip towards the left.

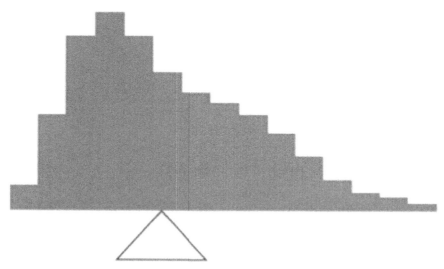

Figure 5. An asymmetric distribution balanced on the tip of a triangle.

The balance point defines one sense of a distribution's center.

Smallest Absolute Deviation

Another way to define the center of a distribution is based on the concept of the sum of the absolute deviations (differences). Consider the distribution made up of the five numbers 2, 3, 4, 9, 16. Let's see how far the distribution is from 10 (picking a number arbitrarily). Table 2 shows the sum of the absolute deviations of these numbers from the number 10.

Table 2. An example of the sum of absolute deviations

Values	Absolute Deviations from 10
2	8
3	7
4	6
9	1
16	6
Sum	28

The first row of the table shows that the absolute value of the difference between 2 and 10 is 8; the second row shows that the absolute difference between 3 and 10 is 7, and similarly for the other rows. When we add up the five absolute deviations, we get 28. So, the sum of the absolute deviations from 10 is 28. Likewise, the sum of the absolute deviations from 5 equals $3 + 2 + 1 + 4 + 11 = 21$. So, the sum of the absolute deviations from 5 is smaller than the sum of the absolute deviations from 10. In this sense, 5 is closer, overall, to the other numbers than is 10.

We are now in a position to define a second measure of central tendency, this time in terms of absolute deviations. Specifically, according to our second definition, the center of a distribution is the number for which the sum of the absolute deviations is smallest. As we just saw, the sum of the absolute deviations from 10 is 28 and the sum of the absolute deviations from 5 is 21. Is there a value for which the sum of the absolute deviations is even smaller than 21? Yes. For these data, there is a value for which the sum of absolute deviations is only 20. See if you can find it.

Smallest Squared Deviation

We shall discuss one more way to define the center of a distribution. It is based on the concept of the sum of squared deviations (differences). Again, consider the distribution of the five numbers 2, 3, 4, 9, 16. Table 3 shows the sum of the squared deviations of these numbers from the number 10.

Table 3. An example of the sum of squared deviations.

Values	Squared Deviations from 10
2	64
3	49
4	36
9	1
16	36
Sum	186

The first row in the table shows that the squared value of the difference between 2 and 10 is 64; the second row shows that the squared difference between 3 and 10 is 49, and so forth. When we add up all these squared deviations, we get 186. Changing the target from 10 to 5, we calculate the sum of the squared deviations from 5 as $9 + 4 + 1 + 16 + 121 = 151$. So, the sum of the squared deviations from 5 is smaller than the sum of the squared deviations from 10. Is there a value for which the sum of the squared deviations is even smaller than 151? Yes, it is possible to reach 134.8. Can you find the target number for which the sum of squared deviations is 134.8?

The target that minimizes the sum of squared deviations provides another useful definition of central tendency (the last one to be discussed in this section). It can be challenging to find the value that minimizes this sum.

Measures of Central Tendency

by David M. Lane

Prerequisites
• Chapter 1: Percentiles
• Chapter 1: Distributions
• Chapter 3: Central Tendency

Learning Objectives
1. Compute mean
2. Compute median
3. Compute mode

In the previous section we saw that there are several ways to define central tendency. This section defines the three most common measures of central tendency: the mean, the median, and the mode. The relationships among these measures of central tendency and the definitions given in the previous section will probably not be obvious to you.

This section gives only the basic definitions of the mean, median and mode. A further discussion of the relative merits and proper applications of these statistics is presented in a later section.

Arithmetic Mean

The arithmetic mean is the most common measure of central tendency. It is simply the sum of the numbers divided by the number of numbers. The symbol "μ" is used for the mean of a population. The symbol "M" is used for the mean of a sample. The formula for μ is shown below:

$$\mu = \frac{\sum X}{N}$$

where $\sum X$ is the sum of all the numbers in the population and N is the number of numbers in the population.

The formula for M is essentially identical:

$$M = \frac{\Sigma X}{N}$$

where ΣX is the sum of all the numbers in the sample and N is the number of numbers in the sample.

As an example, the mean of the numbers 1, 2, 3, 6, 8 is 20/5 = 4 regardless of whether the numbers constitute the entire population or just a sample from the population.

Table 1 shows the number of touchdown (TD) passes thrown by each of the 31 teams in the National Football League in the 2000 season. The mean number of touchdown passes thrown is 20.4516 as shown below.

$$\mu = \frac{\Sigma X}{N} = \frac{634}{31} = 20.4516$$

Table 1. Number of touchdown passes.

37, 33, 33, 32, 29, 28,
28, 23, 22, 22, 22, 21,
21, 21, 20, 20, 19, 19,
18, 18, 18, 18, 16, 15,
14, 14, 14, 12, 12, 9, 6

Although the arithmetic mean is not the only "mean" (there is also a geometric mean), it is by far the most commonly used. Therefore, if the term "mean" is used without specifying whether it is the arithmetic mean, the geometric mean, or some other mean, it is assumed to refer to the arithmetic mean.

Median

The median is also a frequently used measure of central tendency. The median is the midpoint of a distribution: the same number of scores is above the median as below it. For the data in Table 1, there are 31 scores. The 16th highest score (which equals 20) is the median because there are 15 scores below the 16th score and 15 scores above the 16th score. The median can also be thought of as the 50th percentile.

Computation of the Median

When there is an odd number of numbers, the median is simply the middle number. For example, the median of 2, 4, and 7 is 4. When there is an even number of numbers, the median is the mean of the two middle numbers. Thus, the median of the numbers 2, 4, 7, 12 is:

$$\frac{(4 + 7)}{2} = 5.5$$

When there are numbers with the same values, then the formula for the third definition of the 50th percentile should be used.

Mode

The mode is the most frequently occurring value. For the data in Table 1, the mode is 18 since more teams (4) had 18 touchdown passes than any other number of touchdown passes. With continuous data, such as response time measured to many decimals, the frequency of each value is one since no two scores will be exactly the same (see discussion of continuous variables). Therefore the mode of continuous data is normally computed from a grouped frequency distribution. Table 2 shows a grouped frequency distribution for the target response time data. Since the interval with the highest frequency is 600-700, the mode is the middle of that interval (650).

Table 2. Grouped frequency distribution

Range	Frequency
500-600	3
600-700	6
700-800	5
800-900	5
900-1000	0
1000-1100	1

Median and Mean

by David M. Lane

Prerequisites
- Chapter 3: What is Central Tendency
- Chapter 3: Measures of Central Tendency

Learning Objectives
1. State when the mean and median are the same
2. State whether it is the mean or median that minimizes the mean absolute deviation
3. State whether it is the mean or median that minimizes the mean squared deviation
4. State whether it is the mean or median that is the balance point on a balance scale

In the section "What is central tendency," we saw that the center of a distribution could be defined three ways: (1) the point on which a distribution would balance, (2) the value whose average absolute deviation from all the other values is minimized, and (3) the value whose squared difference from all the other values is minimized. The mean is the point on which a distribution would balance, the median is the value that minimizes the sum of absolute deviations, and the mean is the value that minimizes the sum of the squared deviations.

Table 1 shows the absolute and squared deviations of the numbers 2, 3, 4, 9, and 16 from their median of 4 and their mean of 6.8. You can see that the sum of absolute deviations from the median (20) is smaller than the sum of absolute deviations from the mean (22.8). On the other hand, the sum of squared deviations from the median (174) is larger than the sum of squared deviations from the mean (134.8).

Table 1. Absolute and squared deviations from the median of 4 and the mean of 6.8.

Value	Absolute Deviation from Median	Absolute Deviation from Mean	Squared Deviation from Median	Squared Deviation from Mean
2	2	4.8	4	23.04
3	1	3.8	1	14.44
4	0	2.8	0	7.84
9	5	2.2	25	4.84
16	12	9.2	144	84.64
Total	20	22.8	174	134.8

Figure 1 shows that the distribution balances at the mean of 6.8 and not at the median of 4. The relative advantages and disadvantages of the mean and median are discussed in the section "Comparing Measures" later in this chapter.

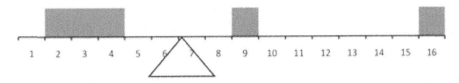

Figure 1. The distribution balances at the mean of 6.8 and not at the median of 4.0.

When a distribution is symmetric, then the mean and the median are the same. Consider the following distribution: 1, 3, 4, 5, 6, 7, 9. The mean and median are both 5. The mean, median, and mode are identical in the bell-shaped normal distribution.

Additional Measures of Central Tendency

by David M. Lane

Prerequisites
- Chapter 1: Percentiles
- Chapter 1: Distributions
- Chapter 3: What is Central Tendency
- Chapter 3: Measures of Central Tendency
- Chapter 3: Mean and Median

Learning Objectives
1. Compute the trimean
2. Compute the geometric mean directly
3. Compute the geometric mean using logs
4. Use the geometric to compute annual portfolio returns
5. Compute a trimmed mean

Although the mean, median, and mode are by far the most commonly used measures of central tendency, they are by no means the only measures. This section defines three additional measures of central tendency: the trimean, the geometric mean, and the trimmed mean. These measures will be discussed again in the section "Comparing Measures of Central Tendency."

Trimean

The trimean is a weighted average of the 25th percentile, the 50th percentile, and the 75th percentile. Letting P25 be the 25th percentile, P50 be the 50th and P75 be the 75th percentile, the formula for the trimean is:

$$Trimean = \frac{(P25 + 2P50 + P75)}{4}$$

Consider the data in Table 2. The 25th percentile is 15, the 50th is 20 and the 75th percentile is 23.

Table 1. Number of touchdown passes.

37, 33, 33, 32, 29, 28, 28, 23, 22, 22, 22, 21, 21, 21, 20,
20, 19, 19, 18, 18, 18, 18, 16, 15, 14, 14, 14, 12, 12, 9, 6

Table 2. Percentiles.

Percentile	Value
25	15
50	20
75	23

The trimean is therefore :

$$\frac{(15 + 2 \times 20 + 23)}{4} = \frac{78}{4} = 19.5$$

Geometric Mean

The geometric mean is computed by multiplying all the numbers together and then taking the nth root of the product. For example, for the numbers 1, 10, and 100, the product of all the numbers is: 1 x 10 x 100 = 1,000. Since there are three numbers, we take the cubed root of the product (1,000) which is equal to 10. The formula for the geometric mean is therefore

$$\left(\prod x\right)^{\frac{1}{N}}$$

where the symbol $\prod$ means to multiply. Therefore, the equation says to multiply all the values of X and then raise the result to the 1/Nth power. Raising a value to the 1/Nth power is, of course, the same as taking the Nth root of the value. In this case, $1000^{1/3}$ is the cube root of 1,000.

The geometric mean has a close relationship with logarithms. Table 3 shows the logs (base 10) of these three numbers. The arithmetic mean of the three logs is 1. The anti-log of this arithmetic mean of 1 is the geometric mean. The anti-log of 1 is $10^1 = 10$. Note that the geometric mean only makes sense if all the numbers are positive.

Table 3. Logarithms.

X	Log10(X)
1	0
10	1
100	2

The geometric mean is an appropriate measure to use for averaging rates. For example, consider a stock portfolio that began with a value of $1,000 and had annual returns of 13%, 22%, 12%, -5%, and -13%. Table 4 shows the value after each of the five years.

Table 4. Portfolio Returns

Year	Return	Value
1	13%	1,130
2	22%	1,379
3	12%	1,544
4	-5%	1,467
5	-13%	1,276

The question is how to compute average annual rate of return. The answer is to compute the geometric mean of the returns. Instead of using the percents, each return is represented as a multiplier indicating how much higher the value is after the year. This multiplier is 1.13 for a 13% return and 0.95 for a 5% loss. The multipliers for this example are 1.13, 1.22, 1.12, 0.95, and 0.87. The geometric mean of these multipliers is 1.05. Therefore, the average annual rate of return is 5%. Table 5 shows how a portfolio gaining 5% a year would end up with the same value ($1,276) as shown in Table 4.

Table 5. Portfolio Returns

Year	Return	Value

1	5%	1,050
2	5%	1,103
3	5%	1,158
4	5%	1,216
5	5%	1,276

Trimmed Mean

To compute a *trimmed mean*, you remove some of the higher and lower scores and compute the mean of the remaining scores. A mean trimmed 10% is a mean computed with 10% of the scores trimmed off: 5% from the bottom and 5% from the top. A mean trimmed 50% is computed by trimming the upper 25% of the scores and the lower 25% of the scores and computing the mean of the remaining scores. The trimmed mean is similar to the median which, in essence, trims the upper 49+% and the lower 49+% of the scores. Therefore the trimmed mean is a hybrid of the mean and the median. To compute the mean trimmed 20% for the touchdown pass data shown in Table 1, you remove the lower 10% of the scores (6, 9, and 12) as well as the upper 10% of the scores (33, 33, and 37) and compute the mean of the remaining 25 scores. This mean is 20.16.

Comparing Measures of Central Tendency

by David M. Lane

Prerequisites
- Chapter 1: Percentiles
- Chapter 1: Distributions
- Chapter 3: What is Central Tendency
- Chapter 3: Measures of Central Tendency
- Chapter 3: Mean and Median

Learning Objectives
1. Understand how the difference between the mean and median is affected by skew
2. State how the measures differ in symmetric distributions
3. State which measure(s) should be used to describe the center of a skewed distribution

How do the various measures of central tendency compare with each other? For symmetric distributions, the mean, median, trimean, and trimmed mean are equal, as is the mode except in bimodal distributions. Differences among the measures occur with skewed distributions. Figure 1 shows the distribution of 642 scores on an introductory psychology test. Notice this distribution has a slight positive skew.

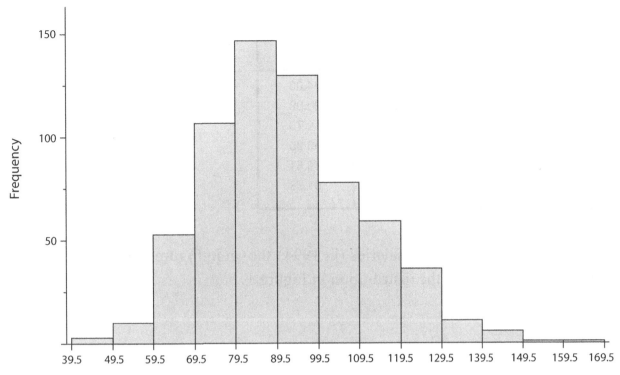

Figure 1. A distribution with a positive skew.

Measures of central tendency are shown in Table 1. Notice they do not differ
greatly, with the exception that the mode is considerably lower than the other
measures. When distributions have a positive skew, the mean is typically higher
than the median, although it may not be in bimodal distributions. For these data,
the mean of 91.58 is higher than the median of 90. Typically the trimean and
trimmed mean will fall between the median and the mean, although in this case,
the trimmed mean is slightly lower than the median. The geometric mean is lower
than all measures except the mode.

Table 1. Measures of central tendency for the test scores.

Measure	Value
Mode	84.00
Median	90.00
Geometric Mean	89.70
Trimean	90.25
Mean trimmed 50%	89.81
Mean	91.58

The distribution of baseball salaries (in 1994) shown in Figure 2 has a much more pronounced skew than the distribution in Figure 1.

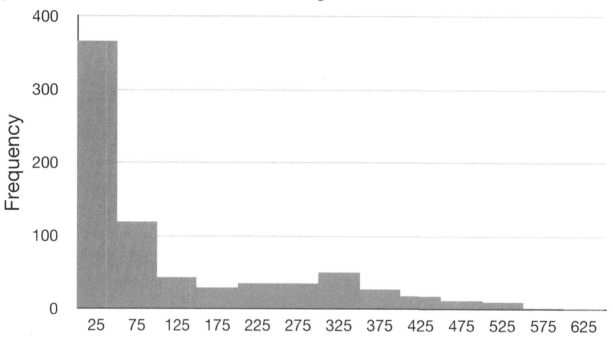

Figure 2. A distribution with a very large positive skew. This histogram
   shows the salaries of major league baseball players (in thousands of
   dollars).

Table 2 shows the measures of central tendency for these data. The large skew results in very different values for these measures. No single measure of central tendency is sufficient for data such as these. If you were asked the very general question: "So, what do baseball players make?" and answered with the mean of $1,183,000, you would not have told the whole story since only about one third of baseball players make that much. If you answered with the mode of $250,000 or the median of \$500,000, you would not be giving any indication that some players make many millions of dollars. Fortunately, there is no need to summarize a distribution with a single number. When the various measures differ, our opinion is that you should report the mean, median, and either the trimean or the mean trimmed 50%. Sometimes it is worth reporting the mode as well. In the media, the median is usually reported to summarize the center of skewed distributions. You will hear about median salaries and median prices of houses sold, etc. This is better than reporting only the mean, but it would be informative to hear more statistics.

Table 2. Measures of central tendency for baseball salaries (in thousands of dollars).

Measure	Value
Mode	250
Median	500
Geometric Mean	555
Trimean	792
Mean trimmed 50%	619
Mean	1,183

Measures of Variability

by David M. Lane

Prerequisites
- Chapter 1: Percentiles
- Chapter 1: Distributions
- Chapter 3: Measures of Central Tendency

Learning Objectives
1. Determine the relative variability of two distributions
2. Compute the range
3. Compute the inter-quartile range
4. Compute the variance in the population
5. Estimate the variance from a sample
6. Compute the standard deviation from the variance

What is Variability?

Variability refers to how "spread out" a group of scores is. To see what we mean by spread out, consider graphs in Figure 1. These graphs represent the scores on two quizzes. The mean score for each quiz is 7.0. Despite the equality of means, you can see that the distributions are quite different. Specifically, the scores on Quiz 1 are more densely packed and those on Quiz 2 are more spread out. The differences among students were much greater on Quiz 2 than on Quiz 1.

Quiz 1

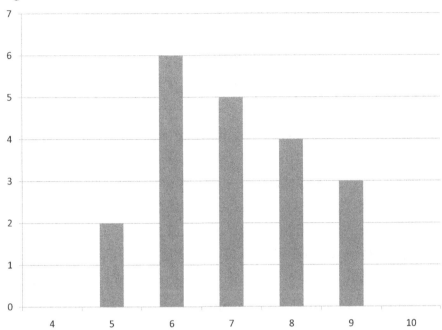

Quiz 2

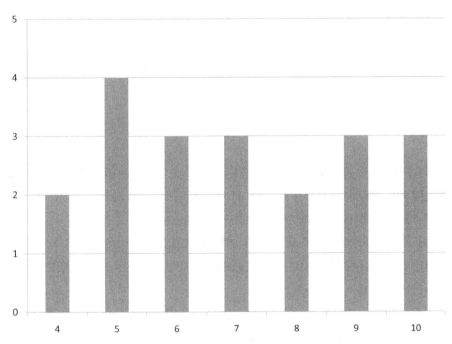

Figure 1. Bar charts of two quizzes.

The terms variability, spread, and dispersion are synonyms, and refer to how spread out a distribution is. Just as in the section on central tendency where we discussed measures of the center of a distribution of scores, in this chapter we will discuss measures of the variability of a distribution. There are four frequently used measures of variability: range, interquartile range, variance, and standard deviation. In the next few paragraphs, we will look at each of these four measures of variability in more detail.

Range

The range is the simplest measure of variability to calculate, and one you have probably encountered many times in your life. The range is simply the highest score minus the lowest score. Let's take a few examples. What is the range of the following group of numbers: 10, 2, 5, 6, 7, 3, 4? Well, the highest number is 10, and the lowest number is 2, so 10 - 2 = 8. The range is 8. Let's take another example. Here's a dataset with 10 numbers: 99, 45, 23, 67, 45, 91, 82, 78, 62, 51. What is the range? The highest number is 99 and the lowest number is 23, so 99 - 23 equals 76; the range is 76. Now consider the two quizzes shown in Figure 1. On Quiz 1, the lowest score is 5 and the highest score is 9. Therefore, the range is 4. The range on Quiz 2 was larger: the lowest score was 4 and the highest score was 10. Therefore the range is 6.

Interquartile Range

The interquartile range (IQR) is the range of the middle 50% of the scores in a distribution. It is computed as follows:

```
IQR = 75th percentile - 25th percentile
```

For Quiz 1, the 75th percentile is 8 and the 25th percentile is 6. The interquartile range is therefore 2. For Quiz 2, which has greater spread, the 75th percentile is 9, the 25th percentile is 5, and the interquartile range is 4. Recall that in the discussion of box plots, the 75th percentile was called the upper hinge and the 25th percentile was called the lower hinge. Using this terminology, the interquartile range is referred to as the H-spread.

A related measure of variability is called the semi-interquartile range. The semi-interquartile range is defined simply as the interquartile range divided by 2. If a distribution is symmetric, the median plus or minus the semi-interquartile range contains half the scores in the distribution.

Variance

Variability can also be defined in terms of how close the scores in the distribution are to the middle of the distribution. Using the mean as the measure of the middle of the distribution, the variance is defined as the average squared difference of the scores from the mean. The data from Quiz 1 are shown in Table 1. The mean score is 7.0. Therefore, the column "Deviation from Mean" contains the score minus 7. The column "Squared Deviation" is simply the previous column squared.

Table 1. Calculation of Variance for Quiz 1 scores.

Scores	Deviation from Mean	Squared Deviation
9	2	4
9	2	4
9	2	4
8	1	1
8	1	1
8	1	1
8	1	1
7	0	0
7	0	0
7	0	0
7	0	0
7	0	0
6	-1	1
6	-1	1
6	-1	1
6	-1	1
6	-1	1
6	-1	1
5	-2	4
5	-2	4
Means		
7	0	1.5

One thing that is important to notice is that the mean deviation from the mean is 0. This will always be the case. The mean of the squared deviations is 1.5. Therefore, the variance is 1.5. Analogous calculations with Quiz 2 show that its variance is 6.7. The formula for the variance is:

$$\sigma^2 = \frac{\Sigma(X - \mu)^2}{N}$$

where σ^2 is the variance, μ is the mean, and N is the number of numbers. For Quiz 1, $\mu = 7$ and $N = 20$.

If the variance in a sample is used to estimate the variance in a population, then the previous formula underestimates the variance and the following formula should be used:

$$s^2 = \frac{\Sigma(X - M)^2}{N - 1}$$

where s^2 is the estimate of the variance and M is the sample mean. Note that M is the mean of a sample taken from a population with a mean of μ. Since, in practice, the variance is usually computed in a sample, this formula is most often used.

Let's take a concrete example. Assume the scores 1, 2, 4, and 5 were sampled from a larger population. To estimate the variance in the population you would compute s^2 as follows:

$$M = \frac{1 + 2 + 4 + 5}{4} = \frac{12}{4} = 3$$

$$s^2 = \frac{(1-3)^2 + (2-3)^2 + (4-3)^2 + (5-3)^2}{4 - 1} = \frac{4 + 1 + 1 + 4}{3} = \frac{10}{3} = 3.333$$

There are alternate formulas that can be easier to use if you are doing your calculations with a hand calculator:

$$\sigma^2 = \frac{\Sigma X^2 - \frac{(\Sigma X)^2}{N}}{N}$$

and

$$s^2 = \frac{\Sigma X^2 - \frac{(\Sigma X)^2}{N}}{N - 1}$$

For this example,

$$\left(\sum X\right)^2 = \frac{(1 + 2 + 4 + 5)^2}{4} = \frac{144}{4} = 36$$

$$\sigma^2 = \frac{(46 - 36)}{4} = 2.5$$

$$s^2 = \frac{(46 - 36)}{3} = 3.333$$

as with the other formula.

Standard Deviation

The standard deviation is simply the square root of the variance. This makes the standard deviations of the two quiz distributions 1.225 and 2.588. The standard deviation is an especially useful measure of variability when the distribution is normal or approximately normal (see Chapter 7) because the proportion of the distribution within a given number of standard deviations from the mean can be calculated. For example, 68% of the distribution is within one standard deviation of the mean and approximately 95% of the distribution is within two standard deviations of the mean. Therefore, if you had a normal distribution with a mean of 50 and a standard deviation of 10, then 68% of the distribution would be between 50 - 10 = 40 and 50 +10 =60. Similarly, about 95% of the distribution would be between 50 - 2 x 10 = 30 and 50 + 2 x 10 = 70. The symbol for the population standard deviation is σ; the symbol for an estimate computed in a sample is s. Figure 2 shows two normal distributions. The red distribution has a mean of 40 and a standard deviation of 5; the blue distribution has a mean of 60 and a standard deviation of 10. For the red distribution, 68% of the distribution is between 45 and 55; for the blue distribution, 68% is between 50 and 70.

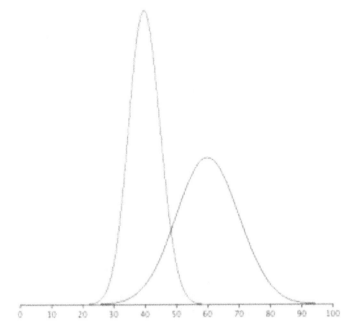

Figure 2. Normal distributions with standard deviations of 5 and 10.

Shapes of Distributions

by David M. Lane

Prerequisites
- Chapter 1: Distributions
- Chapter 3: Measures of Central Tendency
- Chapter 3: Variability

Learning Objectives
1. Compute skew using two different formulas
2. Compute kurtosis

We saw in the section on distributions in Chapter 1 that shapes of distributions can differ in skew and/or kurtosis. This section presents numerical indexes of these two measures of shape.

Skew

Figure 1 shows a distribution with a very large positive skew. Recall that distributions with positive skew have tails that extend to the right.

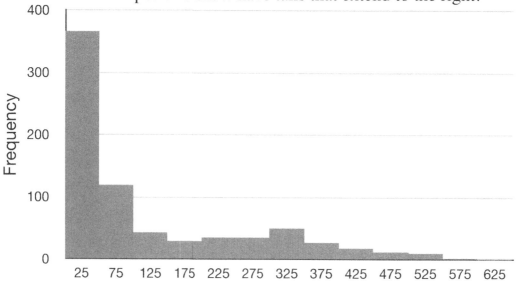

Figure 1. A distribution with a very large positive skew. This histogram shows the salaries of major league baseball players (in thousands of dollars).

Distributions with positive skew normally have larger means than medians. The mean and median of the baseball salaries shown in Figure 1 are $1,183,417 and $500,000 respectively. Thus, for this highly-skewed distribution, the mean is more than twice as high as the median. The relationship between skew and the relative size of the mean and median lead the statistician Pearson to propose the following simple and convenient numerical index of skew:

$$\frac{3(Mean - Median)}{\sigma}$$

The standard deviation of the baseball salaries is 1,390,922. Therefore, Pearson's measure of skew for this distribution is 3(1,183,417 - 500,000)/1,390,922 = 1.47.

Just as there are several measures of central tendency, there is more than one measure of skew. Although Pearson's measure is a good one, the following measure is more commonly used. It is sometimes referred to as the third moment about the mean.

$$\sum \frac{(X - \mu)^3}{\sigma^3}$$

Kurtosis

The following measure of kurtosis is similar to the definition of skew. The value "3" is subtracted to define "no kurtosis" as the kurtosis of a normal distribution. Otherwise, a normal distribution would have a kurtosis of 3.

$$\sum \frac{(X - \mu)^4}{\sigma^4} - 3$$

Effects of Linear Transformations

by David M. Lane

Prerequisites
• Chapter 1: Linear Transformations

Learning Objectives
1. Define a linear transformation
2. Compute the mean of a transformed variable
3. Compute the variance of a transformed variable

This section covers the effects of linear transformations on measures of central tendency and variability. Let's start with an example we saw before in the section that defined linear transformation: temperatures of cities. Table 1 shows the temperatures of 5 cities.

Table 1. Temperatures in 5 cities on 11/16/2002.

City	Degrees Fahrenheit	Degrees Centigrade
Houston	54	12.22
Chicago	37	2.78
Minneapolis	31	-0.56
Miami	78	25.56
Phoenix	70	21.11
Mean	54.000	12.220
Median	54.000	12.220
Variance	330	101.852
SD	18.166	10.092

Recall that to transform the degrees Fahrenheit to degrees Centigrade, we use the formula

```
C = 0.55556F - 17.7778
```

which means we multiply each temperature Fahrenheit by 0.556 and then subtract 17.7778. As you might have expected, you multiply the mean temperature in Fahrenheit by 0.556 and then subtract 17.778 to get the mean in Centigrade. That is, $(0.556)(54) - 17.7778 = 12.22$. The same is true for the median. Note that this relationship holds even if the mean and median are not identical as they are in Table 1.

The formula for the standard deviation is just as simple: the standard deviation in degrees Centigrade is equal to the standard deviation in degrees Fahrenheit times 0.556. Since the variance is the standard deviation squared, the variance in degrees Centigrade is equal to 0.556^2 times the variance in degrees Fahrenheit.

To sum up, if a variable X has a mean of μ, a standard deviation of σ, and a variance of σ^2, then a new variable Y created using the linear transformation

```
Y = bX + A
```

will have a mean of $b\mu+A$, a standard deviation of $b\sigma$, and a variance of $b^2\sigma^2$.

It should be noted that the term "linear transformation" is defined differently in the field of linear algebra. For details, follow this link.

Variance Sum Law I

by David M. Lane

Prerequisites
• Chapter 3: Variance

Learning Objectives
1. Compute the variance of the sum of two uncorrelated variables
2. Compute the variance of the difference between two uncorrelated variables

As you will see in later sections, there are many occasions in which it is important to know the variance of the sum of two variables. Consider the following situation: (a) you have two populations, (b) you sample one number from each population, and (c) you add the two numbers together. The question is, "What is the variance of this sum?" For example, suppose the two populations are the populations of 8-year old males and 8-year-old females in Houston, Texas, and that the variable of interest is memory span. You repeat the following steps thousands of times: (1) sample one male and one female, (2) measure the memory span of each, and (3) sum the two memory spans. After you have done this thousands of times, you compute the variance of the sum. It turns out that the variance of this sum can be computed according to the following formula:

$$\sigma^2_{sum} = \sigma^2_M + \sigma^2_F$$

where the first term is the variance of the sum, the second term is the variance of the males and the third term is the variance of the females. Therefore, if the variances on the memory span test for the males and females respectively were 0.9 and 0.8, respectively, then the variance of the sum would be 1.7.

The formula for the variance of the difference between the two variables (memory span in this example) is shown below. Notice that the expression for the difference is the same as the formula for the sum.

$$\sigma^2_{difference} = \sigma^2_M + \sigma^2_F$$

More generally, the variance sum law can be written as follows:

$$\sigma^2_{X \pm Y} = \sigma^2_X + \sigma^2_Y$$

which is read: "The variance of X plus or minus Y is equal to the variance of X plus the variance of Y."

These formulas for the sum and difference of variables given above only apply when the variables are independent.

In this example, we have thousands of randomly-paired scores. Since the scores are paired randomly, there is no relationship between the memory span of one member of the pair and the memory span of the other. Therefore the two scores are independent. Contrast this situation with one in which thousands of people are sampled and two measures (such as verbal and quantitative SAT) are taken from each. In this case, there would be a relationship between the two variables since higher scores on the verbal SAT are associated with higher scores on the quantitative SAT (although there are many examples of people who score high on one test and low on the other). Thus the two variables are not independent and the variance of the total SAT score would not be the sum of the variances of the verbal SAT and the quantitative SAT. The general form of the variance sum law is presented in a section in the chapter on correlation.

Statistical Literacy

by David M. Lane

Prerequisites
- Chapter 3: Median and Mean

The playbill for the Alley Theatre in Houston wants to appeal to advertisers. They reported the mean household income and the median age of theatergoers.

What do you think?

What might have guided their choice of the mean or median?

> It is likely that they wanted to emphasize that theatergoers had high income but de-emphasize how old they are. The distributions of income and age of theatergoers probably have positive skew. Therefore the mean is probably higher than the median, which results in higher income and lower age than if the median household income and mean age had been presented.

Exercises

Prerequisites
• All material presented in the Summarizing Distributions chapter

1. Make up a dataset of 12 numbers with a positive skew. Use a statistical program to compute the skew. Is the mean larger than the median as it usually is for distributions with a positive skew? What is the value for skew?

2. Repeat Problem 1 only this time make the dataset have a negative skew.

3. Make up three data sets with 5 numbers each that have:

   (a) the same mean but different standard deviations.

   (b) the same mean but different medians.

   (c) the same median but different means.

4. Find the mean and median for the following three variables:

A	B	C
8	4	6
5	4	2
7	6	3
1	3	4
3	4	1

5. A sample of 30 distance scores measured in yards has a mean of 10, a variance of 9, and a standard deviation of 3 (a) You want to convert all your distances from yards to feet, so you multiply each score in the sample by 3. What are the new mean, variance, and standard deviation? (b) You then decide that you only want to look at the distance past a certain point. Thus, after multiplying the original scores by 3, you decide to subtract 4 feet from each of the scores. Now what are the new mean, variance, and standard deviation?

6. You recorded the time in seconds it took for 8 participants to solve a puzzle. These times appear below. However, when the data was entered into the statistical program, the score that was supposed to be 22.1 was entered as 21.2.

You had calculated the following measures of central tendency: the mean, the median, and the mean trimmed 25%. Which of these measures of central tendency will change when you correct the recording error?

Time (seconds)
15.2
18.8
19.3
19.7
20.2
21.8
22.1
29.4

7. For the test scores in question #6, which measures of variability (range, standard deviation, variance) would be changed if the 22.1 data point had been erroneously recorded as 21.2?

8. You know the minimum, the maximum, and the 25th, 50th, and 75th percentiles of a distribution. Which of the following measures of central tendency or variability can you determine?

   mean, median, mode, trimean, geometric mean, range, interquartile range, variance, standard deviation

9. For the numbers 1, 3, 4, 6, and 12:

   Find the value (v) for which $\Sigma(X-v)^2$ is minimized.

   Find the value (v) for which $\Sigma|x-v|$ is minimized.

10. Your younger brother comes home one day after taking a science test. He says that some- one at school told him that "60% of the students in the class scored above the median test grade." What is wrong with this statement? What if he had said "60% of the students scored below the mean?"

11. An experiment compared the ability of three groups of participants to remember briefly- presented chess positions. The data are shown below. The numbers represent the number of pieces correctly remembered from three chess

positions. Compare the performance of each group. Consider spread as well as central tendency.

Non-players	Beginners	Tournament players
22.1	32.5	40.1
22.3	37.1	45.6
26.2	39.1	51.2
29.6	40.5	56.4
31.7	45.5	58.1
33.5	51.3	71.1
38.9	52.6	74.9
39.7	55.7	75.9
43.2	55.9	80.3
43.2	57.7	85.3

12. True/False: A bimodal distribution has two modes and two medians.

13. True/False: The best way to describe a skewed distribution is to report the mean.

14. True/False: When plotted on the same graph, a distribution with a mean of 50 and a standard deviation of 10 will look more spread out than will a distribution with a mean of 60 and a standard deviation of 5.

15. Compare the mean, median, trimean in terms of their sensitivity to extreme scores.

16. If the mean time to respond to a stimulus is much higher than the median time to respond, what can you say about the shape of the distribution of response times?

17. A set of numbers is transformed by taking the log base 10 of each number. The mean of the transformed data is 1.65. What is the geometric mean of the untransformed data?

18. Which measure of central tendency is most often used for returns on investment?

19. The histogram is in balance on the fulcrum. What are the mean, median, and mode of the distribution (approximate where necessary)?

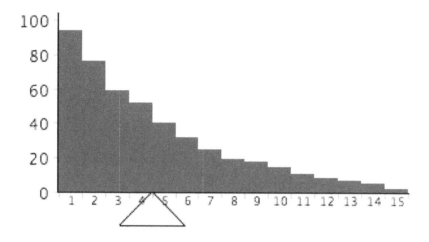

Questions from Case Studies

Angry Moods (AM) case study

20. (AM) Does Anger-Out have a positive skew, a negative skew, or no skew?

21. (AM) What is the range of the Anger-In scores? What is the interquartile range?

22. (AM) What is the overall mean Control-Out score? What is the mean Control-Out score for the athletes? What is the mean Control-Out score for the non-athletes?

23. (AM) What is the variance of the Control-In scores for the athletes? What is the variance of the Control-In scores for the non-athletes?

Flatulence (F) case study

24. (F) Based on a histogram of the variable "perday", do you think the mean or median of this variable is larger? Calculate the mean and median to see if you are right.

Stroop (S) case study

25.(S) Compute the mean for "words".

26. (S#2) Compute the mean and standard deviation for "colors".

Physicians' Reactions (PR) case study

27.(PR) What is the mean expected time spent for the average-weight patients? What is the mean expected time spent for the overweight patients?

28.(PR) What is the difference in means between the groups? By approximately how many standard deviations do the means differ?

Smiles and Leniency (SL) case study

29.(SL) Find the mean, median, standard deviation, and interquartile range for the leniency scores of each of the four groups.

ADHD Treatment (AT) case study

30.(AT) What is the mean number of correct responses of the participants after taking the placebo (0 mg/kg)?

31.(AT) What are the standard deviation and the interquartile range of the d0 condition?

4. Describing Bivariate Data

A dataset with two variables contains what is called bivariate data. This chapter discusses ways to describe the relationship between two variables. For example, you may wish to describe the relationship between the heights and weights of people to determine the extent to which taller people weigh more.

The introductory section gives more examples of bivariate relationships and presents the most common way of portraying these relationships graphically. The next five sections discuss Pearson's correlation, the most common index of the relationship between two variables. The final section, "Variance Sum Law II," makes use of Pearson's correlation to generalize this law to bivariate data.

Introduction to Bivariate Data

by Rudy Guerra and David M. Lane

Prerequisites
- Chapter 1: Variables
- Chapter 1: Distributions
- Chapter 2: Histograms
- Chapter 3: Measures of Central Tendency
- Chapter 3: Variability
- Chapter 3: Shapes of Distributions

Learning Objectives
1. Define "bivariate data"
2. Define "scatter plot"
3. Distinguish between a linear and a nonlinear relationship
4. Identify positive and negative associations from a scatter plot

Measures of central tendency, variability, and spread summarize a single variable by providing important information about its distribution. Often, more than one variable is collected on each individual. For example, in large health studies of populations it is common to obtain variables such as age, sex, height, weight, blood pressure, and total cholesterol on each individual. Economic studies may be interested in, among other things, personal income and years of education. As a third example, most university admissions committees ask for an applicant's high school grade point average and standardized admission test scores (e.g., SAT). In this chapter we consider bivariate data, which for now consists of two quantitative variables for each individual. Our first interest is in summarizing such data in a way that is analogous to summarizing univariate (single variable) data.

By way of illustration, let's consider something with which we are all familiar: age. Let's begin by asking if people tend to marry other people of about the same age. Our experience tells us "yes," but how good is the correspondence? One way to address the question is to look at pairs of ages for a sample of married couples. Table 1 below shows the ages of 10 married couples. Going across the columns we see that, yes, husbands and wives tend to be of about the same age, with men having a tendency to be slightly older than their wives. This is no big surprise, but at least the data bear out our experiences, which is not always the case.

Table 1. Sample of spousal ages of 10 White American Couples.

Husband	36	72	37	36	51	50	47	50	37	41
Wife	35	67	33	35	50	46	47	42	36	41

The pairs of ages in Table 1 are from a dataset consisting of 282 pairs of spousal ages, too many to make sense of from a table. What we need is a way to summarize the 282 pairs of ages. We know that each variable can be summarized by a histogram (see Figure 1) and by a mean and standard deviation (See Table 2).

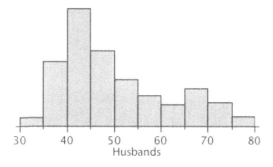

Figure 1. Histograms of spousal ages.

Table 2. Means and standard deviations of spousal ages.

	Mean	Standard Deviation
Husbands	49	11
Wives	47	11

Each distribution is fairly skewed with a long right tail. From Table 1 we see that not all husbands are older than their wives and it is important to see that this fact is lost when we separate the variables. That is, even though we provide summary statistics on each variable, the pairing within couple is lost by separating the variables. We cannot say, for example, based on the means alone what percentage of couples has younger husbands than wives. We have to count across pairs to find this out. Only by maintaining the pairing can meaningful answers be found about couples per se. Another example of information not available from the separate descriptions of husbands and wives' ages is the mean age of husbands with wives of a certain age. For instance, what is the average age of husbands with 45-year-old wives? Finally, we do not know the relationship between the husband's age and the wife's age.

We can learn much more by displaying the bivariate data in a graphical form that maintains the pairing. Figure 2 shows a scatter plot of the paired ages. The x-axis represents the age of the husband and the y-axis the age of the wife.

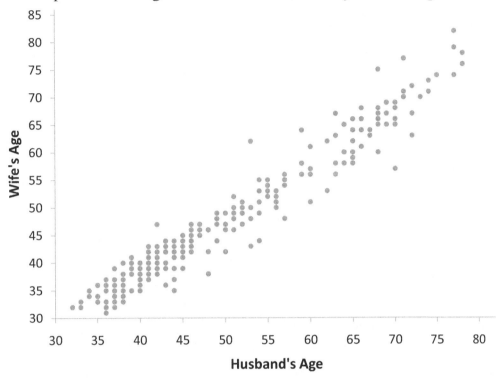

Figure 2. Scatter plot showing wife's age as a function of husband's age.

There are two important characteristics of the data revealed by Figure 2. First, it is clear that there is a strong relationship between the husband's age and the wife's age: the older the husband, the older the wife. When one variable (Y) increases with the second variable (X), we say that X and Y have a positive association. Conversely, when Y decreases as X increases, we say that they have a negative association.

Second, the points cluster along a straight line. When this occurs, the relationship is called a linear relationship.

Figure 3 shows a scatter plot of Arm Strength and Grip Strength from 149 individuals working in physically demanding jobs including electricians, construction and maintenance workers, and auto mechanics. Not surprisingly, the stronger someone's grip, the stronger their arm tends to be. There is therefore a positive association between these variables. Although the points cluster along a line, they are not clustered quite as closely as they are for the scatter plot of spousal age.

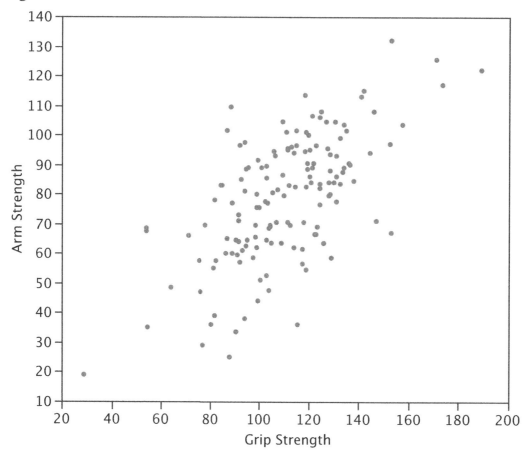

Figure 3. Scatter plot of Grip Strength and Arm Strength.

Not all scatter plots show linear relationships. Figure 4 shows the results of an experiment conducted by Galileo on projectile motion. In the experiment, Galileo rolled balls down an incline and measured how far they traveled as a function of the release height. It is clear from Figure 4 that the relationship between "Release Height" and "Distance Traveled" is not described well by a straight line: If you drew a line connecting the lowest point and the highest point, all of the remaining points would be above the line. The data are better fit by a parabola.

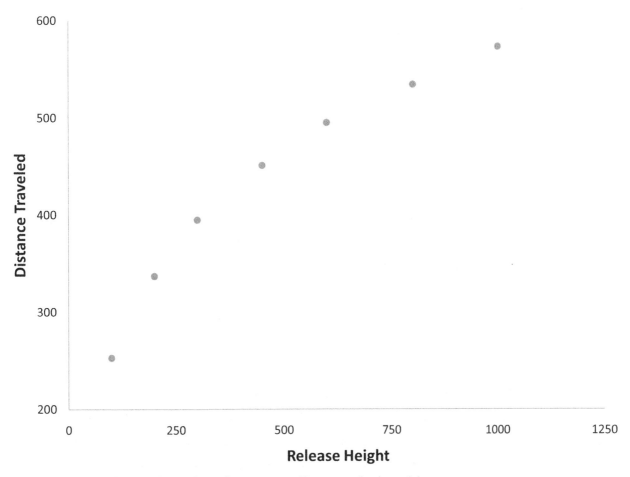

Figure 4. Galileo's data showing a non-linear relationship.

Scatter plots that show linear relationships between variables can differ in several ways including the slope of the line about which they cluster and how tightly the points cluster about the line. A statistical measure of the strength of the relationship between two quantitative variables that takes these factors into account is the subject of the next section.

Values of the Pearson Correlation

by David M. Lane

Prerequisites
• Chapter 4: Introduction to Bivariate Data

Learning Objectives
1. Describe what Pearson's correlation measures
2. Give the symbols for Pearson's correlation in the sample and in the population
3. State the possible range for Pearson's correlation
4. Identify a perfect linear relationship

The Pearson product-moment correlation coefficient is a measure of the strength of the linear relationship between two variables. It is referred to as Pearson's correlation or simply as the correlation coefficient. If the relationship between the variables is not linear, then the correlation coefficient does not adequately represent the strength of the relationship between the variables.

The symbol for Pearson's correlation is "ϱ" when it is measured in the population and "r" when it is measured in a sample. Because we will be dealing almost exclusively with samples, we will use r to represent Pearson's correlation unless otherwise noted.

Pearson's r can range from -1 to 1. An r of -1 indicates a perfect negative linear relationship between variables, an r of 0 indicates no linear relationship between variables, and an r of 1 indicates a perfect positive linear relationship between variables. Figure 1 shows a scatter plot for which r = 1.

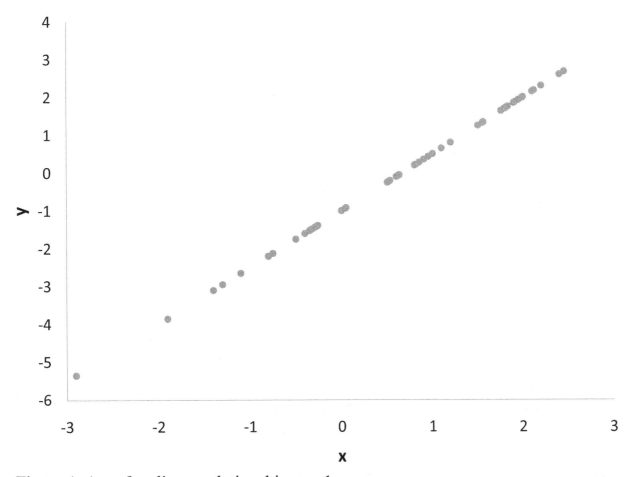

Figure 1. A perfect linear relationship, r = 1.

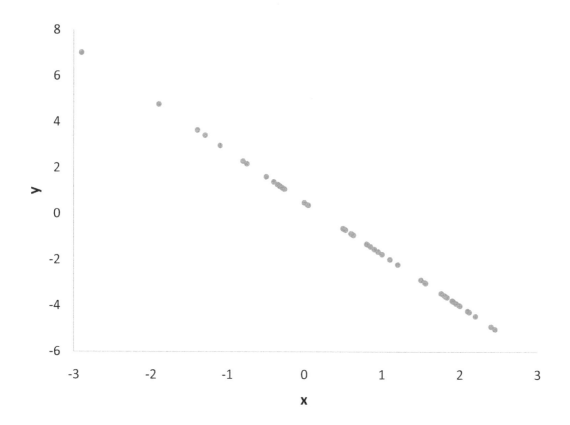

Figure 2. A perfect negative linear relationship, r = -1.

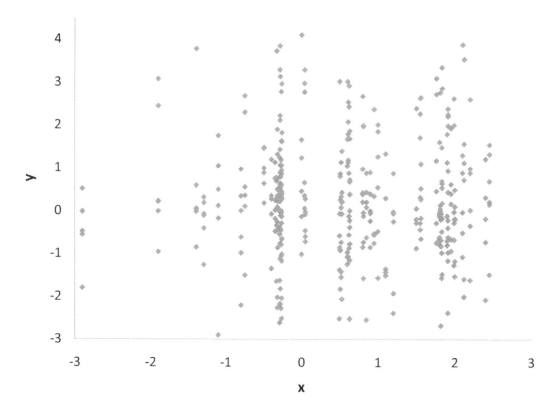

Figure 3. A scatter plot for which r = 0. Notice that there is no relationship
between X and Y.

With real data, you would not expect to get values of r of exactly -1, 0, or 1. The
data for spousal ages shown in Figure 4 and described in the introductory section
has an r of 0.97.

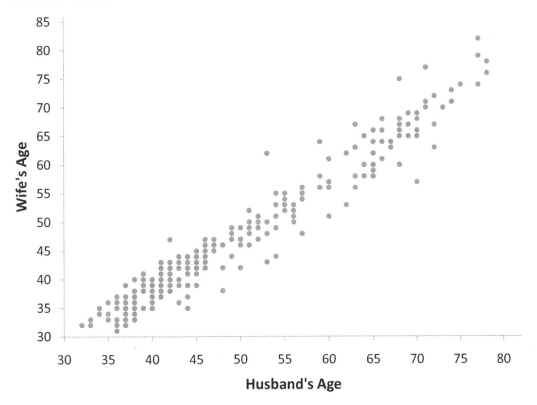

Figure 4. Scatter plot of spousal ages, r = 0.97.

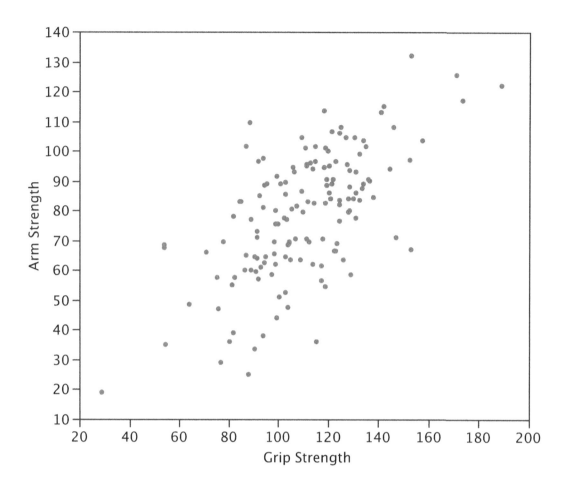

Figure 5. Scatter plot of Grip Strength and Arm Strength, r = 0.63.

The relationship between grip strength and arm strength depicted in Figure 5 (also described in the introductory section) is 0.63.

Properties of Pearson's r

by David M. Lane

Prerequisites
- Chapter 1: Linear Transformations
- Chapter 4: Introduction to Bivariate Data

Learning Objectives
1. State the range of values for Pearson's correlation
2. State the values that represent perfect linear relationships
3. State the relationship between the correlation of Y with X and the correlation of X with Y
4. State the effect of linear transformations on Pearson's correlation

A basic property of Pearson's r is that its possible range is from -1 to 1. A correlation of -1 means a perfect negative linear relationship, a correlation of 0 means no linear relationship, and a correlation of 1 means a perfect positive linear relationship.

Pearson's correlation is symmetric in the sense that the correlation of X with Y is the same as the correlation of Y with X. For example, the correlation of Weight with Height is the same as the correlation of Height with Weight.

A critical property of Pearson's r is that it is unaffected by linear transformations. This means that multiplying a variable by a constant and/or adding a constant does not change the correlation of that variable with other variables. For instance, the correlation of Weight and Height does not depend on whether Height is measured in inches, feet, or even miles. Similarly, adding five points to every student's test score would not change the correlation of the test score with other variables such as GPA.

Computing Pearson's r

by David M. Lane

Prerequisites
• Chapter 1: Summation Notation
• Chapter 4: Introduction to Bivariate Data

Learning Objectives
1. Define X and x
2. State why $\Sigma xy = 0$ when there is no relationship
3. Calculate r

There are several formulas that can be used to compute Pearson's correlation. Some formulas make more conceptual sense whereas others are easier to actually compute. We are going to begin with a formula that makes more conceptual sense.

We are going to compute the correlation between the variables X and Y shown in Table 1. We begin by computing the mean for X and subtracting this mean from all values of X. The new variable is called "x." The variable "y" is computed similarly. The variables x and y are said to be deviation scores because each score is a deviation from the mean. Notice that the means of x and y are both 0. Next we create a new column by multiplying x and y.

Before proceeding with the calculations, let's consider why the sum of the xy column reveals the relationship between X and Y. If there were no relationship between X and Y, then positive values of x would be just as likely to be paired with negative values of y as with positive values. This would make negative values of xy as likely as positive values and the sum would be small. On the other hand, consider Table 1 in which high values of X are associated with high values of Y and low values of X are associated with low values of Y. You can see that positive values of x are associated with positive values of y and negative values of x are associated with negative values of y. In all cases, the product of x and y is positive, resulting in a high total for the xy column. Finally, if there were a negative relationship then positive values of x would be associated with negative values of y and negative values of x would be associated with positive values of y. This would lead to negative values for xy.

Table 1. Calculation of r.

	X	Y	x	y	xy	x^2	y^2
	1	4	-3	-5	15	9	25
	3	6	-1	-3	3	1	9
	5	10	1	1	1	1	1
	5	12	1	3	3	1	9
	6	13	2	4	8	4	16
Total	20	45	0	0	30	16	60
Mean	4	9	0	0	6		

Pearson's r is designed so that the correlation between height and weight is the same whether height is measured in inches or in feet. To achieve this property, Pearson's correlation is computed by dividing the sum of the xy column (Σxy) by the square root of the product of the sum of the x^2 column (Σx^2) and the sum of the y^2 column (Σy^2). The resulting formula is:

$$r = \frac{\Sigma xy}{\sqrt{\Sigma x^2 \, \Sigma y^2}}$$

and therefore

$$r = \frac{30}{\sqrt{(16)(60)}} = \frac{30}{\sqrt{960}} = \frac{30}{30.984} = 0.968$$

An alternative computational formula that avoids the step of computing deviation scores is:

$$r = \frac{\Sigma xy - \frac{\Sigma x \, \Sigma y}{N}}{\sqrt{\left(\Sigma x^2 - \frac{(\Sigma x)^2}{N}\right)}\sqrt{\left(\Sigma y^2 - \frac{(\Sigma y)^2}{N}\right)}}$$

Variance Sum Law II

by David M. Lane

Prerequisites
• Chapter 1: Variance Sum Law I
• Chapter 4: Values of Pearson's Correlation

Learning Objectives
1. State the variance sum law when X and Y are not assumed to be independent
2. Compute the variance of the sum of two variables if the variance of each and their correlation is known
3. Compute the variance of the difference between two variables if the variance of each and their correlation is known

Recall that when the variables X and Y are independent, the variance of the sum or difference between X and Y can be written as follows:

$$\sigma^2_{X \pm Y} = \sigma^2_X + \sigma^2_Y$$

which is read: "The variance of X plus or minus Y is equal to the variance of X plus the variance of Y."

When X and Y are correlated, the following formula should be used:

$$\sigma^2_{X \pm Y} = \sigma^2_X + \sigma^2_Y \pm 2\rho\sigma_X\sigma_Y$$

where ϱ is the correlation between X and Y in the population. For example, if the variance of verbal SAT were 10,000, the variance of quantitative SAT were 11,000 and the correlation between these two tests were 0.50, then the variance of total SAT (verbal + quantitative) would be:

$$\sigma^2_{verbal+quant} = 10,000 + 11,000 + (2)(0.5)\sqrt{10,000}\sqrt{11,000}$$

which is equal to 31,488. The variance of the difference is:

$$\sigma^2_{verbal-quant} = 10,000 + 11,000 - (2)(0.5)\sqrt{10,000}\sqrt{11,000}$$

which is equal to 10,512.

If the variances and the correlation are computed in a sample, then the following notation is used to express the variance sum law:

$$s_{X\pm Y}^2 = s_X^2 + s_Y^2 \pm 2rs_X s_y$$

Statistical Literacy

by David M. Lane

Prerequisites
- Chapter 4: Values of Pearson's Correlation

The graph below showing the relationship between age and sleep is based on a graph that appears on this web page.

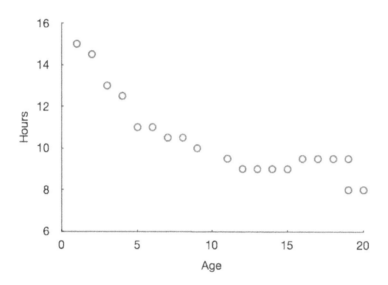

What do you think?

Why might Pearson's correlation not be a good way to describe the relationship?

> Pearson's correlation measures the strength of the linear relationship between two variables. The relationship here is not linear. As age increases, hours slept decreases rapidly at first but then levels off.

Exercises

Prerequisites
• All material presented in the Describing Bivariate Data chapter

1. Describe the relationship between variables A and C. Think of things these variables could represent in real life.

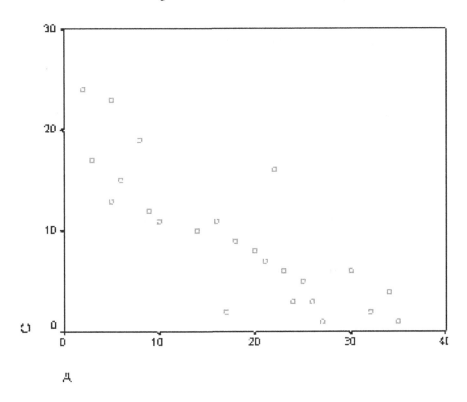

2. Make up a data set with 10 numbers that has a positive correlation.

3. Make up a data set with 10 numbers that has a negative correlation.

4. If the correlation between weight (in pounds) and height (in feet) is 0.58, find: (a) the correlation between weight (in pounds) and height (in yards) (b) the correlation between weight (in kilograms) and height (in meters).

5. Would you expect the correlation between High School GPA and College GPA to be higher when taken from your entire high school class or when taken from only the top 20 students? Why?

6. For a certain class, the relationship between the amount of time spent studying and the test grade earned was examined. It was determined that as the amount of time they studied increased, so did their grades. Is this a positive or negative association?

7. For this same class, the relationship between the amount of time spent studying and the amount of time spent socializing per week was also examined. It was determined that the more hours they spent studying, the fewer hours they spent socializing. Is this a positive or negative association?

8. For the following data:

   a. Find the deviation scores for Variable A that correspond to the raw scores of 2 and 8.

   b. Find the deviation scores for Variable B that correspond to the raw scores of 5 and 4.

   c. Just from looking at these scores, do you think these variables are positively or negatively correlated? Why?

   d. Now calculate the correlation. Were you right?

A	B
2	8
5	5
6	2
8	4
9	1

9. Students took two parts of a test, each worth 50 points. Part A has a variance of 25, and Part B has a variance of 49. The correlation between the test scores is 0.6. (a) If the teacher adds the grades of the two parts together to form a final test grade, what would the variance of the final test grades be? (b) What would the variance of Part A - Part B be?

10. True/False: The correlation in real life between height and weight is r=1.

11. True/False: It is possible for variables to have r=0 but still have a strong association.

12. True/False: Two variables with a correlation of 0.3 have a stronger linear relationship than two variables with a correlation of -0.7.

13. True/False: After polling a certain group of people, researchers found a 0.5 correlation between the number of car accidents per year and the driver's age. This means that older people get in more accidents.

14. True/False: The correlation between R and T is the same as the correlation between T and R.

15. True/False: To examine bivariate data graphically, the best choice is two side by side histograms.

16. True/False: A correlation of r=1.2 is not possible.

Questions from Case Studies

Angry Moods (AM) case study

17. (AM) What is the correlation between the Control-In and Control-Out scores?

18. (AM) Would you expect the correlation between the Anger-Out and Control-Out scores to be positive or negative? Compute this correlation.

Flatulence (F) case study

19. (F) Is there are relationship between the number of male siblings and embarrassment in front of romantic interests? Create a scatterplot and compute r.

Stroop (S) case study

20. (S) Create a scatterplot showing "words" on the X-axis and " colors " on the Y-axis.

21. (S) Compute the correlation between "colors" and "words."

22. (S) Sort the data by color-naming time. Choose only the 23 fastest color-namers.

    (a) What is the new correlation?

    (b) What is the technical term for the finding that this correlation is smaller than the correlation for the full dataset?

Animal Research (AR) case study

23. (AR) What is the overall correlation between the belief that animal research is wrong and belief that animal research is necessary?

ADHD Treatment (AT) case study

24. (AT) What is the correlation between the participants' correct number of responses after taking the placebo and their correct number of responses after taking 0.60 mg/kg of MPH?

5. Probability

Probability is an important and complex field of study. Fortunately, only a few basic issues in probability theory are essential for understanding statistics at the level covered in this book. These basic issues are covered in this chapter.

The introductory section discusses the definitions of probability. This is not as simple as it may seem. The section on basic concepts covers how to compute probabilities in a variety of simple situations. The section on base rates discusses an important but often-ignored factor in determining probabilities.

Remarks on the Concept of "Probability"

by Dan Osherson

Prerequisites
• None

Learning Objectives
1. Define symmetrical outcomes
2. Distinguish between frequentist and subjective approaches
3. Determine whether the frequentist or subjective approach is better suited for a given situation

Inferential statistics is built on the foundation of probability theory, and has been remarkably successful in guiding opinion about the conclusions to be drawn from data. Yet (paradoxically) the very idea of probability has been plagued by controversy from the beginning of the subject to the present day. In this section we provide a glimpse of the debate about the interpretation of the probability concept.

One conception of probability is drawn from the idea of **symmetrical outcomes**. For example, the two possible outcomes of tossing a fair coin seem not to be distinguishable in any way that affects which side will land up or down. Therefore the probability of heads is taken to be 1/2, as is the probability of tails. In general, if there are N symmetrical outcomes, the probability of any given one of them occurring is taken to be 1/N. Thus, if a six-sided die is rolled, the probability of any one of the six sides coming up is 1/6.

Probabilities can also be thought of in terms of **relative frequencies**. If we tossed a coin millions of times, we would expect the proportion of tosses that came up heads to be pretty close to 1/2. As the number of tosses increases, the proportion of heads approaches 1/2. Therefore, we can say that the probability of a head is 1/2.

If it has rained in Seattle on 62% of the last 100,000 days, then the probability of it raining tomorrow might be taken to be 0.62. This is a natural idea but nonetheless unreasonable if we have further information relevant to whether it will rain tomorrow. For example, if tomorrow is August 1, a day of the year on which it seldom rains in Seattle, we should only consider the percentage of the time it rained on August 1. But even this is not enough since the probability of rain on the next August 1 depends on the humidity. (The chances are higher in the presence of high humidity.) So, we should consult only the prior occurrences of

August 1 that had the same humidity as the next occurrence of August 1. Of course, wind direction also affects probability. You can see that our sample of prior cases will soon be reduced to the empty set. Anyway, past meteorological history is misleading if the climate is changing.

For some purposes, probability is best thought of as subjective. Questions such as "What is the probability that Ms. Garcia will defeat Mr. Smith in an upcoming congressional election?" do not conveniently fit into either the symmetry or frequency approaches to probability. Rather, assigning probability 0.7 (say) to this event seems to reflect the speaker's personal opinion --- perhaps his willingness to bet according to certain odds. Such an approach to probability, however, seems to lose the objective content of the idea of chance; probability becomes mere opinion.

Two people might attach different probabilities to the election outcome, yet there would be no criterion for calling one "right" and the other "wrong." We cannot call one of the two people right simply because she assigned higher probability to the outcome that actually transpires. After all, you would be right to attribute probability 1/6 to throwing a six with a fair die, and your friend who attributes 2/3 to this event would be wrong. And you are still right (and your friend is still wrong) even if the die ends up showing a six! The lack of objective criteria for adjudicating claims about probabilities in the subjective perspective is an unattractive feature of it for many scholars.

Like most work in the field, the present text adopts the frequentist approach to probability in most cases. Moreover, almost all the probabilities we shall encounter will be nondogmatic, that is, neither zero nor one. An event with probability 0 has no chance of occurring; an event of probability 1 is certain to occur. It is hard to think of any examples of interest to statistics in which the probability is either 0 or 1. (Even the probability that the Sun will come up tomorrow is less than 1.)

The following example illustrates our attitude about probabilities. Suppose you wish to know what the weather will be like next Saturday because you are planning a picnic. You turn on your radio, and the weather person says, "There is a 10% chance of rain." You decide to have the picnic outdoors and, lo and behold, it rains. You are furious with the weather person. But was she wrong? No, she did not say it would not rain, only that rain was unlikely. She would have been flatly wrong only if she said that the probability is 0 and it subsequently rained. However, if you kept track of her weather predictions over a long period of time and found that it rained on 50% of the days that the weather person said the probability was 0.10, you could say her probability assessments are wrong.

So when is it accurate to say that the probability of rain is 0.10? According to our frequency interpretation, it means that it will rain 10% of the days on which rain is forecast with this probability.

Basic Concepts

by David M. Lane

Prerequisites
- Chapter 5: Introduction to Probability

Learning Objectives
1. Compute probability in a situation where there are equally-likely outcomes
2. Apply concepts to cards and dice
3. Compute the probability of two independent events both occurring
4. Compute the probability of either of two independent events occurring
5. Do problems that involve conditional probabilities
6. Compute the probability that in a room of N people, at least two share a birthday
7. Describe the gambler's fallacy

Probability of a Single Event

If you roll a six-sided die, there are six possible outcomes, and each of these outcomes is equally likely. A six is as likely to come up as a three, and likewise for the other four sides of the die. What, then, is the probability that a one will come up? Since there are six possible outcomes, the probability is 1/6. What is the probability that either a one or a six will come up? The two outcomes about which we are concerned (a one or a six coming up) are called favorable outcomes. Given that all outcomes are equally likely, we can compute the probability of a one or a six using the formula:

$$probability = \frac{Number\ of\ favorable\ outcomes}{Number\ of\ possible\ equally - likely\ outcomes}$$

In this case there are two favorable outcomes and six possible outcomes. So the probability of throwing either a one or six is 1/3. Don't be misled by our use of the term "favorable," by the way. You should understand it in the sense of "favorable to the event in question happening." That event might not be favorable to your well-being. You might be betting on a three, for example.

The above formula applies to many games of chance. For example, what is the probability that a card drawn at random from a deck of playing cards will be an ace? Since the deck has four aces, there are four favorable outcomes; since the deck has 52 cards, there are 52 possible outcomes. The probability is therefore 4/52 = 1/13. What about the probability that the card will be a club? Since there are 13 clubs, the probability is 13/52 = 1/4.

Let's say you have a bag with 20 cherries: 14 sweet and 6 sour. If you pick a cherry at random, what is the probability that it will be sweet? There are 20 possible cherries that could be picked, so the number of possible outcomes is 20. Of these 20 possible outcomes, 14 are favorable (sweet), so the probability that the cherry will be sweet is 14/20 = 7/10. There is one potential complication to this example, however. It must be assumed that the probability of picking any of the cherries is the same as the probability of picking any other. This wouldn't be true if (let us imagine) the sweet cherries are smaller than the sour ones. (The sour cherries would come to hand more readily when you sampled from the bag.) Let us keep in mind, therefore, that when we assess probabilities in terms of the ratio of favorable to all potential cases, we rely heavily on the assumption of equal probability for all outcomes.

Here is a more complex example. You throw 2 dice. What is the probability that the sum of the two dice will be 6? To solve this problem, list all the possible outcomes. There are 36 of them since each die can come up one of six ways. The 36 possibilities are shown in Table 1.

Table 1. 36 possible outcomes.

Die 1	Die 2	Total	Die 1	Die 2	Total	Die 1	Die 2	Total
1	1	2	3	1	4	5	1	6
1	2	3	3	2	5	5	2	7
1	3	4	3	3	6	5	3	8
1	4	5	3	4	7	5	4	9
1	5	6	3	5	8	5	5	10
1	6	7	3	6	9	5	6	11
2	1	3	4	1	5	6	1	7
2	2	4	4	2	6	6	2	8
2	3	5	4	3	7	6	3	9
2	4	6	4	4	8	6	4	10
2	5	7	4	5	9	6	5	11
2	6	8	4	6	10	6	6	12

You can see that 5 of the 36 possibilities total 6. Therefore, the probability is 5/36.

If you know the probability of an event occurring, it is easy to compute the probability that the event does not occur. If P(A) is the probability of Event A, then 1 - P(A) is the probability that the event does not occur. For the last example, the probability that the total is 6 is 5/36. Therefore, the probability that the total is not 6 is 1 - 5/36 = 31/36.

Probability of Two (or more) Independent Events

Events A and B are independent events if the probability of Event B occurring is the same whether or not Event A occurs. Let's take a simple example. A fair coin is tossed two times. The probability that a head comes up on the second toss is 1/2 regardless of whether or not a head came up on the first toss. The two events are (1) first toss is a head and (2) second toss is a head. So these events are independent. Consider the two events (1) "It will rain tomorrow in Houston" and (2) "It will rain tomorrow in Galveston" (a city near Houston). These events are not independent because it is more likely that it will rain in Galveston on days it rains in Houston than on days it does not.

Probability of A and B

When two events are independent, the probability of both occurring is the product of the probabilities of the individual events. More formally, if events A and B are independent, then the probability of both A and B occurring is:

```
P(A and B) = P(A) x P(B)
```

where P(A and B) is the probability of events A and B both occurring, P(A) is the probability of event A occurring, and P(B) is the probability of event B occurring.

If you flip a coin twice, what is the probability that it will come up heads both times? Event A is that the coin comes up heads on the first flip and Event B is that the coin comes up heads on the second flip. Since both P(A) and P(B) equal 1/2, the probability that both events occur is

```
1/2 x 1/2 = 1/4
```

Let's take another example. If you flip a coin and roll a six-sided die, what is the probability that the coin comes up heads and the die comes up 1? Since the two events are independent, the probability is simply the probability of a head (which is 1/2) times the probability of the die coming up 1 (which is 1/6). Therefore, the probability of both events occurring is 1/2 x 1/6 = 1/12.

One final example: You draw a card from a deck of cards, put it back, and then draw another card. What is the probability that the first card is a heart and the second card is black? Since there are 52 cards in a deck and 13 of them are hearts, the probability that the first card is a heart is 13/52 = 1/4. Since there are 26 black cards in the deck, the probability that the second card is black is 26/52 = 1/2. The probability of both events occurring is therefore 1/4 x 1/2 = 1/8.

See the discussion on conditional probabilities later in this section to see how to compute P(A and B) when A and B are not independent.

Probability of A or B

If Events A and B are independent, the probability that either Event A or Event B occurs is:

```
P(A or B) = P(A) + P(B) - P(A and B)
```

In this discussion, when we say "A or B occurs" we include three possibilities:

1. A occurs and B does not occur
2. B occurs and A does not occur
3. Both A and B occur

This use of the word "or" is technically called inclusive or because it includes the case in which both A and B occur. If we included only the first two cases, then we would be using an exclusive or.

(Optional) We can derive the law for P(A-or-B) from our law about P(A-and-B). The event "A-or-B" can happen in any of the following ways:

1. A-and-B happens
2. A-and-not-B happens
3. not-A-and-B happens.

The simple event A can happen if either A-and-B happens or A-and-not-B happens. Similarly, the simple event B happens if either A-and-B happens or not-A-and-B happens. P(A) + P(B) is therefore P(A-and-B) + P(A-and-not-B) + P(A-and-B) + P(not-A-and-B), whereas P(A-or-B) is P(A-and-B) + P(A-and-not-B) + P(not-A-and-B). We can make these two sums equal by subtracting one occurrence of P(A-and-B) from the first. Hence, P(A-or-B) = P(A) + P(B) - P(A-and-B).

Now for some examples. If you flip a coin two times, what is the probability that you will get a head on the first flip or a head on the second flip (or both)? Letting Event A be a head on the first flip and Event B be a head on the second flip, then P(A) = 1/2, P(B) = 1/2, and P(A and B) = 1/4. Therefore,

```
P(A or B) = 1/2 + 1/2 - 1/4 = 3/4.
```

If you throw a six-sided die and then flip a coin, what is the probability that you will get either a 6 on the die or a head on the coin flip (or both)? Using the formula,

$$P(6 \text{ or head}) = P(6) + P(\text{head}) - P(6 \text{ and head})$$
$$= (1/6) + (1/2) - (1/6)(1/2)$$
$$= 7/12$$

An alternate approach to computing this value is to start by computing the probability of not getting either a 6 or a head. Then subtract this value from 1 to compute the probability of getting a 6 or a head. Although this is a complicated method, it has the advantage of being applicable to problems with more than two events. Here is the calculation in the present case. The probability of not getting either a 6 or a head can be recast as the probability of

```
(not getting a 6) AND (not getting a head).
```

This follows because if you did not get a 6 and you did not get a head, then you did not get a 6 or a head. The probability of not getting a six is 1 - 1/6 = 5/6. The probability of not getting a head is 1 - 1/2 = 1/2. The probability of not getting a six and not getting a head is 5/6 x 1/2 = 5/12. This is therefore the probability of not getting a 6 or a head. The probability of getting a six or a head is therefore (once again) 1 - 5/12 = 7/12.

If you throw a die three times, what is the probability that one or more of your throws will come up with a 1? That is, what is the probability of getting a 1 on the first throw OR a 1 on the second throw OR a 1 on the third throw? The easiest way to approach this problem is to compute the probability of

```
NOT getting a 1 on the first throw
AND not getting a 1 on the second throw
AND not getting a 1 on the third throw.
```

The answer will be 1 minus this probability. The probability of not getting a 1 on any of the three throws is 5/6 x 5/6 x 5/6 = 125/216. Therefore, the probability of getting a 1 on at least one of the throws is 1 - 125/216 = 91/216.

Conditional Probabilities

Often it is required to compute the probability of an event given that another event has occurred. For example, what is the probability that two cards drawn at random from a deck of playing cards will both be aces? It might seem that you could use the formula for the probability of two independent events and simply multiply 4/52 x 4/52 = 1/169. This would be incorrect, however, because the two events are not independent. If the first card drawn is an ace, then the probability that the second card is also an ace would be lower because there would only be three aces left in the deck.

Once the first card chosen is an ace, the probability that the second card chosen is also an ace is called the conditional probability of drawing an ace. In this case, the "condition" is that the first card is an ace. Symbolically, we write this as:

```
P(ace on second draw | an ace on the first draw)
```

The vertical bar "|" is read as "given," so the above expression is short for: "The probability that an ace is drawn on the second draw given that an ace was drawn on the first draw." What is this probability? Since after an ace is drawn on the first draw, there are 3 aces out of 51 total cards left. This means that the probability that one of these aces will be drawn is 3/51 = 1/17.

```
If Events A and B are not independent, then
P(A and B) = P(A) x P(B|A).
```

Applying this to the problem of two aces, the probability of drawing two aces from a deck is 4/52 x 3/51 = 1/221.

One more example: If you draw two cards from a deck, what is the probability that you will get the Ace of Diamonds and a black card? There are two ways you can satisfy this condition: (a) You can get the Ace of Diamonds first and then a black card or (b) you can get a black card first and then the Ace of Diamonds. Let's calculate Case A. The probability that the first card is the Ace of Diamonds is 1/52. The probability that the second card is black given that the first card is the Ace of Diamonds is 26/51 because 26 of the remaining 51 cards are black. The probability is therefore 1/52 x 26/51 = 1/102. Now for Case B: the probability that the first card is black is 26/52 = 1/2. The probability that the second card is the Ace of Diamonds given that the first card is black is 1/51. The probability of Case B is therefore 1/2 x 1/51 = 1/102, the same as the probability of Case A. Recall that the probability of A or B is P(A) + P(B) - P(A and B). In this problem, P(A and B) = 0 since a card cannot be the Ace of Diamonds and be a black card. Therefore, the probability of Case A or Case B is 1/102 + 1/102 = 2/102 = 1/51. So, 1/51 is the probability that you will get the Ace of Diamonds and a black card when drawing two cards from a deck.

Birthday Problem

If there are 25 people in a room, what is the probability that at least two of them share the same birthday. If your first thought is that it is 25/365 = 0.068, you will be surprised to learn it is much higher than that. This problem requires the application of the sections on P(A and B) and conditional probability.

This problem is best approached by asking what is the probability that no two people have the same birthday. Once we know this probability, we can simply subtract it from 1 to find the probability that two people share a birthday.

If we choose two people at random, what is the probability that they do not share a birthday? Of the 365 days on which the second person could have a birthday, 364 of them are different from the first person's birthday. Therefore the probability is 364/365. Let's define P2 as the probability that the second person drawn does not share a birthday with the person drawn previously. P2 is therefore 364/365. Now define P3 as the probability that the third person drawn does not share a birthday with anyone drawn previously **given** that there are no previous birthday matches. P3 is therefore a conditional probability. If there are no previous birthday matches, then two of the 365 days have been "used up," leaving 363 non-matching days. Therefore P3 = 363/365. In like manner, P4 = 362/365, P5 = 361/365, and so on up to P25 = 341/365.

In order for there to be no matches, the second person must not match any previous person **and** the third person must not match any previous person, and the fourth person must not match any previous person, etc. Since P(A and B) = P(A)P(B), all we have to do is multiply P2, P3, P4 ...P25 together. The result is 0.431. Therefore the probability of at least one match is 0.569.

Gambler's Fallacy

A fair coin is flipped five times and comes up heads each time. What is the probability that it will come up heads on the sixth flip? The correct answer is, of course, 1/2. But many people believe that a tail is more likely to occur after throwing five heads. Their faulty reasoning may go something like this: "In the long run, the number of heads and tails will be the same, so the tails have some catching up to do."

The error in this reasoning is that the proportion of heads approaches 0.5 but the number of heads does not approach the number of tails. The results of a simulation (external link; requires Java) are shown in Figure 1. (The quality of the image is somewhat low because it was captured from the screen.)

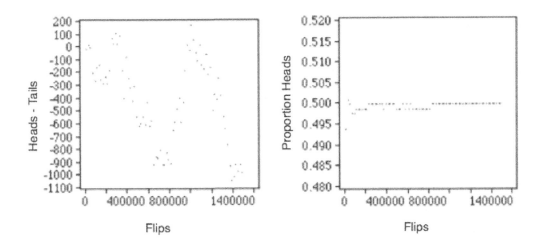

Figure 1. The results of simulating 1,500,000 coin flips. The graph on the left shows the difference between the number of heads and the number of tails as a function of the number of flips. You can see that there is no consistent pattern. After the final flip, there are 968 more tails than heads. The graph on the right shows the proportion of heads. This value goes up and down at the beginning, but converges to 0.5 (rounded to 3 decimal places) before 1,000,000 flips.

Permutations and Combinations

by David M. Lane

Prerequisites
none

Learning Objectives
1. Calculate the probability of two independent events occurring
2. Define permutations and combinations
3. List all permutations and combinations
4. Apply formulas for permutations and combinations

This section covers basic formulas for determining the number of various possible types of outcomes. The topics covered are: (1) counting the number of possible orders, (2) counting using the multiplication rule, (3) counting the number of permutations, and (4) counting the number of combinations.

Possible Orders

Suppose you had a plate with three pieces of candy on it: one green, one yellow, and one red. You are going to pick up these three pieces one at a time. The question is: In how many different orders can you pick up the pieces? Table 1 lists all the possible orders. There are two orders in which red is first: red, yellow, green and red, green, yellow. Similarly, there are two orders in which yellow is first and two orders in which green is first. This makes six possible orders in which the pieces can be picked up.

Table 1. Six Possible Orders.

Number	First	Second	Third
1	red	yellow	green
2	red	green	yellow
3	yellow	red	green
4	yellow	green	red
5	green	red	yellow
6	green	yellow	red

The formula for the number of orders is shown below.

```
Number of orders = n!
```

where n is the number of pieces to be picked up. The symbol "!" stands for factorial. Some examples are:

```
3! = 3 x 2 x 1 = 6
4! = 4 x 3 x 2 x 1 = 24
5! = 5 x 4 x 3 x 2 x 1 = 120
```

This means that if there were 5 pieces of candy to be picked up, they could be picked up in any of 5! = 120 orders.

Multiplication Rule

Imagine a small restaurant whose menu has 3 soups, 6 entrées, and 4 desserts. How many possible meals are there? The answer is calculated by multiplying the numbers to get 3 x 6 x 4 = 72. You can think of it as first there is a choice among 3 soups. Then, for each of these choices there is a choice among 6 entrées resulting in 3 x 6 = 18 possibilities. Then, for each of these 18 possibilities there are 4 possible desserts yielding 18 x 4 = 72 total possibilities.

Permutations

Suppose that there were four pieces of candy (red, yellow, green, and brown) and you were only going to pick up exactly two pieces. How many ways are there of picking up two pieces? Table 2 lists all the possibilities. The first choice can be any of the four colors. For each of these 4 first choices there are 3 second choices. Therefore there are 4 x 3 = 12 possibilities.

Table 2. Twelve Possible Orders.

Number	First	Second
1	red	yellow
2	red	green
3	red	brown
4	yellow	red
5	yellow	green
6	yellow	brown
7	green	red
8	green	yellow
9	green	brown
10	brown	red
11	brown	yellow
12	brown	green

More formally, this question is asking for the number of permutations of four things taken two at a time. The general formula is:

$$_nP_r = \frac{n!}{(n-r)!}$$

where $_nP_r$ is the number of permutations of n things taken r at a time. In other words, it is the number of ways r things can be selected from a group of n things. In this case,

$$_4P_2 = \frac{4!}{(4-2)!} = \frac{4 \text{ x } 3 \text{ x } 2 \text{ x } 1}{2 \text{ x } 1} = 12$$

It is important to note that order counts in permutations. That is, choosing red and then yellow is counted separately from choosing yellow and then red. Therefore permutations refer to the number of ways of choosing rather than the number of possible outcomes. When order of choice is not considered, the formula for combinations is used.

Combinations

Now suppose that you were not concerned with the way the pieces of candy were chosen but only in the final choices. In other words, how many different combinations of two pieces could you end up with? In counting combinations, choosing red and then yellow is the same as choosing yellow and then red because in both cases you end up with one red piece and one yellow piece. Unlike permutations, order does not count. Table 3 is based on Table 2 but is modified so that repeated combinations are given an "x" instead of a number. For example, "yellow then red" has an "x" because the combination of red and yellow was already included as choice number 1. As you can see, there are six combinations of the three colors.

Table 3. Six Combinations.

Number	First	Second
1	red	yellow
2	red	green
3	red	brown
x	yellow	red
4	yellow	green
5	yellow	brown
x	green	red
x	green	yellow
6	green	brown
x	brown	red
x	brown	yellow
x	brown	green

The formula for the number of combinations is shown below where nCr is the number of combinations for n things taken r at a time.

$$_nC_r = \frac{n!}{(n-r)!\,r!}$$

For our example,

$$_4C_2 = \frac{4!}{(4-2)!\,2!} = \frac{4 \times 3 \times 2 \times 1}{(2 \times 1)(2 \times 1)} = 6$$

which is consistent with Table 3.

As an example application, suppose there were six kinds of toppings that one could order for a pizza. How many combinations of exactly 3 toppings could be ordered? Here n = 6 since there are 6 toppings and r = 3 since we are taking 3 at a time. The formula is then:

$$_6C_3 = \frac{6!}{(6-3)!\,3!} = \frac{6 \times 5 \times 4 \times 3 \times 2 \times 1}{(3 \times 2 \times 1)(3 \times 2 \times 1)} = 20.$$

Binomial Distribution

by David M. Lane

Prerequisites
• Chapter 1: Distributions
• Chapter 3: Variability
• Chapter 5: Basic Probability

Learning Objectives
1. Define binomial outcomes
2. Compute the probability of getting X successes in N trials
3. Compute cumulative binomial probabilities
4. Find the mean and standard deviation of a binomial distribution

When you flip a coin, there are two possible outcomes: heads and tails. Each outcome has a fixed probability, the same from trial to trial. In the case of coins, heads and tails each have the same probability of 1/2. More generally, there are situations in which the coin is biased, so that heads and tails have different probabilities. In the present section, we consider probability distributions for which there are just two possible outcomes with fixed probabilities summing to one. These distributions are called binomial distributions.

A Simple Example

The four possible outcomes that could occur if you flipped a coin twice are listed below in Table 1. Note that the four outcomes are equally likely: each has probability 1/4. To see this, note that the tosses of the coin are independent (neither affects the other). Hence, the probability of a head on Flip 1 and a head on Flip 2 is the product of P(H) and P(H), which is 1/2 x 1/2 = 1/4. The same calculation applies to the probability of a head on Flip 1 and a tail on Flip 2. Each is 1/2 x 1/2 = 1/4.

Table 1. Four Possible Outcomes.

Outcome	First Flip	Second Flip
1	Heads	Heads
2	Heads	Tails

3	Tails	Heads
4	Tails	Tails

The four possible outcomes can be classified in terms of the number of heads that come up. The number could be two (Outcome 1), one (Outcomes 2 and 3) or 0 (Outcome 4). The probabilities of these possibilities are shown in Table 2 and in Figure 1. Since two of the outcomes represent the case in which just one head appears in the two tosses, the probability of this event is equal to 1/4 + 1/4 = 1/2. Table 2 summarizes the situation.

Table 2. Probabilities of Getting 0, 1, or 2 Heads.

Number of Heads	Probability
0	1/4
1	1/2
2	1/4

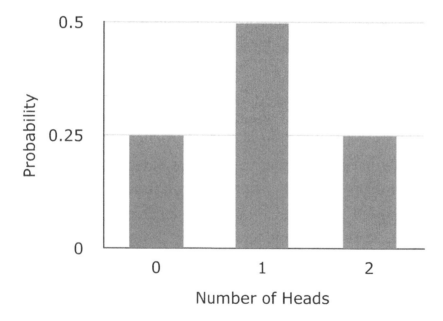

Figure 1. Probabilities of 0, 1, and 2 heads.

Figure 1 is a discrete probability distribution: It shows the probability for each of the values on the X-axis. Defining a head as a "success," Figure 1 shows the probability of 0, 1, and 2 successes for two trials (flips) for an event that has a probability of 0.5 of being a success on each trial. This makes Figure 1 an example of a binomial distribution.

The Formula for Binomial Probabilities

The binomial distribution consists of the probabilities of each of the possible numbers of successes on N trials for independent events that each have a probability of π (the Greek letter pi) of occurring. For the coin flip example, N = 2 and π = 0.5. The formula for the binomial distribution is shown below:

$$P(x) = \frac{N!}{x!\,(N-X)!} \pi^x (1 - \pi)^{N-x}$$

where P(x) is the probability of x successes out of N trials, N is the number of trials, and π is the probability of success on a given trial. Applying this to the coin flip example,

$$P(0) = \frac{2!}{0!\,(2-0)!}(.5^0)(1 - .5)^{2-0} = \frac{2}{2}(1)(.25) = 0.25$$

$$P(1) = \frac{2!}{1!\,(2-1)!}(.5^1)(1 - .5)^{2-1} = \frac{2}{1}(.5)(.5) = 0.50$$

$$P(2) = \frac{2!}{2!\,(2-2)!}(.5^2)(1 - .5)^{2-2} = \frac{2}{2}(.25)(1) = 0.25$$

If you flip a coin twice, what is the probability of getting one or more heads? Since the probability of getting exactly one head is 0.50 and the probability of getting exactly two heads is 0.25, the probability of getting one or more heads is 0.50 + 0.25 = 0.75.

Now suppose that the coin is biased. The probability of heads is only 0.4. What is the probability of getting heads at least once in two tosses? Substituting into the general formula above, you should obtain the answer .64.

Cumulative Probabilities

We toss a coin 12 times. What is the probability that we get from 0 to 3 heads? The answer is found by computing the probability of exactly 0 heads, exactly 1 head, exactly 2 heads, and exactly 3 heads. The probability of getting from 0 to 3 heads is then the sum of these probabilities. The probabilities are: 0.0002, 0.0029, 0.0161, and 0.0537. The sum of the probabilities is 0.073. The calculation of cumulative binomial probabilities can be quite tedious. Therefore we have provided a binomial calculator (external link; requires Java)to make it easy to calculate these probabilities.

Mean and Standard Deviation of Binomial Distributions

Consider a coin-tossing experiment in which you tossed a coin 12 times and recorded the number of heads. If you performed this experiment over and over again, what would the mean number of heads be? On average, you would expect half the coin tosses to come up heads. Therefore the mean number of heads would be 6. In general, the mean of a binomial distribution with parameters N (the number of trials) and π (the probability of success on each trial) is:

$$\mu = N\pi$$

where μ is the mean of the binomial distribution. The variance of the binomial distribution is:

$$\sigma^2 = N\pi(1-\pi)$$

where σ^2 is the variance of the binomial distribution.

Let's return to the coin-tossing experiment. The coin was tossed 12 times, so N = 12. A coin has a probability of 0.5 of coming up heads. Therefore, $\pi = 0.5$. The mean and variance can therefore be computed as follows:

$$\mu = N\pi = (12)(0.5) = 6$$
$$\sigma^2 = N\pi(1-\pi) = (12)(0.5)(1.0 - 0.5) = 3.0.$$

Naturally, the standard deviation (σ) is the square root of the variance (σ^2).

$$\sigma = \sqrt{N\pi(1 - \pi)}$$

Poisson Distribution

by David M. Lane

Prerequisites
• Chapter 1: Logarithms

The Poisson distribution can be used to calculate the probabilities of various numbers of "successes" based on the mean number of successes. In order to apply the Poisson distribution, the various events must be independent. Keep in mind that the term "success" does not really mean success in the traditional positive sense. It just means that the outcome in question occurs.

Suppose you knew that the mean number of calls to a fire station on a weekday is 8. What is the probability that on a given weekday there would be 11 calls? This problem can be solved using the following formula based on the Poisson distribution:

$$p = \frac{e^{-\mu}\mu^{x}}{x!}$$

```
e is the base of natural logarithms (2.7183)
μ is the mean number of "successes"
x is the number of "successes" in question
```

For this example,

$$p = \frac{e^{-8}8^{11}}{11!} = 0.072$$

since the mean is 8 and the question pertains to 11 fires.

The mean of the Poisson distribution is μ. The variance is also equal to μ. Thus, for this example, both the mean and the variance are equal to 8.

Multinomial Distribution

by David M. Lane

Prerequisites
- Chapter 1: Distributions
- Chapter 3: Variability
- Chapter 5: Basic Probability
- Chapter 5: Binomial Distribution

Learning Objectives
1. Define multinomial outcomes
2. Compute probabilities using the multinomial distribution

The binomial distribution allows one to compute the probability of obtaining a given number of binary outcomes. For example, it can be used to compute the probability of getting 6 heads out of 10 coin flips. The flip of a coin is a binary outcome because it has only two possible outcomes: heads and tails. The multinomial distribution can be used to compute the probabilities in situations in which there are more than two possible outcomes. For example, suppose that two chess players had played numerous games and it was determined that the probability that Player A would win is 0.40, the probability that Player B would win is 0.35, and the probability that the game would end in a draw is 0.25. The multinomial distribution can be used to answer questions such as: "If these two chess players played 12 games, what is the probability that Player A would win 7 games, Player B would win 2 games, and the remaining 3 games would be drawn?" The following formula gives the probability of obtaining a specific set of outcomes when there are three possible outcomes for each event:

$$p = \frac{n!}{(n_1!)(n_2!)(n_3!)} p_1^{n_1} p_2^{n_2} p_3^{n_3}$$

where

```
    p is the probility,
    n is the total number of events
```

n_1 is the number of times Outcome 1 occurs,
n_2 is the number of times Outcome 2 occurs,
n_3 is the number of times Outcome 3 occurs,
p_1 is the probability of Outcome 1
p_2 is the probability of Outcome 2, and
p_3 is the probability of Outcome 3.

For the chess example,

```
n  = 12 (12 games are played),
n₁ = 7 (number won by Player A),
n₂ = 2 (number won by Player B),
n₃ = 3 (the number drawn),
p₁ = 0.40 (probability Player A wins)
p₂ = 0.35 (probability Player B wins)
p₃ = 0.25 (probability of a draw)
```

$$p = \frac{12!}{(7!)(2!)(3!)} \cdot .40^7 .35^2 .25^3 = 0.0248$$

The formula for k outcomes is:

$$p = \frac{n!}{(n_1!)(n_2!)...(n_k!)} p_1^{n_1} p_2^{n_2} ... p_k^{n_k}$$

Hypergeometric Distribution

by David M. Lane

Prerequisites
• Chapter 5: Binomial Distribution
• Chapter 5: Permutations and Combinations

The hypergeometric distribution is used to calculate probabilities when sampling without replacement. For example, suppose you first randomly sample one card from a deck of 52. Then, without putting the card back in the deck you sample a second and then (again without replacing cards) a third. Given this sampling procedure, what is the probability that exactly two of the sampled cards will be aces (4 of the 52 cards in the deck are aces). You can calculate this probability using the following formula based on the hypergeometric distribution:

$$p = \frac{{}_kC_x \;\; {}_{(N-k)}C_{(n-x)}}{{}_NC_n}$$

where

```
k is the number of "successes" in the
population
x is the number of "successes" in the sample
N is the size of the population
n is the number sampled
p is the probability of obtaining exactly x
successes
ₖCₓ is the number of combinations of k things
taken x at a time
```

In this example, k = 4 because there are four aces in the deck, x = 2 because the problem asks about the probability of getting two aces, N = 52 because there are 52 cards in a deck, and n = 3 because 3 cards were sampled. Therefore,

$$p = \frac{{}_4C_2 \; {}_{(52-4)}C_{(3-2)}}{{}_{52}C_3}$$

$$p = \frac{\dfrac{4!}{2!2!} \; \dfrac{48!}{47!1!}}{\dfrac{52!}{49!3!}} = 0.013$$

The mean and standard deviation of the hypergeometric distribution are:

$$\text{mean} = \frac{(n)(k)}{N}$$

$$\text{sd} = \sqrt{\frac{(n)(k)(N-k)(N-n)}{N^2(N-1)}}$$

Base Rates

by David M. Lane

Prerequisites
• Chapter 5: Basic Concepts

Learning Objectives
1. Compute the probability of a condition from hits, false alarms, and base rates using a tree diagram
2. Compute the probability of a condition from hits, false alarms, and base rates using Bayes' Theorem

Suppose that at your regular physical exam you test positive for Disease X. Although Disease X has only mild symptoms, you are concerned and ask your doctor about the accuracy of the test. It turns out that the test is 95% accurate. It would appear that the probability that you have Disease X is therefore 0.95. However, the situation is not that simple.

For one thing, more information about the accuracy of the test is needed because there are two kinds of errors the test can make: misses and false positives. If you actually have Disease X and the test failed to detect it, that would be a miss. If you did not have Disease X and the test indicated you did, that would be a false positive. The miss and false positive rates are not necessarily the same. For example, suppose that the test accurately indicates the disease in 99% of the people who have it and accurately indicates no disease in 91% of the people who do not have it. In other words, the test has a miss rate of 0.01 and a false positive rate of 0.09. This might lead you to revise your judgment and conclude that your chance of having the disease is 0.91. This would not be correct since the probability depends on the proportion of people having the disease. This proportion is called the base rate.

Assume that Disease X is a rare disease, and only 2% of people in your situation have it. How does that affect the probability that you have it? Or, more generally, what is the probability that someone who tests positive actually has the disease? Let's consider what would happen if one million people were tested. Out of these one million people, 2% or 20,000 people would have the disease. Of these 20,000 with the disease, the test would accurately detect it in 99% of them. This means that 19,800 cases would be accurately identified. Now let's consider the

98% of the one million people (980,000) who do not have the disease. Since the false positive rate is 0.09, 9% of these 980,000 people will test positive for the disease. This is a total of 88,200 people incorrectly diagnosed.

To sum up, 19,800 people who tested positive would actually have the disease and 88,200 people who tested positive would not have the disease. This means that of all those who tested positive, only

```
19,800/(19,800 + 88,200) = 0.1833
```

of them would actually have the disease. So the probability that you have the disease is not 0.95, or 0.91, but only 0.1833.

These results are summarized in Table 1. The numbers of people diagnosed with the disease are shown in red. Of the one million people tested, the test was correct for 891,800 of those without the disease and for 19,800 with the disease; the test was correct 91% of the time. However, if you look only at the people testing positive (shown in red), only 19,800 (0.1833) of the 88,200 + 19,800 = 108,000 testing positive actually have the disease.

Table 1. Diagnosing Disease X.

True Condition			
No Disease 980,000		Disease 20,000	
Test Result		Test Result	
Positive	Negative	Positive	Negative
88,200	891,800	19,800	200

Bayes' Theorem

This same result can be obtained using Bayes' theorem. Bayes' theorem considers both the prior probability of an event and the diagnostic value of a test to determine the posterior probability of the event. For the current example, the event is that you have Disease X. Let's call this Event D. Since only 2% of people in your situation have Disease X, the prior probability of Event D is 0.02. Or, more formally, $P(D) = 0.02$. If D' represents the probability that Event D is false, then $P(D') = 1 - P(D) = 0.98$.

To define the diagnostic value of the test, we need to define another event: that you test positive for Disease X. Let's call this Event T. The diagnostic value of the test depends on the probability you will test positive given that you actually have the disease, written as P(T|D), and the probability you test positive given that you do not have the disease, written as P(T|D'). Bayes' theorem shown below allows you to calculate P(D|T), the probability that you have the disease given that you test positive for it.

$$P(D|T) = \frac{P(T|D)P(D)}{P(T|D)P(D) + P(T|D')P(D')}$$

The various terms are:

```
P(T|D)   = 0.99
P(T|D')  = 0.09
P(D)     = 0.02
P(D')    = 0.98
```

Therefore,

$$P(D|T) = \frac{(0.99)(0.02)}{(0.99)(0.02) + (0.09)(0.98)} = 0.1833$$

which is the same value computed previously.

Statistical Literacy

by David M. Lane

Prerequisites
- Chapter 5: Base Rates

This <u>webpage</u> gives the FBI list of warning signs for school shooters.

What do you think?

Do you think it is likely that someone showing a majority of these signs would actually shoot people in school?

> Fortunately the vast majority of students do not become shooters. It is necessary to take this base rate information into account in order to compute the probability that any given student will be a shooter. The warning signs are unlikely to be sufficiently predictive to warrant the conclusion that a student will become a shooter. If an action is taken on the basis of these warning signs, it is likely that the student involved would never have become a shooter even without the action.

Exercises

Prerequisites
• All material presented in the Probability Chapter

1. (a) What is the probability of rolling a pair of dice and obtaining a total score of 9 or more? (b) What is the probability of rolling a pair of dice and obtaining a total score of 7?

2. A box contains four black pieces of cloth, two striped pieces, and six dotted pieces. A piece is selected randomly and then placed back in the box. A second piece is selected randomly. What is the probability that:

   a. both pieces are dotted?

   b. the first piece is black and the second piece is dotted?

   c. one piece is black and one piece is striped?

3. A card is drawn at random from a deck. (a) What is the probability that it is an ace or a king? (b) What is the probability that it is either a red card or a black card?

4. The probability that you will win a game is 0.45. (a) If you play the game 80 times, what is the most likely number of wins? (b) What are the mean and variance of a binomial distribution with p = 0.45 and N = 80?

5. A fair coin is flipped 9 times. What is the probability of getting exactly 6 heads?

6. When Susan and Jessica play a card game, Susan wins 60% of the time. If they play 9 games, what is the probability that Jessica will have won more games than Susan?

7. You flip a coin three times. (a) What is the probability of getting heads on only one of your flips? (b) What is the probability of getting heads on at least one flip?

8. A test correctly identifies a disease in 95% of people who have it. It correctly identifies no disease in 94% of people who do not have it. In the population, 3% of the people have the disease. What is the probability that you have the disease if you tested positive?

9. A jar contains 10 blue marbles, 5 red marbles, 4 green marbles, and 1 yellow marble. Two marbles are chosen (without replacement). (a) What is the probability that one will be green and the other red? (b) What is the probability that one will be blue and the other yellow?

10. You roll a fair die five times, and you get a 6 each time. What is the probability that you get a 6 on the next roll?

11. You win a game if you roll a die and get a 2 or a 5. You play this game 60 times.

   a. What is the probability that you win between 5 and 10 times (inclusive)?

   b. What is the probability that you will win the game at least 15 times?

   c. What is the probability that you will win the game at least 40 times?

   d. What is the most likely number of wins.

   e. What is the probability of obtaining the number of wins in d?

   Explain how you got each answer or show your work.

12. In a baseball game, Tommy gets a hit 30% of the time when facing this pitcher. Joey gets a hit 25% of the time. They are both coming up to bat this inning.

   a. What is the probability that Joey or Tommy will get a hit?

   b. What is the probability that neither player gets a hit?

   c. What is the probability that they both get a hit?

13. An unfair coin has a probability of coming up heads of 0.65. The coin is flipped 50 times. What is the probability it will come up heads 25 or fewer times? (Give answer to at least 3 decimal places).

14. You draw two cards from a deck, what is the probability that:

   a. both of them are face cards (king, queen, or jack)?

   b. you draw two cards from a deck and both of them are hearts?

15. True/False: You are more likely to get a pattern of HTHHHTHTTH than HHHHHHHHHTT when you flip a coin 10 times.

16. True/False: Suppose that at your regular physical exam you test positive for a relatively rare disease. You will need to start taking medicine if you have the disease, so you ask your doc- tor about the accuracy of the test. It turns out that the test is 98% accurate. The probability that you have Disease X is therefore 0.98 and the probability that you do not have it is .02. Explain your answer.

Questions from Case Studies

Diet and Health (DH) case study

17. (DH)

    a. What percentage of people on the AHA diet had some sort of illness or death?

    b. What is the probability that if you randomly selected a person on the AHA diet, he or she would have some sort of illness or death?

    c. If 3 people on the AHA diet are chosen at random, what is the probability that they will all be healthy?

18. (DH)

    a. What percentage of people on the Mediterranean diet had some sort of illness or death?

    b. What is the probability that if you randomly selected a person on the Mediterranean diet, he or she would have some sort of illness or death?

    c. What is the probability that if you randomly selected a person on the Mediterranean diet, he or she would have cancer?

    d. If you randomly select five people from the Mediterranean diet, what is the probability that they would all be healthy?

The following questions are from ARTIST (reproduced with permission)

Assessment
Resource
Tools for
Improving
Statistical
Thinking

WEB
Artist

19. Five faces of a fair die are painted black, and one face is painted white. The die is rolled six times. Which of the following results is more likely?

    a. Black side up on five of the rolls; white side up on the other roll

    b. Black side up on all six rolls

    c. a and b are equally likely

20. One of the items on the student survey for an introductory statistics course was "Rate your intelligence on a scale of 1 to 10." The distribution of this variable for the 100 women in the class is presented below. What is the probability of randomly selecting a woman from the class who has an intelligence rating that is LESS than seven (7)?

Intelligence Rating	Count
5	12
6	24
7	38
8	23
9	2
10	1

    a. $(12 + 24)/100 = .36$

    b. $(12 + 24 + 38)/100 = .74$

    c. $38/100 = .38$

    d. $(23 + 2 + 1)/100 = .26$

    e. None of the above.

21. You roll 2 fair six-sided dice. Which of the following outcomes is most likely to occur on the next roll? A. Getting double 3. B. Getting a 3 and a 4. C. They are equally likely. Explain your choice.

22. If Tahnee flips a coin 10 times, and records the results (Heads or Tails), which outcome below is more likely to occur, A or B? Explain your choice.

Throw Number	1	2	3	4	5	6	7	8	9	10
A	H	T	T	H	T	H	H	T	T	T
B	H	T	H	T	H	T	H	T	H	T

23. A bowl has 100 wrapped hard candies in it. 20 are yellow, 50 are red, and 30 are blue. They are well mixed up in the bowl. Jenny pulls out a handful of 10 candies, counts the number of reds, and tells her teacher. The teacher writes the number of red candies on a list. Then, Jenny puts the candies back into the bowl, and mixes them all up again. Four of Jenny's classmates, Jack, Julie, Jason, and Jerry do the same thing. They each pick ten candies, count the reds, and the teacher writes down the number of reds. Then they put the candies back and mix them up again each time. The teacher's list for the number of reds is most likely to be (please select one):

a. 8,9,7,10,9

b. 3,7,5,8,5

c. 5,5,5,5,5

d. 2,4,3,4,3

e. 3,0,9,2,8

24. An insurance company writes policies for a large number of newly-licensed drivers each year. Suppose 40% of these are low-risk drivers, 40% are moderate risk, and 20% are high risk. The company has no way to know which group any individual driver falls in when it writes the policies. None of the low-risk drivers will have an at-fault accident in the next year, but 10% of the moderate-risk and 20% of the high-risk drivers will have such an accident. If a driver has an at-fault accident in the next year, what is the probability that he or she is high-risk?

25. You are to participate in an exam for which you had no chance to study, and for that reason cannot do anything but guess for each question (all questions being of the multiple choice type, so the chance of guessing the correct answer for each question is 1/d, d being the number of options (distractors) per question;

so in case of a 4-choice question, your guess chance is 0.25). Your instructor offers you the opportunity to choose amongst the following exam formats: I. 6 questions of the 4-choice type; you pass when 5 or more answers are correct; II. 5 questions of the 5-choice type; you pass when 4 or more answers are correct; III. 4 questions of the 10-choice type; you pass when 3 or more answers are correct. Rank the three exam formats according to their attractiveness. It should be clear that the format with the highest probability to pass is the most attractive format. Which would you choose and why?

26. Consider the question of whether the home team wins more than half of its games in the National Basketball Association. Suppose that you study a simple random sample of 80 professional basketball games and find that 52 of them are won by the home team.

a. Assuming that there is no home court advantage and that the home team therefore wins 50% of its games in the long run, determine the probability that the home team would win 65% or more of its games in a simple random sample of 80 games.

b. Does the sample information (that 52 of a random sample of 80 games are won by the home team) provide strong evidence that the home team wins more than half of its games in the long run? Explain.

27. A refrigerator contains 6 apples, 5 oranges, 10 bananas, 3 pears, 7 peaches, 11 plums, and 2 mangos.

a. Imagine you stick your hand in this refrigerator and pull out a piece of fruit at random. What is the probability that you will pull out a pear?

b. Imagine now that you put your hand in the refrigerator and pull out a piece of fruit. You decide you do not want to eat that fruit so you put it back into the refrigerator and pull out another piece of fruit. What is the probability that the first piece of fruit you pull out is a banana and the second piece you pull out is an apple?

c. What is the probability that you stick your hand in the refrigerator one time and pull out a mango or an orange?

6. Research Design

A. Scientific Method

B. Measurement

C. Basics of Data Collection

D. Sampling Bias

E. Experimental Designs

F. Causation

G. Exercises

Scientific Method

by David M. Lane

Prerequisites
• none

This section contains a brief discussion of the most important principles of the scientific method. A thorough treatment of the philosophy of science is beyond the scope of this work.

One of the hallmarks of the scientific method is that it depends on empirical data. To be a proper scientific investigation, the data must be collected systematically. However, scientific investigation does not necessarily require experimentation in the sense of manipulating variables and observing the results. Observational studies in the fields of astronomy, developmental psychology, and ethology are common and provide valuable scientific information.

Theories and explanations are very important in science. Theories in science can never be proved since one can never be 100% certain that a new empirical finding inconsistent with the theory will never be found.

Scientific theories must be potentially disconfirmable. If a theory can accommodate all possible results then it is not a scientific theory. Therefore, a scientific theory should lead to testable hypotheses. If a hypothesis is disconfirmed, then the theory from which the hypothesis was deduced is incorrect. For example, the secondary reinforcement theory of attachment states that an infant becomes attached to its parent by means of a pairing of the parent with a primary reinforcer (food). It is through this "secondary reinforcement" that the child-parent bond forms. The secondary reinforcement theory has been disconfirmed by numerous experiments. Perhaps the most notable is one in which infant monkeys were fed by a surrogate wire mother while a surrogate cloth mother was available. The infant monkeys formed no attachment to the wire monkeys and frequently clung to the cloth surrogate mothers (Harlow, 1958).

If a hypothesis derived from a theory is confirmed, then the theory has survived a test and it becomes more useful and better thought of by the researchers in the field. A theory is not confirmed when correct hypotheses are derived from it.

A key difference between scientific explanations and faith-based explanations is simply that faith-based explanations are based on faith and do not need to be testable. This does not mean that an explanation that cannot be tested is incorrect in some cosmic sense. It just means that it is not a scientific explanation.

The method of investigation in which a hypothesis is developed from a theory and then confirmed or disconfirmed involves deductive reasoning. However, deductive reasoning does not explain where the theory came from in the first place. In general, a theory is developed by a scientist who is aware of many empirical findings on a topic of interest. Then, through a generally poorly understood process called "induction," the scientist develops a way to explain all or most of the findings within a relatively simple framework or theory.

An important attribute of a good scientific theory is that it is parsimonious. That is, that it is simple in the sense that it uses relatively few constructs to explain many empirical findings. A theory that is so complex that it has as many assumptions as it has predictions is not very valuable.

Although strictly speaking, disconfirming an hypothesis deduced from a theory disconfirms the theory, it rarely leads to the abandonment of the theory. Instead, the theory will probably be modified to accommodate the inconsistent finding. If the theory has to be modified over and over to accommodate new findings, the theory generally becomes less and less parsimonious. This can lead to discontent with the theory and the search for a new theory. If a new theory is developed that can explain the same facts in a more parsimonious way, then the new theory will eventually supersede the old theory.

Measurement

by David M. Lane

Prerequisites
- Values of Pearson's Correlation
- Variance Sum Law
- Chapter 3: Measures of Variability

Learning Objectives
1. Define reliability
2. Describe reliability in terms of true scores and error
3. Compute reliability from the true score and error variance
4. Define the standard error of measurement and state why it is valuable
5. State the effect of test length on reliability
6. Distinguish between reliability and validity
7. Define three types of validity
8. State the how reliability determines the upper limit to validity

The measurement of psychological attributes such as self-esteem can be complex. A good measurement scale should be both reliable and valid. These concepts will be discussed in turn.

Reliability

The notion of reliability revolves around whether you would get at least approximately the same result if you measure something twice with the same measurement instrument. A common way to define reliability is the correlation between parallel forms of a test. Letting "test" represent a parallel form of the test, the symbol $r_{test,test}$ is used to denote the reliability of the test.

True Scores and Error

Assume you wish to measure a person's mean response time to the onset of a stimulus. For simplicity, assume that there is no learning over tests which, of course, is not really true. The person is given 1,000 trials on the task and you obtain the response time on each trial.

The mean response time over the 1,000 trials can be thought of as the person's "true" score, or at least a very good approximation of it. Theoretically, the true score is the mean that would be approached as the number of trials increases indefinitely.

An individual response time can be thought of as being composed of two parts: the true score and the error of measurement. Thus if the person's true score were 345 and their response on one of the trials were 358, then the error of measurement would be 13. Similarly, if the response time were 340, the error of measurement would be -5.

Now consider the more realistic example of a class of students taking a 100-point true/false exam. Let's assume that each student knows the answer to some of the questions and has no idea about the other questions. For the sake of simplicity, we are assuming there is no partial knowledge of any of the answers and for a given question a student either knows the answer or guesses. Finally, assume the test is scored such that a student receives one point for a correct answer and loses a point for an incorrect answer. In this example, a student's true score is the number of questions they know the answer to and their error score is their score on the questions they guessed on. For example, assume a student knew 90 of the answers and guessed correctly on 7 of the remaining 10 (and therefore incorrectly on 3). Their true score would be 90 since that is the number of answers they knew. Their error score would be 7 - 3 = 4 and therefore their actual test score would be 90 + 4.

Every test score can be thought of as the sum of two independent components, the true score and the error score. This can be written as:

$$y_{test} = y_{true} + y_{error}$$

The following expression follows directly from the Variance Sum Law:

$$\sigma_{Test}^2 = \sigma_{True}^2 + \sigma_{error}^2$$

Reliability in Terms of True Scores and Error

It can be shown that the reliability of a test, $r_{test,test}$, is the ratio of true-score variance to test-score variance. This can be written as:

$$r_{test,test} = \frac{\sigma^2_{True}}{\sigma^2_{Test}} = \frac{\sigma^2_{True}}{\sigma^2_{True} + \sigma^2_{error}}$$

It is important to understand the implications of the role the variance of true scores plays in the definition of reliability: If a test were given in two populations for which the variance of the true scores differed, the reliability of the test would be higher in the population with the higher true-score variance. Therefore, reliability is not a property of a test per se but the reliability of a test in a given population.

Assessing Error of Measurement

The reliability of a test does not show directly how close the test scores are to the true scores. That is, it does not reveal how much a person's test score would vary across parallel forms of the test. By definition, the mean over a large number of parallel tests would be the true score. The standard deviation of a person's test scores would indicate how much the test scores vary from the true score. This standard deviation is called the standard error of measurement. In practice, it is not practical to give a test over and over to the same person and/or assume that there are no practice effects. Instead, the following formula is used to estimate the standard error of measurement.

$$S_{measurement} = S_{test}\sqrt{1 - r_{test,test}}$$

where $S_{measurement}$ is the standard error of measurement, S_{test} is the standard deviation of the test scores, and $r_{test,test}$ is the reliability of the test. Taking the extremes, if the reliability is 0, then the standard error of measurement is equal to the standard deviation of the test; if the reliability is perfect (1.0) then the standard error of measurement is 0.

Increasing Reliability

It is important to make measures as reliable as is practically possible. Suppose an investigator is studying the relationship between spatial ability and a set of other variables. The higher the reliability of the test of spatial ability, the higher the correlations will be. Similarly, if an experimenter seeks to determine whether a particular exercise regiment decreases blood pressure, the higher the reliability of the measure of blood pressure, the more sensitive the experiment. More precisely, the higher the reliability the higher the power of the experiment. Power is covered in detail in Chapter 13. Finally, if a test is being used to select students for college admission or employees for jobs, the higher the reliability of the test the stronger will be the relationship to the criterion.

Two basic ways of increasing reliability are (1) to improve the quality of the items and (2) to increase the number of items. Items that are either too easy so that almost everyone gets them correct or too difficult so that almost no one gets them correct are not good items: they provide very little information. In most contexts, items which about half the people get correct are the best (other things being equal).

Items that do not correlate with other items can usually be improved. Sometimes the item is confusing or ambiguous.

Increasing the number of items increases reliability in the manner shown by the following formula:

$$r_{new,new} = \frac{kr_{test,test}}{1 + (k-1)r_{test,test}}$$

where k is the factor by which the test length is increased, $r_{new,new}$ is the reliability of the new longer test, and $r_{test,test}$ is the current reliability. For example, if a test with 50 items has a reliability of .70 then the reliability of a test that is 1.5 times longer (75 items) would be calculated as follows

$$r_{new,new} = \frac{(1.5)(0.70)}{1 + (1.5-1)(0.70)}$$

which equals 0.78. Thus increasing the number of items from 50 to 75 would increase the reliability from 0.70 to 0.78.

It is important to note that this formula assumes the new items have the same characteristics as the old items. Obviously adding poor items would not increase the reliability as expected and might even decrease the reliability.

Validity

The validity of a test refers to whether the test measures what it is supposed to measure. The three most common types of validity are face validity, empirical validity, and construct validity. We consider these types of validity below.

Face Validity

A test's face validity refers to whether the test appears to measure what it is supposed to measure. That is, does the test "on its face" appear to measure what it is supposed to be measuring. An Asian history test consisting of a series of questions about Asian history would have high face validity. If the test included primarily questions about American history then it would have little or no face validity as a test of Asian history.

Predictive Validity

Predictive validity (sometimes called empirical validity) refers to a test's ability to predict a relevant behavior. For example, the main way in which SAT tests are validated is by their ability to predict college grades. Thus, to the extent these tests are successful at predicting college grades they are said to possess predictive validity.

Construct Validity

Construct validity is more difficult to define. In general, a test has construct validity if its pattern of correlations with other measures is in line with the construct it is purporting to measure. Construct validity can be established by showing a test has both convergent and divergent validity. A test has convergent validity if it correlates with other tests that are also measures of the construct in question. Divergent validity is established by showing the test does not correlate highly with tests of other constructs. Of course, some constructs may overlap so the establishment of convergent and divergent validity can be complex.

To take an example, suppose one wished to establish the construct validity of a new test of spatial ability. Convergent and divergent validity could be established by showing the test correlates relatively highly with other measures of spatial ability but less highly with tests of verbal ability or social intelligence.

Reliability and Predictive Validity

The reliability of a test limits the size of the correlation between the test and other measures. In general, the correlation of a test with another measure will be lower than the test's reliability. After all, how could a test correlate with something else as high as it correlates with a parallel form of itself? Theoretically it is possible for a test to correlate as high as the square root of the reliability with another measure. For example, if a test has a reliability of 0.81 then it could correlate as high as 0.90 with another measure. This could happen if the other measure were a perfectly reliable test of the same construct as the test in question. In practice, this is very unlikely.

A correlation above the upper limit set by reliabilities can act as a red flag. For example, Vul, Harris, Winkielman, and Paschler (2009) found that in many studies the correlations between various fMRI activation patterns and personality measures were higher than their reliabilities would allow. A careful examination of these studies revealed serious flaws in the way the data were analyzed.

Basics of Data Collection

by Heidi Zeimer

Prerequisites

• None

Learning Objectives

1. Describe how a variable such as height should be recorded

2. Choose a good response scale for a questionnaire

Most statistical analyses require that your data be in numerical rather than verbal form (you can't punch letters into your calculator). Therefore, data collected in verbal form must be coded so that it is represented by numbers. To illustrate, consider the data in Table 1.

Table 1. Example Data

Student Name	Hair Color	Gender	Major	Height	Computer Experience
Norma	Brown	Female	Psychology	5'4"	Lots
Amber	Blonde	Female	Social Science	5'7"	Very little
Paul	Blonde	Male	History	6'1"	Moderate
Christopher	Black	Male	Biology	5'10"	Lots
Sonya	Brown	Female	Psychology	5'4"	Little

Can you conduct statistical analyses on the above data or must you re-code it in some way? For example, how would you go about computing the average height of the 5 students. You cannot enter students' heights in their current form into a statistical program -- the computer would probably give you an error message because it does not understand notation such as 5'4". One solution is to change all the numbers to inches. So, 5'4" becomes (5 x 12) + 4 = 64, and 6'1" becomes (6 x 12) + 1 = 73, and so forth. In this way, you are converting height in feet and inches to simply height in inches. From there, it is very easy to ask a statistical program to calculate the mean height in inches for the 5 students.

You may ask, "Why not simply ask subjects to write their height in inches in the first place?" Well, the number one rule of data collection is to ask for information in such a way as it will be most accurately reported. Most people know their height in feet and inches and cannot quickly and accurately convert it into inches "on the fly." So, in order to preserve data accuracy, it is best for researchers to make the necessary conversions.

Let's take another example. Suppose you wanted to calculate the mean amount of computer experience for the five students shown in Table 1. One way would be to convert the verbal descriptions to numbers as shown in Table 2. Thus, "Very Little" would be converted to "1" and "Little" would be converted to "2."

Table 2. Conversion of verbal descriptions to numbers

1	2	3	4	5
Very Little	Little	Moderate	Lots	Very Lots

Measurement Examples

Example #1: How much information should I record?

Say you are volunteering at a track meet at your college, and your job is to record each runner's time as they pass the finish line for each race. Their times are shown in large red numbers on a digital clock with eight digits to the right of the decimal point, and you are told to record the entire number in your tablet. Thinking eight decimal places is a bit excessive, you only record runners' times to one decimal place. The track meet begins, and runner number one finishes with a time of 22.93219780 seconds. You dutifully record her time in your tablet, but only to one decimal place, that is 22.9. Race number two finishes and you record 32.7 for the winning runner. The fastest time in Race number three is 25.6. Race number four winning time is 22.9, Race number five is.... But wait! You suddenly realize your mistake; you now have a tie between runner one and runner four for the title of Fastest Overall Runner! You should have recorded more information from the digital clock -- that information is now lost, and you cannot go back in time and record running times to more decimal places.

The point is that you should think very carefully about the scales and specificity of information needed in your research before you begin collecting data. If you believe you might need additional information later but are not sure, measure it; you can always decide to not use some of the data, or "collapse" your data down to lower scales if you wish, but you cannot expand your data set to include more information after the fact. In this example, you probably would not need to record eight digits to the right of the decimal point. But recording only one decimal digit is clearly too few.

Example #2

Pretend for a moment that you are teaching five children in middle school (yikes!), and you are trying to convince them that they must study more in order to earn better grades. To prove your point, you decide to collect actual data from their recent math exams, and, toward this end, you develop a questionnaire to measure their study time and subsequent grades. You might develop a questionnaire which looks like the following:

1. Please write your name: _____

2. Please indicate how much you studied for this math exam:
   a lot..............moderate................little

3. Please circle the grade you received on the math exam:
   A B C D F

Given the above questionnaire, your obtained data might look like the following:

Name	Amount Studied	Grade
John	Little	C
Sally	Moderate	B
Alexander	Lots	A
Linda	Moderate	A
Thomas	Little	B

Eyeballing the data, it seems as if the children who studied more received better grades, but it's difficult to tell. "Little," "lots," and "B," are imprecise, qualitative terms. You could get more precise information by asking specifically how many hours they studied and their exact score on the exam. The data then might look as follows:

Name	Hours studied	% Correct

John	5	71
Sally	9	83
Alexander	13	97
Linda	12	91
Thomas	7	85

Of course, this assumes the students would know how many hours they studied. Rather than trust the students' memories, you might ask them to keep a log of their study time as they study.

Sampling Bias

by David M. Lane

Prerequisites
• Inferential Statistics (including sampling)

Learning Objectives
1. Recognize sampling bias
2. Distinguish among self-selection bias, undercoverage bias, and survivorship bias

Descriptions of various types of sampling such as *simple random sampling* and *stratified random sampling* are covered in the inferential statistics section of Chapter 1. This section discusses various types of sampling biases including self-selection bias and survivorship bias. Examples of other sampling biases that are not easily categorized will also be given.

It is important to keep in mind that sampling bias refers to the method of sampling, not the sample itself. There is no guarantee that random sampling will result in a sample representative of the population just as not every sample obtained using a biased sampling method will be greatly non-representative of the population.

Self-Selection Bias

Imagine that a university newspaper ran an ad asking for students to volunteer for a study in which intimate details of their sex lives would be discussed. Clearly the sample of students who would volunteer for such a study would not be representative of the students at the university. Similarly, an online survey about computer use is likely to attract people more interested in technology than is typical. In both of these examples, people who "self-select" themselves for the experiment are likely to differ in important ways from the population the experimenter wishes to draw conclusions about. Many of the admittedly "non-scientific" polls taken on television or web sites suffer greatly from self-selection bias.

A self-selection bias can result when the non-random component occurs after the potential subject has enlisted in the experiment. Considering again the hypothetical experiment in which subjects are to be asked intimate details of their sex lives, assume that the subjects did not know what the experiment was going to be about until they showed up. Many of the subjects would then likely leave the experiment resulting in a biased sample.

Undercoverage Bias

A common type of sampling bias is to sample too few observations from a segment of the population. A commonly-cited example of undercoverage is the poll taken by the Literary Digest in 1936 that indicated that Landon would win an election against Roosevelt by a large margin when, in fact, it was Roosevelt who won by a large margin. A common explanation is that poorer people were undercovered because they were less likely to have telephones and that this group was more likely to support Roosevelt.

A detailed analysis by Squire (1988) showed that it was not just an undercoverage bias that resulted in the faulty prediction of the election results. He concluded that, in addition to the undercoverage described above, there was a nonresponse bias (a form of self-selection bias) such that those favoring Landon were more likely to return their survey than were those favoring Roosevelt.

Survivorship Bias

Survivorship bias occurs when the observations recorded at the end of the investigation are a non-random set of those present at the beginning of the investigation. Gains in stock funds is an area in which survivorship bias often plays a role. The basic problem is that poorly-performing funds are often either eliminated or merged into other funds. Suppose one considers a sample of stock funds that exist in the present and then calculates the mean 10-year appreciation of those funds. Can these results be validly generalized to other stock funds of the same type? The problem is that the poorly-performing stock funds that are not still in existence (did not survive for 10 years) are not included. Therefore, there is a bias toward selecting better-performing funds. There is good evidence that this survivorship bias is substantial (Malkiel, 1995).

In World War II, the statistician Abraham Wald analyzed the distribution of hits from anti-aircraft fire on aircraft returning from missions. The idea was that this information would be useful for deciding where to place extra armor. A naive approach would be to put armor at locations that were frequently hit to reduce the damage there. However, this would ignore the survivorship bias occurring because only a subset of aircraft return. Wald's approach was the opposite: if there were few hits in a certain location on returning planes, then hits in that location were likely to bring a plane down. Therefore, he recommended that locations without hits on the returning planes should be given extra armor. A detailed and mathematical description of Wald's work can be found in Mangel and Samaniego (1984.)

Experimental Designs

by David M. Lane

Prerequisites
• Chapter 1: Variables

Learning Objectives

1. Distinguish between between-subject and within-subject designs
2. State the advantages of within-subject designs
3. Define "multi-factor design" and "factorial design"
4. Identify the levels of a variable in an experimental design
5. Describe when counterbalancing is used

There are many ways an experiment can be designed. For example, subjects can all be tested under each of the treatment conditions or a different group of subjects can be used for each treatment. An experiment might have just one *independent variable* or it might have several. This section describes basic experimental designs and their advantages and disadvantages.

Between-Subjects Designs

In a *between-subjects* design, the various experimental treatments are given to different groups of subjects. For example, in the *"Teacher Ratings"* case study, subjects were randomly divided into two groups. Subjects were all told they were going to see a video of an instructor's lecture after which they would rate the quality of the lecture. The groups differed in that the subjects in one group were told that prior teaching evaluations indicated that the instructor was charismatic whereas subjects in the other group were told that the evaluations indicated the instructor was punitive. In this experiment, the *independent variable* is "Condition" and has two levels (charismatic teacher and punitive teacher). It is a *between-subjects* variable because different subjects were used for the two levels of the independent variable: subjects were in either the "charismatic teacher" or the "punitive teacher" condition. Thus the comparison of the charismatic-teacher condition with the punitive-teacher condition is a comparison between the subjects in one condition with the subjects in the other condition.

The two conditions were treated exactly the same except for the instructions they received. Therefore, it would appear that any difference between conditions should be attributed to the treatments themselves. However, this ignores the possibility of chance differences between the groups. That is, by chance, the raters in one condition might have, on average, been more lenient than the raters in the other condition. Randomly assigning subjects to treatments ensures that all differences between conditions are chance differences; it does not ensure there will be no differences. The key question, then, is how to distinguish real differences from chance differences. The field of inferential statistics answers just this question. The inferential statistics applicable to testing the difference between the means of the two conditions covered in Chapter 12. Analyzing the data from this experiment reveals that the ratings in the charismatic-teacher condition were higher than those in the punitive-teacher condition. Using *inferential statistics*, it can be calculated that the probability of finding a difference as large or larger than the one obtained if the treatment had no effect is only 0.018. Therefore it seems likely that the treatment had an effect and it is not the case that all differences were chance differences.

Independent variables often have several levels. For example, in the "Smiles and Leniency" case study, the independent variable is "type of smile" and there are four levels of this independent variable: (1) false smile, (2) felt smile, (3) miserable smile, and (4) a neutral control. Keep in mind that although there are four levels, there is only one independent variable. Designs with more than one independent variable are considered next.

Multi-Factor Between-Subject Designs

In the "*Bias Against Associates of the Obese*" experiment, the qualifications of potential job applicants were judged. Each applicant was accompanied by an associate. The experiment had two independent variables: the weight of the associate (obese or average) and the applicant's relationship to the associate (girl friend or acquaintance). This design can be described as an Associate's Weight (2) x Associate's Relationship (2) *factorial design*. The numbers in parentheses represent the number of levels of the independent variable. The design was a factorial design because all four combinations of associate's weight and associate's relationship were included. The dependent variable was a rating of the applicant's qualifications (on a 9-point scale).

If two separate experiments had been conducted, one to test the effect of Associate's Weight and one to test the effect of Associate's Relationship then there would be no way to assess whether the effect of Associate's Weight depended on the Associate's Relationship. One might imagine that the Associate's Weight would have a larger effect if the associate were a girl friend rather than merely an acquaintance. A factorial design allows this question to be addressed. When the effect of one variable does differ depending on the level of the other variable then it is said that there is an *interaction* between the variables.

Factorial designs can have three or more independent variables. In order to be a between-subjects design there must be a separate group of subjects for each combination of the levels of the independent variables.

Within-Subjects Designs

A within-subjects design differs from a between-subjects design in that the same subjects perform at all levels of the *independent variable*. For example consider the "*ADHD Treatment*" case study. In this experiment, subjects diagnosed as having attention deficit disorder were each tested on a delay of gratification task after receiving methylphenidate (MPH). All subjects were tested four times, once after receiving one of the four doses. Since each subject was tested under each of the four levels of the independent variable "dose," the design is a *within-subjects design* and dose is a *within-subjects variable*. Within-subjects designs are sometimes called *repeated-measures designs*.

Counterbalancing

In a within-subject design it is important not to *confound* the order in which a task is performed with the experimental treatment. For example, consider the problem that would have occurred if, in the ADHD study, every subject had received the doses in the same order starting with the lowest and continuing to the highest. It is not unlikely that experience with the delay of gratification task would have an effect. If practice on this task leads to better performance, then it would appear that higher doses caused the better performance when, in fact, it was the practice that caused the better performance.

One way to address this problem is to *counterbalance* the order of presentations. In other words, subjects would be given the doses in different orders in such a way that each dose was given in each sequential position an equal number of times. An example of counterbalancing is shown in Table 1.

Table 1. Counterbalanced order for four subjects.

Subject	0 mg/kg	.15 mg/kg	.30 mg/kg	.60 mg/kg
1	First	Second	Third	Fourth
2	Second	Third	Fourth	First
3	Third	Fourth	First	Second
4	Fourth	First	Second	Third

It should be kept in mind that counterbalancing is not a satisfactory solution if there are complex dependencies between which treatment precedes which and the dependent variable. In these cases, it is usually better to use a between-subjects design than a within-subjects design.

Advantage of Within-Subjects Designs

An advantage of within-subjects designs is that individual differences in subjects' overall levels of performance are controlled. This is important because subjects invariably will differ greatly from one another. In an experiment on problem solving, some subjects will be better than others regardless of the condition they are in. Similarly, in a study of blood pressure some subjects will have higher blood pressure than others regardless of the condition. Within-subjects designs control these individual differences by comparing the scores of a subject in one condition to the scores of the same subject in other conditions. In this sense each subject serves as his or her own control. This typically gives within-subjects designs considerably more *power* than between-subjects designs. That is, this makes within-subjects designs more able to detect an effect of the independent variable than are between-subjects designs.

Within-subjects designs are often called "repeated-measures" designs since repeated measurements are taken for each subject. Similarly, a within-subject variable can be called a repeated-measures factor.

Complex Designs

Designs can contain combinations of between-subject and within-subject variables. For example, the "*Weapons and Aggression*" case study has one between-subject variable (gender) and two within-subject variables (the type of priming word and the type of word to be responded to).

Causation

by David M. Lane

Prerequisites
- Chapter 1: What are Statistics
- Chapter 3: Measures of Variability
- Chapter 4: Pearson's Correlation
- Chapter 6: Experimental Designs

Learning Objectives
1. Explain how experimentation allows causal inferences
2. Explain the role of unmeasured variables
3. Explain the "third-variable" problem
4. Explain how causation can be inferred in non-experimental designs

The concept of causation is a complex one in the philosophy of science. Since a full coverage of this topic is well beyond the scope of this text, we focus on two specific topics: (1) the establishment of causation in experiments and (2) the establishment of causation in non-experimental designs.

Establishing Causation in Experiments

Consider a simple experiment in which subjects are *sampled randomly* from a *population* and then *assigned randomly* to either the experimental group or the control group. Assume the condition means on the *dependent variable* differed. Does this mean the treatment caused the difference?

To make this discussion more concrete, assume that the experimental group received a drug for insomnia, the control group received a placebo, and the dependent variable was the number of minutes the subject slept that night. An obvious obstacle to inferring causality is that there are many unmeasured variables that affect how many hours someone sleeps. Among them are how much stress the person is under, physiological and genetic factors, how much caffeine they consumed, how much sleep they got the night before, etc. Perhaps differences between the groups on these factors are responsible for the difference in the number of minutes slept.

At first blush it might seem that the random assignment eliminates differences in unmeasured variables. However, this is not the case. Random assignment ensures that differences on unmeasured variables are chance differences. It does not ensure that there are no differences. Perhaps, by chance, many subjects in the control group were under high stress and this stress made it more difficult to fall asleep. The fact that the greater stress in the control group was due to chance does not mean it could not be responsible for the difference between the control and the experimental groups. In other words, the observed difference in "minutes slept" could have been due to a chance difference between the control group and the experimental group rather than due to the drug's effect.

This problem seems intractable since, by definition, it is impossible to measure an "unmeasured variable" just as it is impossible to measure and control all variables that affect the dependent variable. However, although it is impossible to assess the effect of any single unmeasured variable, it is possible to assess the combined effects of all unmeasured variables. Since everyone in a given condition is treated the same in the experiment, differences in their scores on the dependent variable must be due to the unmeasured variables. Therefore, a measure of the differences among the subjects within a condition is a measure of the sum total of the effects of the unmeasured variables. The most common measure of differences is the variance. By using the within-condition variance to assess the effects of unmeasured variables, statistical methods determine the probability that these unmeasured variables could produce a difference between conditions as large or larger than the difference obtained in the experiment. If that probability is low, then it is inferred (that's why they call it *inferential statistics*) that the treatment had an effect and that the differences are not entirely due to chance. Of course, there is always some nonzero probability that the difference occurred by chance so total certainty is not a possibility.

Causation in Non-Experimental Designs

It is almost a cliché that correlation does not mean causation. The main fallacy in inferring causation from correlation is called the *"third-variable problem"* and means that a third variable is responsible for the correlation between two other variables. An excellent example used by Li (1975) to illustrate this point is the positive correlation in Taiwan in the 1970's between the use of contraception and the number of electric appliances in one's house. Of course, using contraception does not induce you to buy electrical appliances or vice versa. Instead, the third variable of education level affects both.

Does the possibility of a third-variable problem make it impossible to draw causal inferences without doing an experiment? One approach is to simply assume that you do not have a third-variable problem. This approach, although common, is not very satisfactory. However, be aware that the assumption of no third-variable problem may be hidden behind a complex causal model that contains sophisticated and elegant mathematics.

A better though, admittedly more difficult approach, is to find converging evidence. This was the approach taken to conclude that smoking causes cancer. The analysis included converging evidence from retrospective studies, prospective studies, lab studies with animals, and theoretical understandings of cancer causes.

A second problem is determining the direction of causality. A correlation between two variables does not indicate which variable is causing which. For example, Reinhart and Rogoff (2010) found a strong correlation between public debt and GDP growth. Although some have argued that public debt slows growth, most evidence supports the alternative that slow growth increases public debt.

Statistical Literacy

by David M. Lane

Prerequisites
- Chapter 6: Causation

A low level of HDL have long been known to be a risk factor for heart disease. Taking niacin has been shown to increase HDL levels and has been recommended for patients with low levels of HDL. The assumption of this recommendation is that niacin causes HDL to increase thus causing a lower risk for heart disease.

What do you think?

What experimental design involving niacin would test whether the relationship between HDL and heart disease is causal?

> You could randomly assign patients with low levels of HDL to a condition in which they received niacin or to one in which they did not. A finding that niacin increased HDL without decreasing heart disease would cast doubt on the causal relationship. This is exactly what was found in a study conducted by the NIH. See the description of the results here.

References

Harlow, H. (1958) The nature of love. *American Psychologist, 13,* 673-685.

Li, C. (1975) *Path analysis: A primer.* Boxwood Press, Pacific Grove. CA .

Malkiel, B. G. (1995) Returns from investing in equity mutual funds 1971 to 1991. *The Journal of Finance, 50,* 549-572.

Mangel, M. & Samaniego, F. J. (1984) Abraham Wald's work on aircraft survivability. *Journal of the American Statistical Association, 79,* 259-267.

Reinhart, C. M. and Rogoff, K. S. (2010). Growth in a Time of Debt. Working Paper 15639, National Bureau of Economic Research, http://www.nber.org/papers/w15639

Squire, P. (1988) Why the 1936 Literary Digest poll failed. *Public Opinion Quarterly, 52,* 125-133.

Vul, E., Harris, C., Winkielman, P., & Paschler, H. (2009) Puzzlingly High Correlations in fMRI Studies of Emotion, Personality, and Social Cognition. *Perspectives on Psychological Science, 4,* 274-290.

Exercises

1. To be a scientific theory, the theory must be potentially _____.

2. What is the difference between a faith-based explanation and a scientific explanation?

3. What does it mean for a theory to be parsimonious?

4. Define reliability in terms of parallel forms.

5. Define true score.

6. What is the reliability if the true score variance is 80 and the test score variance is 100?

7. What statistic relates to how close a score on one test will be to a score on a parallel form?

8. What is the effect of test length on the reliability of a test?

9. Distinguish between predictive validity and construct validity.

10. What is the theoretical maximum correlation of a test with a criterion if the test has a reliability of .81?

11. An experiment solicits subjects to participate in a highly stressful experiment. What type of sampling bias is likely to occur?

12. Give an example of survivorship bias not presented in this text.

13. Distinguish "between-subject" variables from "within-subjects" variables.

14. Of the variables "gender" and "trials," which is likely to be a between-subjects variable and which a within-subjects variable?

15. Define interaction.

16. What is counterbalancing used for?

17. How does randomization deal with the problem of pre-existing differences between groups?

18. Give an example of the "third-variable problem" other than those in this text.

7. Normal Distributions

A. Introduction

B. History

C. Areas of Normal Distributions

D. Standard Normal

E. Exercises

Most of the statistical analyses presented in this book are based on the bell-shaped or normal distribution. The introductory section defines what it means for a distribution to be normal and presents some important properties of normal distributions. The interesting history of the discovery of the normal distribution is described in the second section. Methods for calculating probabilities based on the normal distribution are described in Areas of Normal Distributions. A frequently used normal distribution is called the Standard Normal distribution and is described in the section with that name. The binomial distribution can be approximated by a normal distribution. The section Normal Approximation to the Binomial shows this approximation.

Introduction to Normal Distributions

by David M. Lane

Prerequisites
- Chapter 1: Distributions
- Chapter 3: Central Tendency
- Chapter 3: Variability

Learning Objectives
1. Describe the shape of normal distributions
2. State 7 features of normal distributions

The normal distribution is the most important and most widely used distribution in statistics. It is sometimes called the "bell curve," although the tonal qualities of such a bell would be less than pleasing. It is also called the "Gaussian curve" after the mathematician Karl Friedrich Gauss. As you will see in the section on the history of the normal distribution, although Gauss played an important role in its history, de Moivre first discovered the normal distribution.

Strictly speaking, it is not correct to talk about "the normal distribution" since there are many normal distributions. Normal distributions can differ in their means and in their standard deviations. Figure 1 shows three normal distributions. The green (left-most) distribution has a mean of -3 and a standard deviation of 0.5, the distribution in red (the middle distribution) has a mean of 0 and a standard deviation of 1, and the distribution in black (right-most) has a mean of 2 and a standard deviation of 3. These as well as all other normal distributions are symmetric with relatively more values at the center of the distribution and relatively few in the tails.

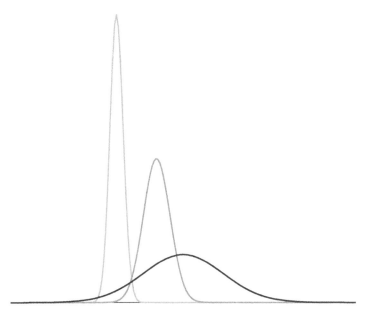

Figure 1. Normal distributions differing in mean and standard deviation.

The density of the normal distribution (the height for a given value on the x-axis) is shown below. The parameters μ and σ are the mean and standard deviation, respectively, and define the normal distribution. The symbol e is the base of the natural logarithm and π is the constant pi.

$$\frac{1}{\sqrt{2\pi\sigma^2}}e^{\frac{-(x-\mu)^2}{2\sigma^2}}$$

Since this is a non-mathematical treatment of statistics, do not worry if this expression confuses you. We will not be referring back to it in later sections.

Seven features of normal distributions are listed below. These features are illustrated in more detail in the remaining sections of this chapter.

1. Normal distributions are symmetric around their mean.

2. The mean, median, and mode of a normal distribution are equal.

3. The area under the normal curve is equal to 1.0.

4. Normal distributions are denser in the center and less dense in the tails.

5. Normal distributions are defined by two parameters, the mean (μ) and the standard deviation (σ).

6. 68% of the area of a normal distribution is within one standard deviation of the mean.

7. Approximately 95% of the area of a normal distribution is within two standard deviations of the mean.

History of the Normal Distribution

by David M. Lane

Prerequisites
- Chapter 1: Distributions
- Chapter 3: Central Tendency
- Chapter 3: Variability
- Chapter 5: Binomial Distribution

Learning Objectives

1. Name the person who discovered the normal distribution and state the problem he applied it to

2. State the relationship between the normal and binomial distributions

3. State who related the normal distribution to errors

4. Describe briefly the central limit theorem

5. State who was the first to prove the central limit theorem

In the chapter on probability, we saw that the binomial distribution could be used to solve problems such as "If a fair coin is flipped 100 times, what is the probability of getting 60 or more heads?" The probability of exactly x heads out of N flips is computed using the formula:

$$P(x) = \frac{N!}{x!\,(N-x)!} \pi^x (1 - \pi)^{N-x}$$

where x is the number of heads (60), N is the number of flips (100), and π is the probability of a head (0.5). Therefore, to solve this problem, you compute the probability of 60 heads, then the probability of 61 heads, 62 heads, etc., and add up all these probabilities. Imagine how long it must have taken to compute binomial probabilities before the advent of calculators and computers.

Abraham de Moivre, an 18th century statistician and consultant to gamblers, was often called upon to make these lengthy computations. de Moivre noted that when the number of events (coin flips) increased, the shape of the binomial distribution approached a very smooth curve. Binomial distributions for 2, 4, 12, and 24 flips are shown in Figure 1.

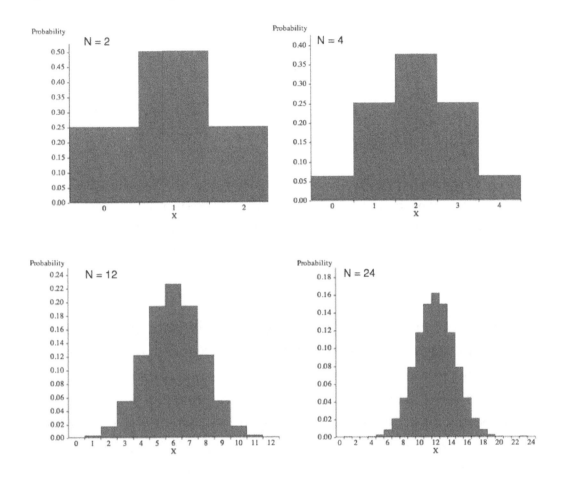

Figure 1. Examples of binomial distributions. The heights of the blue bars
  represent the probabilities.

de Moivre reasoned that if he could find a mathematical expression for this curve, he would be able to solve problems such as finding the probability of 60 or more heads out of 100 coin flips much more easily. This is exactly what he did, and the curve he discovered is now called the "normal curve."

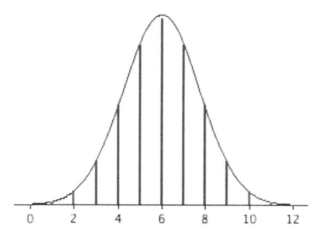

Figure 2. The normal approximation to the binomial distribution for 12 coin flips. The smooth curve is the normal distribution. Note how well it approximates the binomial probabilities represented by the heights of the blue lines.

The importance of the normal curve stems primarily from the fact that the distributions of many natural phenomena are at least approximately normally distributed. One of the first applications of the normal distribution was to the analysis of errors of measurement made in astronomical observations, errors that occurred because of imperfect instruments and imperfect observers. Galileo in the 17th century noted that these errors were symmetric and that small errors occurred more frequently than large errors. This led to several hypothesized distributions of errors, but it was not until the early 19th century that it was discovered that these errors followed a normal distribution. Independently, the mathematicians Adrain in 1808 and Gauss in 1809 developed the formula for the normal distribution and showed that errors were fit well by this distribution.

This same distribution had been discovered by Laplace in 1778 when he derived the extremely important central limit theorem, the topic of a later section of this chapter. Laplace showed that even if a distribution is not normally distributed, the means of repeated samples from the distribution would be very nearly normally distributed, and that the larger the sample size, the closer the distribution of means would be to a normal distribution.

Most statistical procedures for testing differences between means assume normal distributions. Because the distribution of means is very close to normal, these tests work well even if the original distribution is only roughly normal.

Quételet was the first to apply the normal distribution to human characteristics. He noted that characteristics such as height, weight, and strength were normally distributed.

Areas Under Normal Distributions

by David M. Lane

Prerequisites
- Chapter 1: Distributions
- Chapter 3: Central Tendency
- Chapter 3: Variability
- Chapter 7: Introduction to Normal Distributions

Learning Objectives
1. State the proportion of a normal distribution within 1 standard deviation of the mean
2. State the proportion of a normal distribution that is more than 1.96 standard deviations from the mean
3. Use the normal calculator to calculate an area for a given X"
4. Use the normal calculator to calculate X for a given area

Areas under portions of a normal distribution can be computed by using calculus. Since this is a non-mathematical treatment of statistics, we will rely on computer programs and tables to determine these areas. Figure 1 shows a normal distribution with a mean of 50 and a standard deviation of 10. The shaded area between 40 and 60 contains 68% of the distribution.

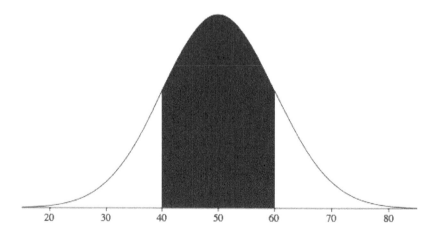

Figure 1. Normal distribution with a mean of 50 and standard deviation of 10. 68% of the area is within one standard deviation (10) of the mean (50).

Figure 2 shows a normal distribution with a mean of 100 and a standard deviation of 20. As in Figure 1, 68% of the distribution is within one standard deviation of the mean.

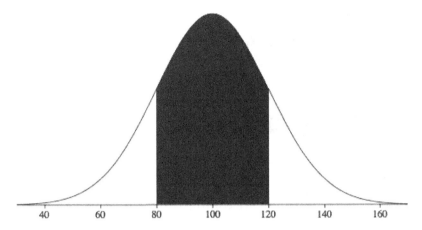

Figure 2. Normal distribution with a mean of 100 and standard deviation of 20. 68% of the area is within one standard deviation (20) of the mean (100).

The normal distributions shown in Figures 1 and 2 are specific examples of the general rule that 68% of the area of any normal distribution is within one standard deviation of the mean.

Figure 3 shows a normal distribution with a mean of 75 and a standard deviation of 10. The shaded area contains 95% of the area and extends from 55.4 to 94.6. For all normal distributions, 95% of the area is within 1.96 standard deviations of the mean. For quick approximations, it is sometimes useful to round off and use 2 rather than 1.96 as the number of standard deviations you need to extend from the mean so as to include 95% of the area.

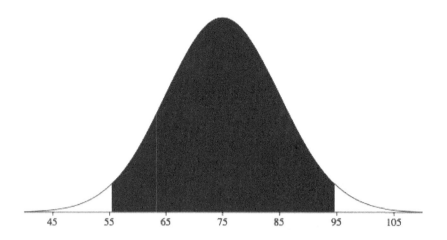

Figure 3. A normal distribution with a mean of 75 and a standard deviation
of 10. 95% of the area is within 1.96 standard deviations of the mean.

Areas under the normal distribution can be calculated with this online calculator.

Standard Normal Distribution

by David M. Lane

Prerequisites
• Chapter 3: Effects of Linear Transformations
• Chapter 7: Introduction to Normal Distributions

Learning Objectives
1. State the mean and standard deviation of the standard normal distribution
2. Use a Z table
3. Use the normal calculator
4. Transform raw data to Z scores

As discussed in the introductory section, normal distributions do not necessarily have the same means and standard deviations. A normal distribution with a mean of 0 and a standard deviation of 1 is called a standard normal distribution.

Areas of the normal distribution are often represented by tables of the standard normal distribution. A portion of a table of the standard normal distribution is shown in Table 1.

Table 1. A portion of a table of the standard normal distribution.

Z	Area below
-2.5	0.0062
-2.49	0.0064
-2.48	0.0066
-2.47	0.0068
-2.46	0.0069
-2.45	0.0071
-2.44	0.0073
-2.43	0.0075
-2.42	0.0078
-2.41	0.008
-2.4	0.0082

-2.39	0.0084
-2.38	0.0087
-2.37	0.0089
-2.36	0.0091
-2.35	0.0094
-2.34	0.0096
-2.33	0.0099
-2.32	0.0102

The first column titled "Z" contains values of the standard normal distribution; the second column contains the area below Z. Since the distribution has a mean of 0 and a standard deviation of 1, the Z column is equal to the number of standard deviations below (or above) the mean. For example, a Z of -2.5 represents a value 2.5 standard deviations below the mean. The area below Z is 0.0062.

The same information can be obtained using the following Java applet. Figure 1 shows how it can be used to compute the area below a value of -2.5 on the standard normal distribution. Note that the mean is set to 0 and the standard deviation is set to 1.

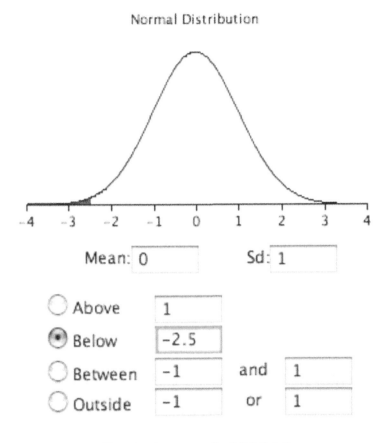

Figure 1. An example from the applet.

A value from any normal distribution can be transformed into its corresponding value on a standard normal distribution using the following formula:

```
Z = (X - μ)/σ
```

where Z is the value on the standard normal distribution, X is the value on the original distribution, μ is the mean of the original distribution, and σ is the standard deviation of the original distribution.

As a simple application, what portion of a normal distribution with a mean of 50 and a standard deviation of 10 is below 26? Applying the formula, we obtain

```
Z = (26 - 50)/10 = -2.4.
```

From Table 1, we can see that 0.0082 of the distribution is below -2.4. There is no need to transform to Z if you use the applet as shown in Figure 2.

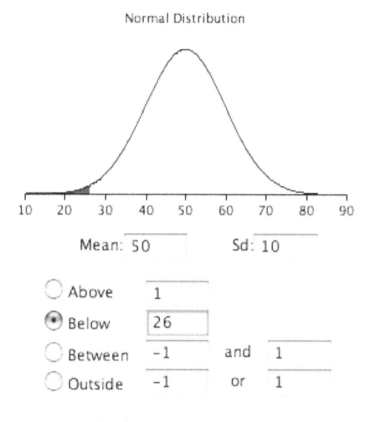

Figure 2. Area below 26 in a normal distribution with a mean of 50 and a standard deviation of 10.

If all the values in a distribution are transformed to Z scores, then the distribution will have a mean of 0 and a standard deviation of 1. This process of transforming a distribution to one with a mean of 0 and a standard deviation of 1 is called standardizing the distribution.

Normal Approximation to the Binomial

by David M. Lane

Prerequisites
- Chapter 5: Binomial Distribution
- Chapter 7: History of the Normal Distribution
- Chapter 7: Areas of Normal Distributions

Learning Objectives
1. State the relationship between the normal distribution and the binomial distribution
2. Use the normal distribution to approximate the binomial distribution
3. State when the approximation is adequate

In the section on the history of the normal distribution, we saw that the normal distribution can be used to approximate the binomial distribution. This section shows how to compute these approximations.

Let's begin with an example. Assume you have a fair coin and wish to know the probability that you would get 8 heads out of 10 flips. The binomial distribution has a mean of $\mu = N\pi = (10)(0.5) = 5$ and a variance of $\sigma^2 = N\pi(1-\pi) = (10)(0.5)(0.5) = 2.5$. The standard deviation is therefore 1.5811. A total of 8 heads is $(8 - 5)/1.5811 = 1.897$ standard deviations above the mean of the distribution. The question then is, "What is the probability of getting a value exactly 1.897 standard deviations above the mean?" You may be surprised to learn that the answer is 0: The probability of any one specific point is 0. The problem is that the binomial distribution is a discrete probability distribution, whereas the normal distribution is a continuous distribution.

The solution is to round off and consider any value from 7.5 to 8.5 to represent an outcome of 8 heads. Using this approach, we figure out the area under a normal curve from 7.5 to 8.5. The area in green in Figure 1 is an approximation of the probability of obtaining 8 heads.

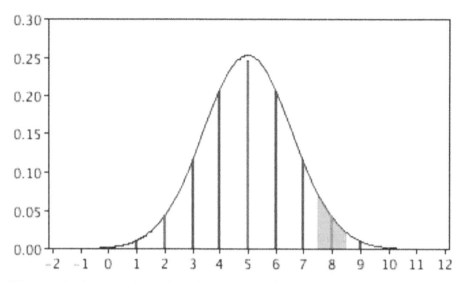

Figure 1. Approximating the probability of 8 heads with the normal distribution.

The solution is therefore to compute this area. First we compute the area below 8.5, and then subtract the area below 7.5.

     The results of using the normal area calculator to find the area below 8.5 are shown in Figure 2. The results for 7.5 are shown in Figure 3.

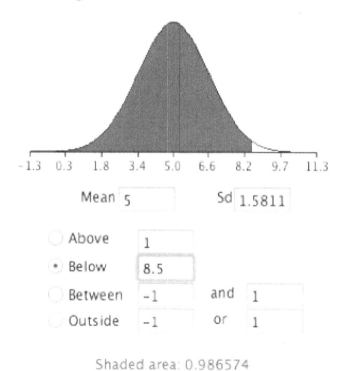

Figure 2. Area below 8.5

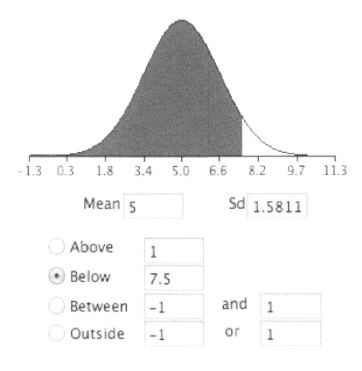

Figure 3. Area below 7.5.

The difference between the areas is 0.044, which is the approximation of the binomial probability. For these parameters, the approximation is very accurate. The demonstration in the next section allows you to explore its accuracy with different parameters.

If you did not have the normal area calculator, you could find the solution using a table of the standard normal distribution (a Z table) as follows:
1. Find a Z score for 8.5 using the formula $Z = (8.5 - 5)/1.5811 = 2.21$.
2. Find the area below a Z of $2.21 = 0.987$.
3. Find a Z score for 7.5 using the formula $Z = (7.5 - 5)/1.5811 = 1.58$.
4. Find the area below a Z of $1.58 = 0.943$.
5. Subtract the value in step 4 from the value in step 2 to get 0.044.

The same logic applies when calculating the probability of a range of outcomes. For example, to calculate the probability of 8 to 10 flips, calculate the area from 7.5 to 10.5.

The accuracy of the approximation depends on the values of N and π. A rule of thumb is that the approximation is good if both Nπ and N(1-π) are both greater than 10.

Statistical Literacy

by David M. Lane

Prerequisites
- Chapter 7: Areas Under the Normal Distribution
- Chapter 7: Shapes of Distributions

Risk analyses often are based on the assumption of normal distributions. Critics have said that extreme events in reality are more frequent than would be expected assuming normality. The assumption has even been called a "Great Intellectual Fraud."

A recent article discussing how to protect investments against extreme events defined "tail risk" as "A tail risk, or extreme shock to financial markets, is technically defined as an investment that moves more than three standard deviations from the mean of a normal distribution of investment returns."

What do you think?

Tail risk can be evaluated by assuming a normal distribution and computing the probability of such an event. Is that how "tail risk" should be evaluated?

> Events more than three standard deviations from the mean are very rare for normal distributions. However, they are not as rare for other distributions such as highly-skewed distributions. If the normal distribution is used to assess the probability of tail events defined this way, then the "tail risk" will be underestimated.

Exercises

Prerequisites
• All material presented in the Normal Distributions chapter

1. If scores are normally distributed with a mean of 35 and a standard deviation of 10, what percent of the scores is:

   a. greater than 34?

   b. smaller than 42?

   c. between 28 and 34?

2. What are the mean and standard deviation of the standard normal distribution? (b) What would be the mean and standard deviation of a distribution created by multiplying the standard normal distribution by 8 and then adding 75?

3. The normal distribution is defined by two parameters. What are they?

4. What proportion of a normal distribution is within one standard deviation of the mean? (b) What proportion is more than 2.0 standard deviations from the mean? (c) What proportion is between 1.25 and 2.1 standard deviations above the mean?

5. A test is normally distributed with a mean of 70 and a standard deviation of 8. (a) What score would be needed to be in the 85th percentile? (b) What score would be needed to be in the 22nd percentile?

6. Assume a normal distribution with a mean of 70 and a standard deviation of 12. What limits would include the middle 65% of the cases?

7. A normal distribution has a mean of 20 and a standard deviation of 4. Find the Z scores for the following numbers: (a) 28 (b) 18 (c) 10 (d) 23

8. Assume the speed of vehicles along a stretch of I-10 has an approximately normal distribution with a mean of 71 mph and a standard deviation of 8 mph.

   a. The current speed limit is 65 mph. What is the proportion of vehicles less than or equal to the speed limit?

   b. What proportion of the vehicles would be going less than 50 mph?

c. A new speed limit will be initiated such that approximately 10% of vehicles will be over the speed limit. What is the new speed limit based on this criterion?

d. In what way do you think the actual distribution of speeds differs from a normal distribution?

9. A variable is normally distributed with a mean of 120 and a standard deviation of 5. One score is randomly sampled. What is the probability it is above 127?

10. You want to use the normal distribution to approximate the binomial distribution. Explain what you need to do to find the probability of obtaining exactly 7 heads out of 12 flips.

11. A group of students at a school takes a history test. The distribution is normal with a mean of 25, and a standard deviation of 4. (a) Everyone who scores in the top 30% of the distribution gets a certificate. What is the lowest score someone can get and still earn a certificate? (b) The top 5% of the scores get to compete in a statewide history contest. What is the lowest score someone can get and still go onto compete with the rest of the state?

12. Use the normal distribution to approximate the binomial distribution and find the probability of getting 15 to 18 heads out of 25 flips. Compare this to what you get when you calculate the probability using the binomial distribution. Write your answers out to four decimal places.

13. True/false: For any normal distribution, the mean, median, and mode will be equal.

14. True/false: In a normal distribution, 11.5% of scores are greater than $Z = 1.2$.

15. True/false: The percentile rank for the mean is 50% for any normal distribution.

16. True/false: The larger the n, the better the normal distribution approximates the binomial distribution.

17. True/false: A Z-score represents the number of standard deviations above or below the mean.

18. True/false: Abraham de Moivre, a consultant to gamblers, discovered the normal distribution when trying to approximate the binomial distribution to make his computations easier.

Answer questions 19 - 21 based on the graph below:

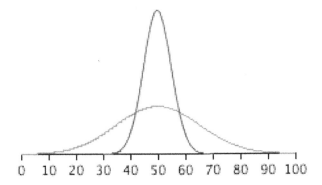

19. True/false: The standard deviation of the blue distribution shown below is about 10.

20. True/false: The red distribution has a larger standard deviation than the blue distribution.

21. True/false: The red distribution has more area underneath the curve than the blue distribution does.

Questions from Case Studies

Angry Moods (AM) case study

22. For this problem, use the Anger Expression (AE) scores.

    a. Compute the mean and standard deviation.

    b. Then, compute what the 25th, 50th and 75th percentiles would be if the distribution were normal.

    c. Compare the estimates to the actual 25th, 50th, and 75th percentiles.

Physicians' Reactions (PR) case study

23. (PR) For this problem, use the time spent with the overweight patients. (a) Compute the mean and standard deviation of this distribution. (b) What is the probability that if you chose an overweight participant at random, the doctor would have spent 31 minutes or longer with this person? (c) Now assume this distribution is normal (and has the same mean and standard deviation). Now what is the probability that if you chose an overweight participant at random, the doctor would have spent 31 minutes or longer with this person?

The following questions are from ARTIST (reproduced with permission)

Assessment
Resource
Tools for
   Improving
Statistical
Thinking

24. A set of test scores are normally distributed. Their mean is 100 and standard deviation is 20. These scores are converted to standard normal z scores. What would be the mean and median of this distribution?

   a. 0
   b. 1
   c. 50
   d. 100

25. Suppose that weights of bags of potato chips coming from a factory follow a normal distribution with mean 12.8 ounces and standard deviation .6 ounces. If the manufacturer wants to keep the mean at 12.8 ounces but adjust the standard deviation so that only 1% of the bags weigh less than 12 ounces, how small does he/she need to make that standard deviation?

26. A student received a standardized (z) score on a test that was -.57. What does this score tell about how this student scored in relation to the rest of the class? Sketch a graph of the normal curve and shade in the appropriate area.

27. Suppose you take 50 measurements on the speed of cars on Interstate 5, and that these measurements follow roughly a Normal distribution. Do you expect the standard deviation of these 50 measurements to be about 1 mph, 5 mph, 10 mph, or 20 mph? Explain.

28. Suppose that combined verbal and math SAT scores follow a normal distribution with mean 896 and standard deviation 174. Suppose further that Peter finds out that he scored in the top 3% of SAT scores. Determine how high Peter's score must have been.

29. Heights of adult women in the United States are normally distributed with a population mean of $\mu = 63.5$ inches and a population standard deviation of $\sigma = 2.5$. A medical re- searcher is planning to select a large random sample of adult women to participate in a future study. What is the standard value, or z-value, for an adult woman who has a height of 68.5 inches?

30. An automobile manufacturer introduces a new model that averages 27 miles per gallon in the city. A person who plans to purchase one of these new cars wrote the manufacturer for the details of the tests, and found out that the standard deviation is 3 miles per gallon. Assume that in-city mileage is approximately normally distributed.

    a. What is the probability that the person will purchase a car that averages less than 20 miles per gallon for in-city driving?

    b. What is the probability that the person will purchase a car that averages between 25 and 29 miles per gallon for in-city driving?

8. Advanced Graphs

A. Q-Q Plots
B. Contour Plots
C. 3D Plots

Quantile-Quantile (q-q) Plots

by David Scott

Prerequisites
- Chapter 1: Distributions
- Chapter 1: Percentiles
- Chapter 2: Histograms
- Chapter 4: Introduction to Bivariate Data
- Chapter 7: Introduction to Normal Distributions

Learning Objectives
1. State what q-q plots are used for.
2. Describe the shape of a q-q plot when the distributional assumption is met.
3. Be able to create a normal q-q plot.

Introduction

The quantile-quantile or q-q plot is an exploratory graphical device used to check the validity of a distributional assumption for a data set. In general, the basic idea is to compute the theoretically expected value for each data point based on the distribution in question. If the data indeed follow the assumed distribution, then the points on the q-q plot will fall approximately on a straight line.

Before delving into the details of q-q plots, we first describe two related graphical methods for assessing distributional assumptions: the histogram and the cumulative distribution function (CDF). As will be seen, q-q plots are more general than these alternatives.

Assessing Distributional Assumptions

As an example, consider data measured from a physical device such as the spinner depicted in Figure 1. The red arrow is spun around the center, and when the arrow stops spinning, the number between 0 and 1 is recorded. Can we determine if the spinner is fair?

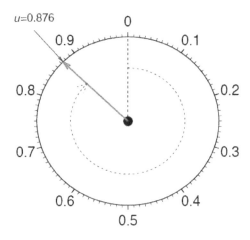

Figure 1. A physical device that gives samples from a uniform distribution.

If the spinner is fair, then these numbers should follow a uniform distribution. To investigate whether the spinner is fair, spin the arrow n times, and record the measurements by $\{\mu_1, \mu_2, ..., \mu_n\}$. In this example, we collect n = 100 samples. The histogram provides a useful visualization of these data. In Figure 2, we display three different histograms on a probability scale. The histogram should be flat for a uniform sample, but the visual perception varies depending on whether the histogram has 10, 5, or 3 bins. The last histogram looks flat, but the other two histograms are not obviously flat. It is not clear which histogram we should base our conclusion on.

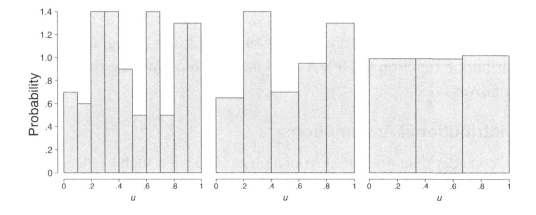

Figure 2. Three histograms of a sample of 100 uniform points.

Alternatively, we might use the cumulative distribution function (CDF), which is denoted by $F(\mu)$. The CDF gives the probability that the spinner gives a value less than or equal to μ, that is, the probability that the red arrow lands in the interval $[0, \mu]$. By simple arithmetic, $F(\mu) = \mu$, which is the diagonal straight line $y = x$. The CDF based upon the sample data is called the empirical CDF (ECDF), is denoted by

$$\hat{F}_n(\mu)$$

and is defined to be the fraction of the data less than or equal to μ; that is,

$$\hat{F}_n(u) = \frac{\# \; u_i \le u}{n}.$$

In general, the ECDF takes on a ragged staircase appearance.

For the spinner sample analyzed in Figure 2, we computed the ECDF and CDF, which are displayed in Figure 3. In the left frame, the ECDF appears close to the line $y = x$, shown in the middle frame. In the right frame, we overlay these two curves and verify that they are indeed quite close to each other. Observe that we do not need to specify the number of bins as with the histogram.

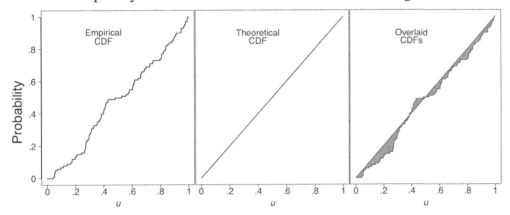

Figure 3. The empirical and theoretical cumulative distribution functions of a sample of 100 uniform points.

q-q plot for uniform data

The q-q plot for uniform data is very similar to the empirical CDF graphic, except with the axes reversed. The q-q plot provides a visual comparison of the sample quantiles to the corresponding theoretical quantiles. In general, if the points in a q-q plot depart from a straight line, then the assumed distribution is called into question.

Here we define the qth quantile of a batch of n numbers as a number ξ_q such that a fraction q x n of the sample is less than ξ_q, while a fraction (1 - q) x n of the sample is greater than ξ_q. The best known quantile is the median, $\xi_{0.5}$, which is located in the middle of the sample.

Consider a small sample of 5 numbers from the spinner

$$\mu_1 = 0.41, \quad \mu_2 = 0.24, \quad \mu_3 = 0.59, \quad \mu_4 = 0.03, \quad \mu_5 = 0.67.$$

Based upon our description of the spinner, we expect a uniform distribution to model these data. If the sample data were "perfect," then on average there would be an observation in the middle of each of the 5 intervals: 0 to .2, .2 to .4, .4 to .6, and so on. Table 1 shows the 5 data points (sorted in ascending order) and the theoretically expected value of each based on the assumption that the distribution is uniform (the middle of the interval).

Table 1. Computing the Expected Quantile Values.

Data (μ)	Rank (i)	Middle of the ith Interval
0.03	1	0.1
0.24	2	0.3
0.41	3	0.5
0.59	4	0.7
0.67	5	0.9

The theoretical and empirical CDFs are shown in Figure 4 and the q-q plot is shown in the left frame of Figure 5.

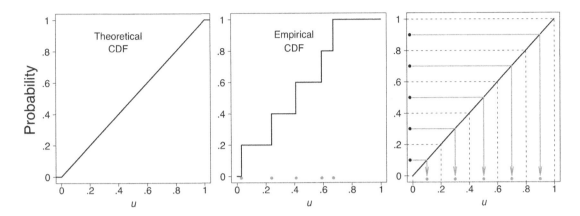

Figure 4. The theoretical and empirical CDFs of a small sample of 5 uniform points, together with the expected values of the 5 points (red dots in the right frame).

In general, we consider the full set of sample quantiles to be the sorted data values

$$\mu_{(1)} < \mu_{(2)} < \mu_{(3)} < \cdots < \mu_{(n-1)} < \mu_{(n)} ,$$

where the parentheses in the subscript indicate the data have been ordered. Roughly speaking, we expect the first ordered value to be in the middle of the interval (0, 1/n), the second to be in the middle of the interval (1/n, 2/n), and the last to be in the middle of the interval ((n - 1)/n, 1). Thus, we take as the theoretical quantile the value

$$\xi_q = q \approx \frac{i - 0.5}{n} ,$$

where q corresponds to the ith ordered sample value. We subtract the quantity 0.5 so that we are exactly in the middle of the interval ((i - 1)/n, i/n). These ideas are depicted in the right frame of Figure 4 for our small sample of size n = 5.

We are now prepared to define the q-q plot precisely. First, we compute the n expected values of the data, which we pair with the n data points sorted in ascending order. For the uniform density, the q-q plot is composed of the n ordered pairs

$$\left(\frac{i-0.5}{n}, u_{(i)}\right), \qquad \text{for } i = 1, 2, \ldots, n.$$

This definition is slightly different from the ECDF, which includes the points $(u_{(i)},$ $i/n)$. In the left frame of Figure 5, we display the q-q plot of the 5 points in Table 1. In the right two frames of Figure 5, we display the q-q plot of the same batch of numbers used in Figure 2. In the final frame, we add the diagonal line y = x as a point of reference.

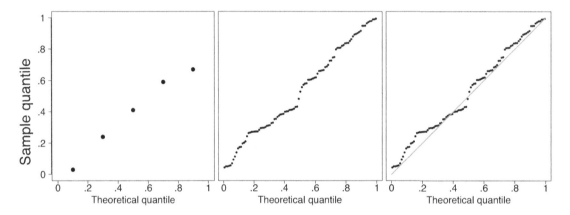

Figure 5. (Left) q-q plot of the 5 uniform points. (Right) q-q plot of a sample
of 100 uniform points.

The sample size should be taken into account when judging how close the q-q plot is to the straight line. We show two other uniform samples of size n = 10 and n = 1000 in Figure 6. Observe that the q-q plot when n = 1000 is almost identical to the line y = x, while such is not the case when the sample size is only n = 10.

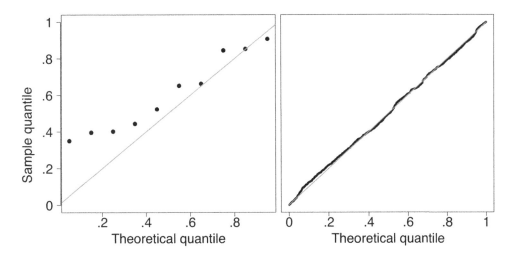

Figure 6. q-q plots of a sample of 10 and 1000 uniform points.

In Figure 7, we show the q-q plots of two random samples that are not uniform. In both examples, the sample quantiles match the theoretical quantiles only at the median and at the extremes. Both samples seem to be symmetric around the median. But the data in the left frame are closer to the median than would be expected if the data were uniform. The data in the right frame are further from the median than would be expected if the data were uniform.

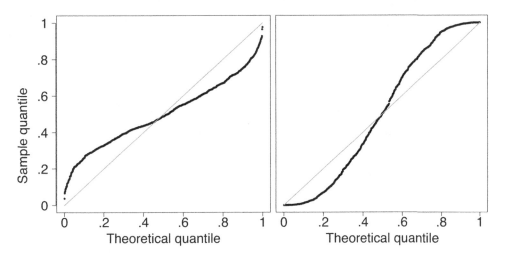

Figure 7. q-q plots of two samples of size 1000 that are not uniform.

In fact, the data were generated in the R language from beta distributions with parameters $a = b = 3$ on the left and $a = b = 0.4$ on the right. In Figure 8 we display histograms of these two data sets, which serve to clarify the true shapes of the densities. These are clearly non-uniform.

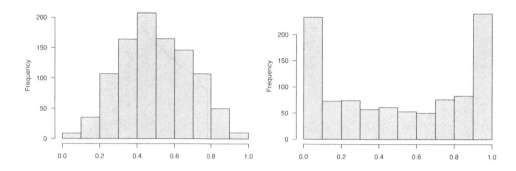

Figure 8. Histograms of the two non-uniform data sets.

q-q plot for normal data

The definition of the q-q plot may be extended to any continuous density. The q-q plot will be close to a straight line if the assumed density is correct. Because the cumulative distribution function of the uniform density was a straight line, the q-q plot was very easy to construct. For data that are not uniform, the theoretical quantiles must be computed in a different manner.

Let $\{z_1, z_2, ..., z_n\}$ denote a random sample from a normal distribution with mean $\mu = 0$ and standard deviation $\sigma = 1$. Let the ordered values be denoted by

$$z_{(1)} < z_{(2)} < z_{(3)} < \ ... \ < z_{(n-1)} < z_{(n)}.$$

These n ordered values will play the role of the sample quantiles.

Let us consider a sample of 5 values from a distribution to see how they compare with what would be expected for a normal distribution. The 5 values in ascending order are shown in the first column of Table 2.

Table 2. Computing the Expected Quantile Values for Normal Data.
of the Two Non-Uniform Data Sets.

Data (z)	Rank (i)	Middle of the ith Interval	z
-1.96	1	0.1	-1.28
-0.78	2	0.3	-0.52
0.31	3	0.5	0
1.15	4	0.7	0.52
1.62	5	0.9	1.28

Just as in the case of the uniform distribution, we have 5 intervals. However, with a normal distribution the theoretical quantile is not the middle of the interval but rather the inverse of the normal distribution for the middle of the interval. Taking the first interval as an example, we want to know the z value such that 0.1 of the area in the normal distribution is below z. This can be computed using the Inverse Normal Calculator as shown in Figure 9. Simply set the "Shaded Area" field to the middle of the interval (0.1) and click on the "Below" button. The result is -1.28. Therefore, 10% of the distribution is below a z value of -1.28.

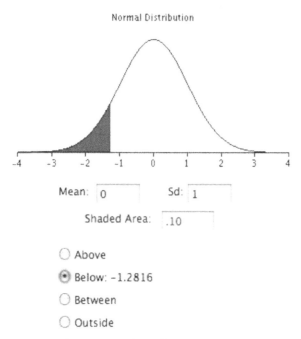

Figure 9. Example of the Inverse Normal Calculator for finding a value of the expected quantile from a normal distribution.

The q-q plot for the data in Table 2 is shown in the left frame of Figure 11.

In general, what should we take as the corresponding theoretical quantiles? Let the cumulative distribution function of the normal density be denoted by $\Phi(z)$. In the previous example, $\Phi(-1.28) = 0.10$ and $\Phi(0.00) = 0.50$. Using the quantile notation, if ξ_q is the qth quantile of a normal distribution, then

$$\Phi(\xi_q) = q.$$

That is, the probability a normal sample is less than ξ_q is in fact just q.

Consider the first ordered value, $z_{(1)}$. What might we expect the value of $\Phi(z_{(1)})$ to be? Intuitively, we expect this probability to take on a value in the interval (0, 1/n). Likewise, we expect $\Phi(z_{(2)})$ to take on a value in the interval (1/n, 2/n). Continuing, we expect $\Phi(z_{(n)})$ to fall in the interval ((n - 1)/n, 1/n). Thus, the theoretical quantile we desire is defined by the inverse (not reciprocal) of the normal CDF. In particular, the theoretical quantile corresponding to the empirical quantile $z_{(i)}$ should be

$$\Phi^{-1}\left(\frac{i - 0.5}{n}\right) \qquad \text{for } i = 1, 2, \ldots, n.$$

The empirical CDF and theoretical quantile construction for the small sample given in Table 2 are displayed in Figure 10. For the larger sample of size 100, the first few expected quantiles are -2.576, -2.170, and -1.960.

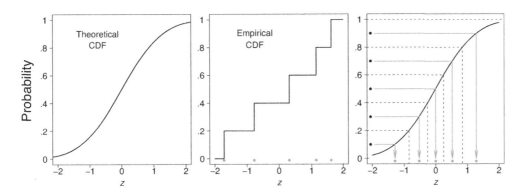

Figure 10. The empirical CDF of a small sample of 5 normal points, together with the expected values of the 5 points (red dots in the right frame).

In the left frame of Figure 11, we display the q-q plot of the small normal sample given in Table 2. The remaining frames in Figure 11 display the q-q plots of normal random samples of size n = 100 and n = 1000. As the sample size increases, the points in the q-q plots lie closer to the line y = x.

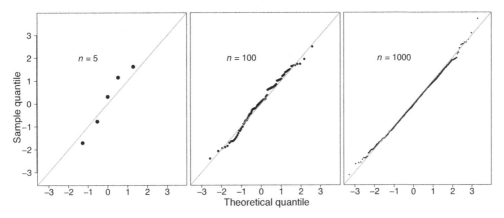

Figure 11. q-q plots of normal data.

As before, a normal q-q plot can indicate departures from normality. The two most common examples are skewed data and data with heavy tails (large kurtosis). In

Figure 12 we show normal q-q plots for a chi-squared (skewed) data set and a Student's-t (kurtotic) data set, both of size n = 1000. The data were first standardized. The red line is again y = x. Notice, in particular, that the data from the t distribution follow the normal curve fairly closely until the last dozen or so points on each extreme.

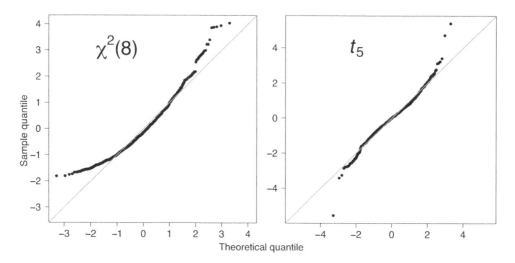

Figure 12. q-q plots for standardized non-normal data (n = 1000).

q-q plots for normal data with general mean and scale

Our previous discussion of q-q plots for normal data all assumed that our data were standardized. One approach to constructing q-q plots is to first standardize the data and then proceed as described previously. An alternative is to construct the plot directly from raw data.

In this section we present a general approach for data that are not standardized. Why did we standardize the data in Figure 12? The q-q plot is comprised of the n points

$$\left(\Phi^{-1}\left(\frac{i - 0.5}{n} \right), z_{(i)} \right) \qquad \text{for } i = 1, 2, \ldots, n.$$

If the original data $\{z_i\}$ are normal, but have an arbitrary mean μ and standard deviation σ, then the line y = x will not match the expected theoretical quantile. Clearly, the linear transformation

$$\mu + \sigma \xi_q$$

would provide the qth theoretical quantile on the transformed scale. In practice, with a new data set

$$\{x_1, x_2, \ldots, x_n\} ,$$

the normal q-q plot would consist of the n points

Instead of plotting the line y = x as a reference line, the line

$$y = M + s \cdot x$$

should be composed, where M and s are the sample moments (mean and standard deviation) corresponding to the theoretical moments μ and σ. Alternatively, if the data are standardized, then the line y = x would be appropriate, since now the sample mean would be 0 and the sample standard deviation would be 1.

Example: SAT Case Study

The SAT case study followed the academic achievements of 105 college students majoring in computer science. The first variable is their verbal SAT score and the second is their grade point average (GPA) at the university level. Before we compute inferential statistics using these variables, we should check if their distributions are normal. In Figure 13, we display the q-q plots of the verbal SAT and university GPA variables.

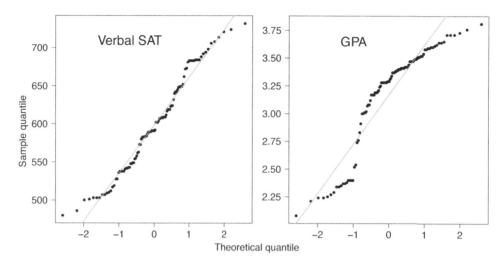

Figure 13. q-q plots for the student data (n = 105).

The verbal SAT seems to follow a normal distribution reasonably well, except in the extreme tails. However, the university GPA variable is highly non-normal. Compare the GPA q-q plot to the simulation in the right frame of Figure 7. These figures are very similar, except for the region where x ≈ -1. To follow these ideas, we computed histograms of the variables and their scatter diagram in Figure 14. These figures tell quite a different story. The university GPA is bimodal, with about 20% of the students falling into a separate cluster with a grade of C. The scatter diagram is quite unusual. While the students in this cluster all have below average verbal SAT scores, there are as many students with low SAT scores whose GPAs were quite respectable. We might speculate as to the cause(s): different distractions, different study habits, but it would only be speculation. But observe that the raw correlation between verbal SAT and GPA is a rather high 0.65, but when we exclude the cluster, the correlation for the remaining 86 students falls a little to 0.59.

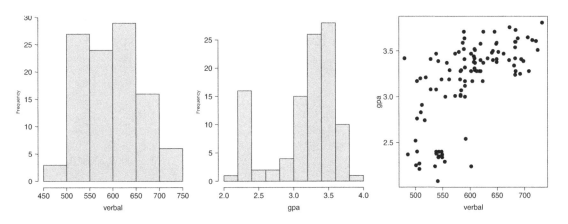

Figure 14. Histograms and scatter diagram of the verbal SAT and GPA
variables for the 105 students.

Discussion

Parametric modeling usually involves making assumptions about the shape of data, or the shape of residuals from a regression fit. Verifying such assumptions can take many forms, but an exploration of the shape using histograms and q-q plots is very effective. The q-q plot does not have any design parameters such as the number of bins for a histogram.

In an advanced treatment, the q-q plot can be used to formally test the null hypothesis that the data are normal. This is done by computing the correlation coefficient of the n points in the q-q plot. Depending upon n, the null hypothesis is rejected if the correlation coefficient is less than a threshold. The threshold is already quite close to 0.95 for modest sample sizes.

We have seen that the q-q plot for uniform data is very closely related to the empirical cumulative distribution function. For general density functions, the so-called probability integral transform takes a random variable X and maps it to the interval (0, 1) through the CDF of X itself, that is,

$$Y = F_X(X)$$

which has been shown to be a uniform density. This explains why the q-q plot on standardized data is always close to the line y = x when the model is correct. Finally, scientists have used special graph paper for years to make relationships linear (straight lines). The most common example used to be semi-log paper, on which points following the formula $y = ae^{bx}$ appear linear. This follows of course since $\log(y) = \log(a) + bx$, which is the equation for a straight line. The q-q plots may be thought of as being "probability graph paper" that makes a plot of the ordered data values into a straight line. Every density has its own special probability graph paper.

Contour Plots

by David Lane

Prerequisites
• none

Learning Objectives
1. Describe a contour plot.
2. Interpret a contour plot

Contour plots portray data for three variables in two dimensions. The plot contains a number of contour lines. Each contour line is shown in an X-Y plot and has a constant value on a third variable. Consider the Figure 1 that contains data on the fat, non-sugar carbohydrates, and calories present in a variety of breakfast cereals. Each line shows the carbohydrate and fat levels for cereals with the same number of calories. Note that the number of calories is not determined exactly by the fat and non-sugar carbohydrates since cereals also differ in sugar and protein.

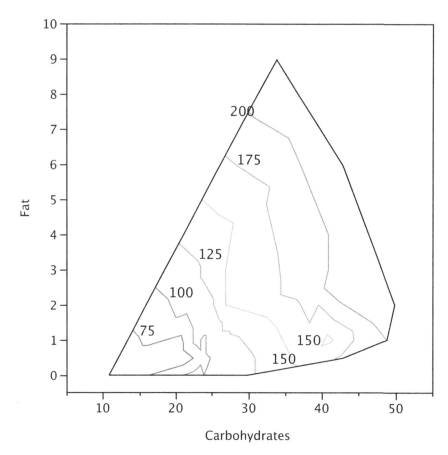

Figure 1. A contour plot showing calories as a function of fat and carbohydrates.

An alternative way to draw the plot is shown in Figure 2. The areas with the same number of calories are shaded.

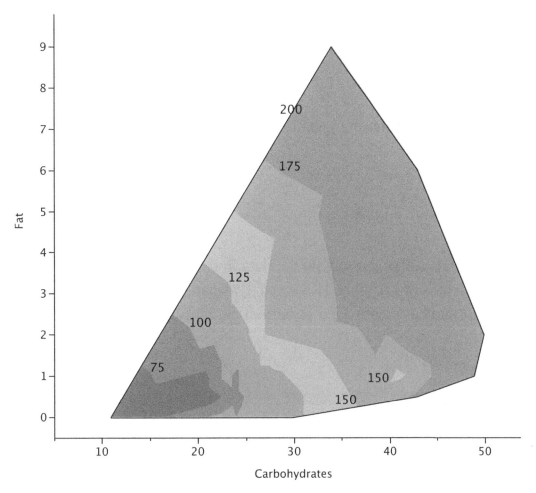

Figure 2. A contour plot showing calories as a function of fat and carbohydrates with areas shaded. An area represents values less than or equal to the label to the right of the area.

3D Plots

by David Lane

Prerequisites
• Chapter 4: Introduction to Bivariate Data

Learning Objectives
1. Describe a 3D Plot.
2. Give an example of the value of a 3D plot.

Just as two-dimensional scatter plots show the data in two dimensions, 3D plots show data in three dimensions. Figure 1 shows a 3D scatter plot of the fat, non-sugar carbohydrates, and calories from a variety of cereal types.

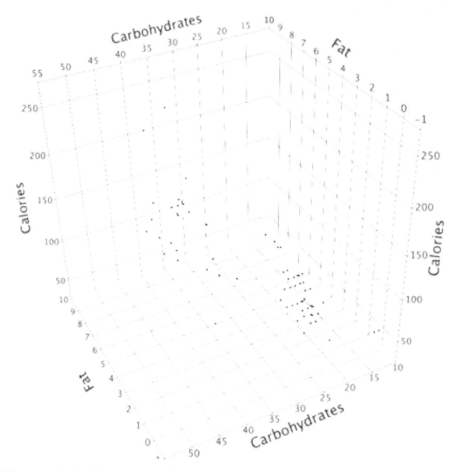

Figure 1. A 3D scatter plot showing fat, non-sugar carbohydrates, and calories from a variety of cereal types.

Many statistical packages allow you to rotate the axes interactively to view the data from a different vantage point. Figure 2 is an example.

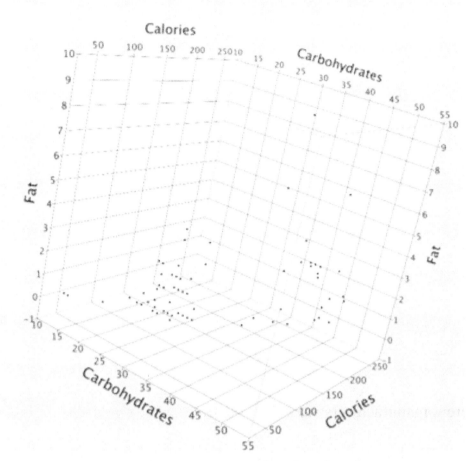

Figure 2. An alternative 3D scatter plot showing fat, non-sugar carbohydrates, and calories.

A fourth dimension can be represented as long as it is represented as a nominal variable. Figure 3 represents the different manufacturers by using different colors.

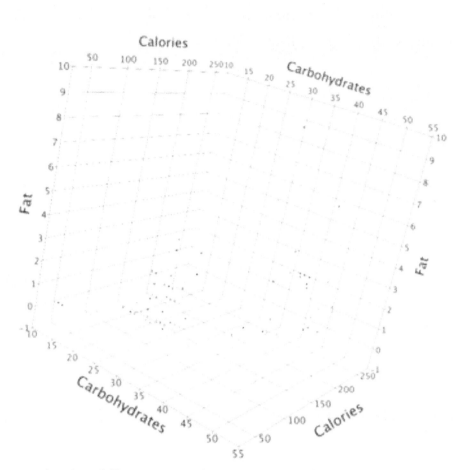

Figure 3. The different manufacturers are color coded.

Interactively rotating 3D plots can sometimes reveal aspects of the data not otherwise apparent. Figure 4 shows data from a pseudo random number generator. Figure 4 does not show anything systematic and the random number generator appears to generate data with properties similar to those of true random numbers.

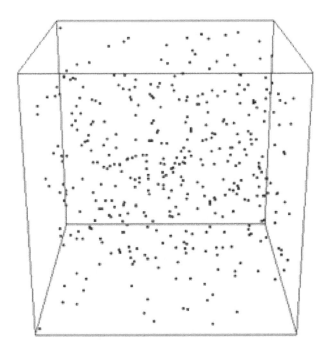

Figure 4. A 3D scatter plot showing 400 values of X, Y, and Z from a pseudo random number generator.

Figure 5 shows a different perspective on these data. Clearly they were not generated by a random process.

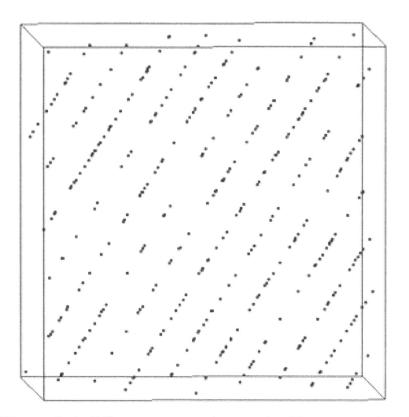

Figure 5. A different perspective on the 3D scatter plot showing 400 values of X, Y, and Z from a pseudo random number generator.

Figures 4 and 5 are reproduced with permission from <u>R snippets</u> by Bogumil Kaminski.

Statistical Literacy

by David M. Lane

Prerequisites
- Chapter 8: Contour Plots

This web page portrays altitudes in the United States.

What do you think?

What part of the state of Texas (North, South, East, or West) contains the highest elevation?

West Texas

Exercises

1. What are Q-Q plots useful for?

2. For the following data, plot the theoretically expected z score as a function of the actual z score (a Q-Q plot).

0	0.5	0.8	1.3	2.1
0	0.6	0.9	1.4	2.1
0	0.6	1	1.4	2.1
0	0.6	1	1.5	2.1
0	0.6	1.1	1.6	2.1
0	0.6	1.1	1.7	2.1
0.1	0.6	1.2	1.7	2.3
0.1	0.6	1.2	1.7	2.5
0.1	0.6	1.2	1.8	2.7
0.1	0.6	1.2	1.8	3
0.1	0.7	1.2	1.9	4.2
0.2	0.7	1.2	1.9	5
0.2	0.8	1.3	2	5.7
0.3	0.8	1.3	2	12.4
0.3	0.8	1.3	2	15.2
0.4	0.8	1.3	2.1	

3. For the data in problem 2, describe how the data differ from a normal distribution.

4. For the "SAT and College GPA" case study data, create a contour plot looking at College GPA as a function of Math SAT and High School GPA. Naturally, you should use a computer to do this.

5. For the "SAT and College GPA" case study data, create a 3D plot using the variables College GPA, Math SAT, and High School GPA. Naturally, you should use a computer to do this.

9. Sampling Distributions

Prerequisites
• none

A. Introduction
B. Sampling Distribution of the Mean
C. Sampling Distribution of Difference Between Means
D. Sampling Distribution of Pearson's r
E. Sampling Distribution of a Proportion
F. Exercises

The concept of a sampling distribution is perhaps the most basic concept in inferential statistics. It is also a difficult concept because a sampling distribution is a theoretical distribution rather than an empirical distribution.

The introductory section defines the concept and gives an example for both a discrete and a continuous distribution. It also discusses how sampling distributions are used in inferential statistics.

The remaining sections of the chapter concern the sampling distributions of important statistics: the Sampling Distribution of the Mean, the Sampling Distribution of the Difference Between Means, the Sampling Distribution of r, and the Sampling Distribution of a Proportion.

Introduction to Sampling Distributions

by David M. Lane

Prerequisites
• Chapter 1: Distributions
• Chapter 1: Inferential Statistics

Learning Objectives
1. Define inferential statistics
2. Graph a probability distribution for the mean of a discrete variable
3. Describe a sampling distribution in terms of "all possible outcomes"
4. Describe a sampling distribution in terms of repeated sampling
5. Describe the role of sampling distributions in inferential statistics
6. Define the standard error of the mean

Suppose you randomly sampled 10 people from the population of women in Houston, Texas, between the ages of 21 and 35 years and computed the mean height of your sample. You would not expect your sample mean to be equal to the mean of all women in Houston. It might be somewhat lower or it might be somewhat higher, but it would not equal the population mean exactly. Similarly, if you took a second sample of 10 people from the same population, you would not expect the mean of this second sample to equal the mean of the first sample.

Recall that inferential statistics concern generalizing from a sample to a population. A critical part of inferential statistics involves determining how far sample statistics are likely to vary from each other and from the population parameter. (In this example, the sample statistics are the sample means and the population parameter is the population mean.) As the later portions of this chapter show, these determinations are based on sampling distributions.

Discrete Distributions

We will illustrate the concept of sampling distributions with a simple example. Figure 1 shows three pool balls, each with a number on it. Suppose two of the balls are selected randomly (with replacement) and the average of their numbers is computed. All possible outcomes are shown below in Table 1.

Figure 1. The pool balls.

Table 1. All possible outcomes when two balls are sampled with replacement.

Outcome	Ball 1	Ball 2	Mean
1	1	1	1
2	1	2	1.5
3	1	3	2
4	2	1	1.5
5	2	2	2
6	2	3	2.5
7	3	1	2
8	3	2	2.5
9	3	3	3

Notice that all the means are either 1.0, 1.5, 2.0, 2.5, or 3.0. The frequencies of these means are shown in Table 2. The relative frequencies are equal to the frequencies divided by nine because there are nine possible outcomes.

Table 2. Frequencies of means for N = 2.

Mean	Frequency	Relative Frequency
1	1	0.111
1.5	2	0.222
2	3	0.333
2.5	2	0.222
3	1	0.111

Figure 2 shows a relative frequency distribution of the means based on Table 2. This distribution is also a probability distribution since the Y-axis is the probability of obtaining a given mean from a sample of two balls in addition to being the relative frequency.

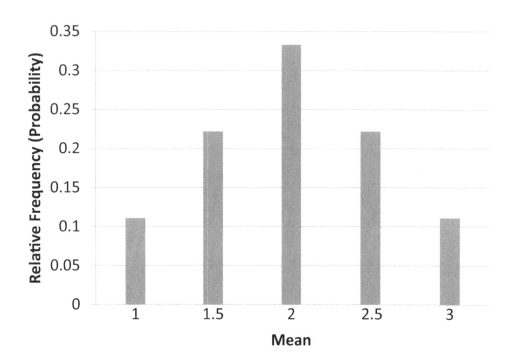

Figure 2. Distribution of means for N = 2.

The distribution shown in Figure 2 is called the sampling distribution of the mean. Specifically, it is the sampling distribution of the mean for a sample size of 2 (N = 2). For this simple example, the distribution of pool balls and the sampling distribution are both discrete distributions. The pool balls have only the values 1, 2, and 3, and a sample mean can have one of only five values shown in Table 2.

There is an alternative way of conceptualizing a sampling distribution that will be useful for more complex distributions. Imagine that two balls are sampled (with replacement) and the mean of the two balls is computed and recorded. Then this process is repeated for a second sample, a third sample, and eventually thousands of samples. After thousands of samples are taken and the mean computed for each, a relative frequency distribution is drawn. The more samples, the closer the relative frequency distribution will come to the sampling distribution shown in Figure 2. As the number of samples approaches infinity, the relative frequency distribution will approach the sampling distribution. This means that you can conceive of a sampling distribution as being a relative frequency distribution based on a very large number of samples. To be strictly correct, the relative frequency distribution approaches the sampling distribution as the number of samples approaches infinity.

It is important to keep in mind that every statistic, not just the mean, has a sampling distribution. For example, Table 3 shows all possible outcomes for the range of two numbers (larger number minus the smaller number). Table 4 shows the frequencies for each of the possible ranges and Figure 3 shows the sampling distribution of the range.

Table 3. All possible outcomes when two balls are sampled with replacement.

Outcome	Ball 1	Ball 2	Range
1	1	1	0
2	1	2	1
3	1	3	2
4	2	1	1
5	2	2	0
6	2	3	1
7	3	1	2
8	3	2	1
9	3	3	0

Table 4. Frequencies of ranges for N = 2.

Range	Frequency	Relative Frequency
0	3	0.333
1	4	0.444
2	2	0.222

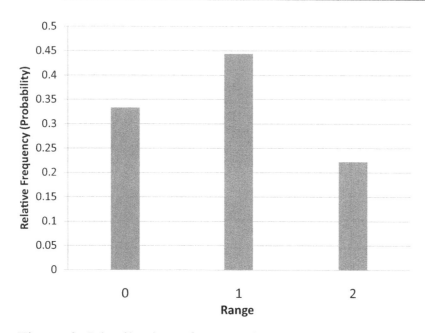

Figure 3. Distribution of ranges for N = 2.

It is also important to keep in mind that there is a sampling distribution for various sample sizes. For simplicity, we have been using N = 2. The sampling distribution of the range for N = 3 is shown in Figure 4.

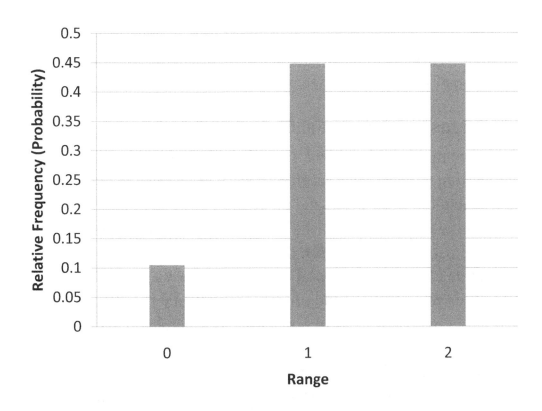

Figure 4. Distribution of ranges for N = 3.

Continuous Distributions

In the previous section, the population consisted of three pool balls. Now we will consider sampling distributions when the population distribution is continuous. What if we had a thousand pool balls with numbers ranging from 0.001 to 1.000 in equal steps? (Although this distribution is not really continuous, it is close enough to be considered continuous for practical purposes.) As before, we are interested in the distribution of means we would get if we sampled two balls and computed the mean of these two balls. In the previous example, we started by computing the mean for each of the nine possible outcomes. This would get a bit tedious for this example since there are 1,000,000 possible outcomes (1,000 for the first ball x 1,000 for the second). Therefore, it is more convenient to use our second conceptualization of sampling distributions which conceives of sampling distributions in terms of relative frequency distributions. Specifically, the relative frequency distribution that would occur if samples of two balls were repeatedly taken and the mean of each sample computed.

When we have a truly continuous distribution, it is not only impractical but actually impossible to enumerate all possible outcomes. Moreover, in continuous distributions, the probability of obtaining any single value is zero. Therefore, as discussed in the section "Distributions" in Chapter 1, these values are called probability densities rather than probabilities.

Sampling Distributions and Inferential Statistics

As we stated in the beginning of this chapter, sampling distributions are important for inferential statistics. In the examples given so far, a population was specified and the sampling distribution of the mean and the range were determined. In practice, the process proceeds the other way: you collect sample data, and from these data you estimate parameters of the sampling distribution. This knowledge of the sampling distribution can be very useful. For example, knowing the degree to which means from different samples would differ from each other and from the population mean would give you a sense of how close your particular sample mean is likely to be to the population mean. Fortunately, this information is directly available from a sampling distribution. The most common measure of how much sample means differ from each other is the standard deviation of the sampling distribution of the mean. This standard deviation is called the standard error of the mean. If all the sample means were very close to the population mean, then the standard error of the mean would be small. On the other hand, if the sample means varied considerably, then the standard error of the mean would be large.

To be specific, assume your sample mean were 125 and you estimated that the standard error of the mean were 5 (using a method shown in a later section). If you had a normal distribution, then it would be likely that your sample mean would be within 10 units of the population mean since most of a normal distribution is within two standard deviations of the mean.

Keep in mind that all statistics have sampling distributions, not just the mean. In later sections we will be discussing the sampling distribution of the variance, the sampling distribution of the difference between means, and the sampling distribution of Pearson's correlation, among others.

Sampling Distribution of the Mean

by David M. Lane

Prerequisites
• Chapter 3: Variance Sum Law I
• Chapter 9: Introduction to Sampling Distributions

Learning Objectives
1. State the mean and variance of the sampling distribution of the mean
2. Compute the standard error of the mean
3. State the central limit theorem

The sampling distribution of the mean was defined in the section introducing sampling distributions. This section reviews some important properties of the sampling distribution of the mean.

Mean

The mean of the sampling distribution of the mean is the mean of the population from which the scores were sampled. Therefore, if a population has a mean μ, then the mean of the sampling distribution of the mean is also μ. The symbol μ_M is used to refer to the mean of the sampling distribution of the mean. Therefore, the formula for the mean of the sampling distribution of the mean can be written as:

$$\mu_M = \mu$$

Variance

The variance of the sampling distribution of the mean is computed as follows:

$$\sigma_m^2 = \frac{\sigma^2}{N}$$

That is, the variance of the sampling distribution of the mean is the population variance divided by N, the sample size (the number of scores used to compute a mean). Thus, the larger the sample size, the smaller the variance of the sampling distribution of the mean.

(optional paragraph) This expression can be derived very easily from the variance sum law. Let's begin by computing the variance of the sampling distribution of the

307

sum of three numbers sampled from a population with variance σ^2. The variance of the sum would be $\sigma^2 + \sigma^2 + \sigma^2$. For N numbers, the variance would be $N\sigma^2$. Since the mean is 1/N times the sum, the variance of the sampling distribution of the mean would be $1/N^2$ times the variance of the sum, which equals σ^2/N.

The standard error of the mean is the standard deviation of the sampling distribution of the mean. It is therefore the square root of the variance of the sampling distribution of the mean and can be written as:

$$\sigma_m = \frac{\sigma}{\sqrt{N}}$$

The standard error is represented by a σ because it is a standard deviation. The subscript (M) indicates that the standard error in question is the standard error of the mean.

Central Limit Theorem

The central limit theorem states that:

> *Given a population with a finite mean μ and a finite non-zero variance σ^2, the sampling distribution of the mean approaches a normal distribution with a mean of μ and a variance of σ^2/N as N, the sample size, increases.*

The expressions for the mean and variance of the sampling distribution of the mean are not new or remarkable. What is remarkable is that regardless of the shape of the parent population, the sampling distribution of the mean approaches a normal distribution as N increases. If you have used the "Central Limit Theorem Demo," (external link; requires Java) you have already seen this for yourself. As a reminder, Figure 1 shows the results of the simulation for N = 2 and N = 10. The parent population was a uniform distribution. You can see that the distribution for N = 2 is far from a normal distribution. Nonetheless, it does show that the scores are denser in the middle than in the tails. For N = 10 the distribution is quite close to a normal distribution. Notice that the means of the two distributions are the same, but that the spread of the distribution for N = 10 is smaller.

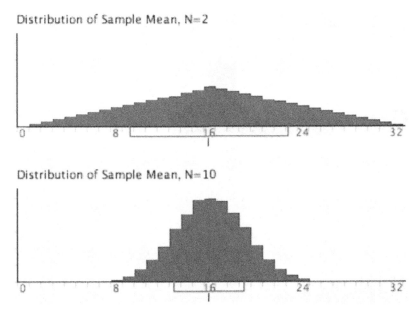

Figure 1. A simulation of a sampling distribution. The parent population is
    uniform. The blue line under "16" indicates that 16 is the mean. The
    red line extends from the mean plus and minus one standard deviation.

Figure 2 shows how closely the sampling distribution of the mean approximates a
normal distribution even when the parent population is very non-normal. If you
look closely you can see that the sampling distributions do have a slight positive
skew. The larger the sample size, the closer the sampling distribution of the mean
would be to a normal distribution.

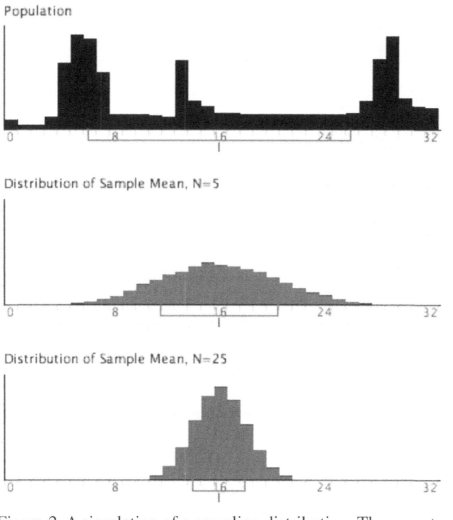

Figure 2. A simulation of a sampling distribution. The parent population is very non-normal.

Sampling Distribution of Difference Between Means

by David M. Lane

Prerequisites
- Chapter 3: Variance Sum Law I
- Chapter 9: Sampling Distributions
- Chapter 9: Sampling Distribution of the Mean

Learning Objectives
1. State the mean and variance of the sampling distribution of the difference between means
2. Compute the standard error of the difference between means
3. Compute the probability of a difference between means being above a specified value

Statistical analyses are very often concerned with the difference between means. A typical example is an experiment designed to compare the mean of a control group with the mean of an experimental group. Inferential statistics used in the analysis of this type of experiment depend on the sampling distribution of the difference between means.

The sampling distribution of the difference between means can be thought of as the distribution that would result if we repeated the following three steps over and over again: (1) sample n_1 scores from Population 1 and n_2 scores from Population 2, (2) compute the means of the two samples (M_1 and M_2), and (3) compute the difference between means, $M_1 - M_2$. The distribution of the differences between means is the sampling distribution of the difference between means.

As you might expect, the mean of the sampling distribution of the difference between means is:

$$\mu_{M_1-M_2} = \mu_1 - \mu_2$$

which says that the mean of the distribution of differences between sample means is equal to the difference between population means. For example, say that the mean test score of all 12-year-olds in a population is 34 and the mean of 10-year-olds is 25. If numerous samples were taken from each age group and the mean difference computed each time, the mean of these numerous differences between sample means would be 34 - 25 = 9.

From the variance sum law, we know that:

$$\sigma^2_{M_1-M_2} = \sigma^2_{M_1} + \sigma^2_{M_2}$$

which says that the variance of the sampling distribution of the difference between means is equal to the variance of the sampling distribution of the mean for Population 1 plus the variance of the sampling distribution of the mean for Population 2. Recall the formula for the variance of the sampling distribution of the mean:

$$\sigma^2_M = \frac{\sigma^2}{N}$$

Since we have two populations and two samples sizes, we need to distinguish between the two variances and sample sizes. We do this by using the subscripts 1 and 2. Using this convention, we can write the formula for the variance of the sampling distribution of the difference between means as:

$$\sigma^2_{M_1-M_2} = \frac{\sigma^2_1}{n_1} + \frac{\sigma^2_2}{n_2}$$

Since the standard error of a sampling distribution is the standard deviation of the sampling distribution, the standard error of the difference between means is:

$$\sigma_{M_1-M_2} = \sqrt{\frac{\sigma^2_1}{n_1} + \frac{\sigma^2_2}{n_2}}$$

Just to review the notation, the symbol on the left contains a sigma (σ), which means it is a standard deviation. The subscripts M_1 - M_2 indicate that it is the standard deviation of the sampling distribution of M_1 - M_2.

Now let's look at an application of this formula. Assume there are two species of green beings on Mars. The mean height of Species 1 is 32 while the mean height of Species 2 is 22. The variances of the two species are 60 and 70, respectively, and the heights of both species are normally distributed. You randomly sample 10 members of Species 1 and 14 members of Species 2. What is the probability that the mean of the 10 members of Species 1 will exceed the mean of the 14 members of Species 2 by 5 or more? Without doing any calculations, you probably know that the probability is pretty high since the difference in population means is 10. But what exactly is the probability?

First, let's determine the sampling distribution of the difference between means. Using the formulas above, the mean is

$$\mu_{M_1-M_2} = 32 - 22 = 10$$

The standard error is:

$$\sigma_{M_1-M_2} = \sqrt{\frac{60}{10} + \frac{70}{14}} = 3.317$$

The sampling distribution is shown in Figure 1. Notice that it is normally distributed with a mean of 10 and a standard deviation of 3.317. The area above 5 is shaded blue.

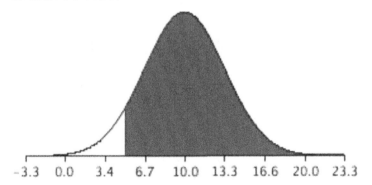

-3.3   0.0   3.4   6.7   10.0   13.3   16.6   20.0   23.3

Figure 1. The sampling distribution of the difference between means.

The last step is to determine the area that is shaded blue. Using either a Z table or the normal calculator, the area can be determined to be 0.934. Thus the probability that the mean of the sample from Species 1 will exceed the mean of the sample from Species 2 by 5 or more is 0.934.

As shown below, the formula for the standard error of the difference between means is much simpler if the sample sizes and the population variances are equal. When the variances and samples sizes are the same, there is no need to use the subscripts 1 and 2 to differentiate these terms.

$$\sigma_{M_1-M_2} = \sqrt{\frac{\sigma_1^2}{n_1} + \frac{\sigma_2^2}{n_2}} = \sqrt{\frac{\sigma^2}{n} + \frac{\sigma^2}{n}} = \sqrt{\frac{2\sigma^2}{n}}$$

This simplified version of the formula can be used for the following problem: The mean height of 15-year-old boys (in cm) is 175 and the variance is 64. For girls, the mean is 165 and the variance is 64. If eight boys and eight girls were sampled, what is the probability that the mean height of the sample of girls would be higher than the mean height of the sample of boys? In other words, what is the probability that the mean height of girls minus the mean height of boys is greater than 0?

As before, the problem can be solved in terms of the sampling distribution of the difference between means (girls - boys). The mean of the distribution is 165 - 175 = -10. The standard deviation of the distribution is:

$$\sigma_{M_1-M_2} = \sqrt{\frac{2\sigma^2}{n}} = \sqrt{\frac{(2)(64)}{8}} = 4$$

A graph of the distribution is shown in Figure 2. It is clear that it is unlikely that the mean height for girls would be higher than the mean height for boys since in the population boys are quite a bit taller. Nonetheless it is not inconceivable that the girls' mean could be higher than the boys' mean.

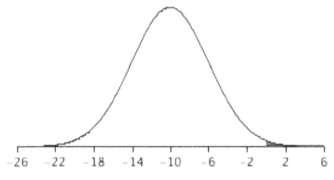

Figure 2. Sampling distribution of the difference between mean heights.

A difference between means of 0 or higher is a difference of 10/4 = 2.5 standard deviations above the mean of -10. The probability of a score 2.5 or more standard deviations above the mean is 0.0062.

Sampling Distribution of Pearson's r

by David M. Lane

Prerequisites
- Chapter 4: Values of the Pearson Correlation
- Chapter 9: Introduction to Sampling Distributions

Learning Objectives
1. State how the shape of the sampling distribution of r deviates from normality
2. Transform r to z'
3. Compute the standard error of z'
4. Calculate the probability of obtaining an r above a specified value

Assume that the correlation between quantitative and verbal SAT scores in a given population is 0.60. In other words, $\varrho = 0.60$. If 12 students were sampled randomly, the sample correlation, r, would not be exactly equal to 0.60. Naturally different samples of 12 students would yield different values of r. The distribution of values of r after repeated samples of 12 students is the sampling distribution of r.

The shape of the sampling distribution of r for the above example is shown in Figure 1. You can see that the sampling distribution is not symmetric: it is negatively skewed. The reason for the skew is that r cannot take on values greater than 1.0 and therefore the distribution cannot extend as far in the positive direction as it can in the negative direction. The greater the value of ϱ, the more pronounced the skew.

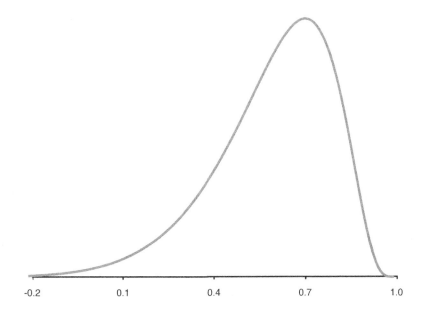

Figure 1. The sampling distribution of r for N = 12 and ϱ = 0.60.

Figure 2 shows the sampling distribution for ϱ = 0.90. This distribution has a very short positive tail and a long negative tail.

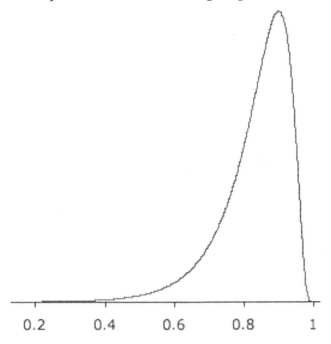

Figure 2. The sampling distribution of r for N = 12 and ρ = 0.90.

Referring back to the SAT example, suppose you wanted to know the probability that in a sample of 12 students, the sample value of r would be 0.75 or higher. You might think that all you would need to know to compute this probability is the mean and standard error of the sampling distribution of r. However, since the sampling distribution is not normal, you would still not be able to solve the problem. Fortunately, the statistician Fisher developed a way to transform r to a variable that is normally distributed with a known standard error. The variable is called z' and the formula for the transformation is given below.

$$z' = 0.5 \ln[(1+r)/(1-r)]$$

The details of the formula are not important here since normally you will use either a table or calculator (external link) to do the transformation. What is important is that z' is normally distributed and has a standard error of

$$\frac{1}{\sqrt{N-3}}$$

where N is the number of pairs of scores.

Let's return to the question of determining the probability of getting a sample correlation of 0.75 or above in a sample of 12 from a population with a correlation of 0.60. The first step is to convert both 0.60 and 0.75 to their z' values, which are 0.693 and 0.973, respectively. The standard error of z' for N = 12 is 0.333. Therefore, the question is reduced to the following: given a normal distribution with a mean of 0.693 and a standard deviation of 0.333, what is the probability of obtaining a value of 0.973 or higher? The answer can be found directly from the normal calculator (external link) to be 0.20. Alternatively, you could use the formula:

$$z = (X - \mu)/\sigma = (0.973 - 0.693)/0.333 = 0.841$$

and use a table to find that the area above 0.841 is 0.20.

Sampling Distribution of p

by David M. Lane

Prerequisites
- Chapter 5: Binomial Distribution
- Chapter 7: Normal Approximation to the Binomial
- Chapter 9: Introduction to Sampling Distributions

Learning Objectives
1. Compute the mean and standard deviation of the sampling distribution of p
2. State the relationship between the sampling distribution of p and the normal distribution

Assume that in an election race between Candidate A and Candidate B, 0.60 of the voters prefer Candidate A. If a random sample of 10 voters were polled, it is unlikely that exactly 60% of them (6) would prefer Candidate A. By chance the proportion in the sample preferring Candidate A could easily be a little lower than 0.60 or a little higher than 0.60. The sampling distribution of p is the distribution that would result if you repeatedly sampled 10 voters and determined the proportion (p) that favored Candidate A.

The sampling distribution of p is a special case of the sampling distribution of the mean. Table 1 shows a hypothetical random sample of 10 voters. Those who prefer Candidate A are given scores of 1 and those who prefer Candidate B are given scores of 0. Note that seven of the voters prefer candidate A so the sample proportion (p) is

$$p = 7/10 = 0.70$$

As you can see, p is the mean of the 10 preference scores.

Table 1. Sample of voters.

Voter	Preference
1	1
2	0
3	1
4	1
5	1
6	0
7	1
8	0
9	1
10	1

The distribution of p is closely related to the binomial distribution. The binomial distribution is the distribution of the total number of successes (favoring Candidate A, for example), whereas the distribution of p is the distribution of the mean number of successes. The mean, of course, is the total divided by the sample size, N. Therefore, the sampling distribution of p and the binomial distribution differ in that p is the mean of the scores (0.70) and the binomial distribution is dealing with the total number of successes (7).

The binomial distribution has a mean of

$$\mu = N\pi$$

Dividing by N to adjust for the fact that the sampling distribution of p is dealing with means instead of totals, we find that the mean of the sampling distribution of p is:

$$\mu_p = \pi$$

The standard deviation of the binomial distribution is:

$$\sqrt{N\pi(1-\pi)}$$

Dividing by N because p is a mean not a total, we find the standard error of p:

$$\sigma_p = \frac{\sqrt{N\pi(1-\pi)}}{N} = \sqrt{\frac{\pi(1-\pi)}{N}}$$

Returning to the voter example, $\pi = 0.60$ (Don't confuse $\pi = 0.60$, the population proportion, with p = 0.70, the sample proportion) and N = 10. Therefore, the mean of the sampling distribution of p is 0.60. The standard error is

$$\sigma_p = \sqrt{\frac{0.60(1-.60)}{10}} = 0.155$$

The sampling distribution of p is a discrete rather than a continuous distribution. For example, with an N of 10, it is possible to have a p of 0.50 or a p of 0.60, but not a p of 0.55.

The sampling distribution of p is approximately normally distributed if N is fairly large and π is not close to 0 or 1. A rule of thumb is that the approximation is good if both $N\pi$ and $N(1-\pi)$ are greater than 10. The sampling distribution for the voter example is shown in Figure 1. Note that even though $N(1-\pi)$ is only 4, the approximation is quite good.

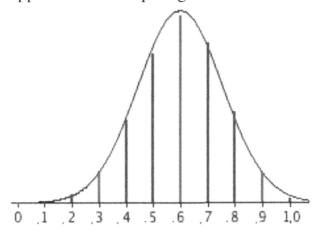

Figure 1. The sampling distribution of p. Vertical bars are the probabilities; the smooth curve is the normal approximation.

Statistical Literacy

by David M. Lane

Prerequisites
- Chapter 9: Introduction
- Chapter 9: Sampling Distribution of the Mean

The monthly jobs report always gets a lot of attention. Presidential candidates refer to the report when it favors their position. Referring to the August 2012 report in which only 96,000 jobs were created, Republican presidential challenger Mitt Romney stated "the weak jobs report is devastating news for American workers and American families ... a harsh indictment of the president's handling of the economy." When the September 2012 report was released showing 114,000 jobs were created (and the previous report was revised upwards), some supporters of Romney claimed the data were tampered with for political reasons. The most famous statement, "Unbelievable jobs numbers...these Chicago guys will do anything..can't debate so change numbers," was made by former Chairman and CEO of General Electric.

What do you think?

The standard error of the monthly estimate is 100,000. Given that, what do you think of the difference between the two job reports?

> The difference between the two reports is very small given that the standard error is 100,000. It is not sensible to take any single jobs report too seriously.

Exercises

Prerequisites
All material presented in the Sampling Distributions chapter

1. A population has a mean of 50 and a standard deviation of 6. (a) What are the mean and standard deviation of the sampling distribution of the mean for N = 16? (b) What are the mean and standard deviation of the sampling distribution of the mean for N = 20?

2. Given a test that is normally distributed with a mean of 100 and a standard deviation of 12, find:

    a. the probability that a single score drawn at random will be greater than 110

    b. the probability that a sample of 25 scores will have a mean greater than 105

    c. the probability that a sample of 64 scores will have a mean greater than 105

    d. the probability that the mean of a sample of 16 scores will be either less than 95 or greater than 105

3. What term refers to the standard deviation of a sampling distribution?

4. (a) If the standard error of the mean is 10 for N = 12, what is the standard error of the mean for N = 22? (b) If the standard error of the mean is 50 for N = 25, what is it for N = 64?

5. A questionnaire is developed to assess women's and men's attitudes toward using animals in research. One question asks whether animal research is wrong and is answered on a 7-point scale. Assume that in the population, the mean for women is 5, the mean for men is 4, and the standard deviation for both groups is 1.5. Assume the scores are normally distributed. If 12 women and 12 men are selected randomly, what is the probability that the mean of the women will be more than 2 points higher than the mean of the men?

6. If the correlation between reading achievement and math achievement in the population of fifth graders were 0.60, what would be the probability that in a sample of 28 students, the sample correlation coefficient would be greater than 0.65?

7. If numerous samples of N = 15 are taken from a uniform distribution and a relative frequency distribution of the means is drawn, what would be the shape of the frequency distribution?

8. A normal distribution has a mean of 20 and a standard deviation of 10. Two scores are sampled randomly from the distribution and the second score is subtracted from the first. What is the probability that the difference score will be greater than 5? Hint: Read the Variance Sum Law section of Chapter 3.

9. What is the shape of the sampling distribution of r? In what way does the shape depend on the size of the population correlation?

10. If you sample one number from a standard normal distribution, what is the probability it will be 0.5?

11. A variable is normally distributed with a mean of 120 and a standard deviation of 5. Four scores are randomly sampled. What is the probability that the mean of the four scores is above 127?

12. The correlation between self-esteem and extraversion is .30. A sample of 84 is taken. a. What is the probability that the correlation will be less than 0.10? b. What is the probability that the correlation will be greater than 0.25?

13. The mean GPA for students in School A is 3.0; the mean GPA for students in School B is 2.8. The standard deviation in both schools is 0.25. The GPAs of both schools are normally distributed. If 9 students are randomly sampled from each school, what is the probability that:

a. the sample mean for School A will exceed that of School B by 0.5 or more?

b. the sample mean for School B will be greater than the sample mean for School A?

14. In a city, 70% of the people prefer Candidate A. Suppose 30 people from this city were sampled.

a. What is the mean of the sampling distribution of p?

b. What is the standard error of p?

c. What is the probability that 80% or more of this sample will prefer Candidate A?

15. When solving problems where you need the sampling distribution of r, what is the reason for converting from r to z'?

16. In the population, the mean SAT score is 1000. Would you be more likely (or equally likely) to get a sample mean of 1200 if you randomly sampled 10 students or if you randomly sampled 30 students? Explain.

17. True/false: The standard error of the mean is smaller when N = 20 than when N = 10.

18. True/false: The sampling distribution of r = .8 becomes normal as N increases.

19. True/false: You choose 20 students from the population and calculate the mean of their test scores. You repeat this process 100 times and plot the distribution of the means. In this case, the sample size is 100.

20. True/false: In your school, 40% of students watch TV at night. You randomly ask 5 students every day if they watch TV at night. Every day, you would find that 2 of the 5 do watch TV at night.

21. True/false: The median has a sampling distribution.

22. True/false: Refer to the figure below. The population distribution is shown in black, and its corresponding sampling distribution of the mean for N = 10 is labeled "A."

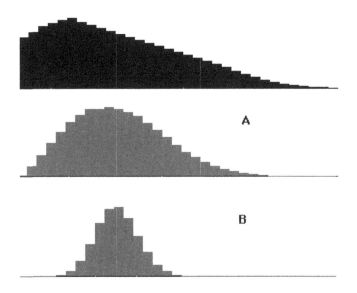

A

B

Questions from Case Studies

Angry Moods (AM) case study

23. (AM)

    a. How many men were sampled?
    b. How many women were sampled?

24. (AM) What is the mean difference between men and women on the Anger-Out scores?

25. (AM) Suppose in the population, the Anger-Out score for men is two points higher than it is for women. The population variances for men and women are both 20. Assume the Anger- Out scores for both genders are normally distributed. Given this information about the population parameters:

    (a) What is the mean of the sampling distribution of the difference between means?

    (b) What is the standard error of the difference between means?

    (c) What is the probability that you would have gotten this mean difference (see #24) or less in your sample?

Animal Research (AR) case study

26. (AR) How many people were sampled to give their opinions on animal research?

27. (AR) What is the correlation in this sample between the belief that animal research is wrong and belief that animal research is necessary?

28. (AR) Suppose the correlation between the belief that animal research is wrong and the belief that animal research is necessary is -.68 in the population.

(a) Convert -.68 to z'.

(b) Find the standard error of this sampling distribution.

(c) Assuming the data used in this study was randomly sampled, what is the probability that you would get this correlation or stronger (closer to -1)?

10. Estimation

One of the major applications of statistics is estimating population parameters from sample statistics. For example, a poll may seek to estimate the proportion of adult residents of a city that support a proposition to build a new sports stadium. Out of a random sample of 200 people, 106 say they support the proposition. Thus in the sample, 0.53 of the people supported the proposition. This value of 0.53 is called a point estimate of the population proportion. It is called a point estimate because the estimate consists of a single value or point.

The concept of degrees of freedom and its relationship to estimation is discussed in Section B. "Characteristics of Estimators" discusses two important concepts: bias and precision.

Point estimates are usually supplemented by interval estimates called confidence intervals. Confidence intervals are intervals constructed using a method that contains the population parameter a specified proportion of the time. For example, if the pollster used a method that contains the parameter 95% of the time it is used, he or she would arrive at the following 95% confidence interval: $0.46 < \pi < 0.60$. The pollster would then conclude that somewhere between 0.46 and 0.60 of the population supports the proposal. The media usually reports this type of result by saying that 53% favor the proposition with a margin of error of 7%. The sections on confidence intervals show how to compute confidence intervals for a variety of parameters.

Introduction to Estimation

by David M. Lane

Prerequisites
- Chapter 3 Measures of Central Tendency
- Chapter 3: Variability

Learning Objectives
1. Define statistic
2. Define parameter
3. Define point estimate
4. Define interval estimate
5. Define margin of error

One of the major applications of statistics is estimating population parameters from sample statistics. For example, a poll may seek to estimate the proportion of adult residents of a city that support a proposition to build a new sports stadium. Out of a random sample of 200 people, 106 say they support the proposition. Thus in the sample, 0.53 of the people supported the proposition. This value of 0.53 is called a point estimate of the population proportion. It is called a point estimate because the estimate consists of a single value or point.

Point estimates are usually supplemented by interval estimates called confidence intervals. Confidence intervals are intervals constructed using a method that contains the population parameter a specified proportion of the time. For example, if the pollster used a method that contains the parameter 95% of the time it is used, he or she would arrive at the following 95% confidence interval: $0.46 < \pi < 0.60$. The pollster would then conclude that somewhere between 0.46 and 0.60 of the population supports the proposal. The media usually reports this type of result by saying that 53% favor the proposition with a margin of error of 7%.

In an experiment on memory for chess positions, the mean recall for tournament players was 63.8 and the mean for non-players was 33.1. Therefore a point estimate of the difference between population means is 30.7. The 95% confidence interval on the difference between means extends from 19.05 to 42.35. You will see how to compute this kind of interval in another section.

Degrees of Freedom

by David M. Lane

Prerequisites
• Chapter 3: Measures of Variability
• Chapter 10: Introduction to Estimation

Learning Objectives
1. Define degrees of freedom
2. Estimate the variance from a sample of 1 if the population mean is known
3. State why deviations from the sample mean are not independent
4. State the general formula for degrees of freedom in terms of the number of values and the number of estimated parameters
5. Calculate s^2

Some estimates are based on more information than others. For example, an estimate of the variance based on a sample size of 100 is based on more information than an estimate of the variance based on a sample size of 5. The degrees of freedom (df) of an estimate is the number of independent pieces of information on which the estimate is based.

As an example, let's say that we know that the mean height of Martians is 6 and wish to estimate the variance of their heights. We randomly sample one Martian and find that its height is 8. Recall that the variance is defined as the mean squared deviation of the values from their population mean. We can compute the squared deviation of our value of 8 from the population mean of 6 to find a single squared deviation from the mean. This single squared deviation from the mean $(8-6)^2 = 4$ is an estimate of the mean squared deviation for all Martians. Therefore, based on this sample of one, we would estimate that the population variance is 4. This estimate is based on a single piece of information and therefore has 1 df. If we sampled another Martian and obtained a height of 5, then we could compute a second estimate of the variance, $(5-6)^2 = 1$. We could then average our two estimates (4 and 1) to obtain an estimate of 2.5. Since this estimate is based on two independent pieces of information, it has two degrees of freedom. The two estimates are independent because they are based on two independently and randomly selected Martians. The estimates would not be independent if after sampling one Martian, we decided to choose its brother as our second Martian.

As you are probably thinking, it is pretty rare that we know the population mean when we are estimating the variance. Instead, we have to first estimate the population mean (μ) with the sample mean (M). The process of estimating the mean affects our degrees of freedom as shown below.

Returning to our problem of estimating the variance in Martian heights, let's assume we do not know the population mean and therefore we have to estimate it from the sample. We have sampled two Martians and found that their heights are 8 and 5. Therefore M, our estimate of the population mean, is

```
M = (8+5)/2 = 6.5.
```

We can now compute two estimates of variance:

```
Estimate 1 = (8-6.5)2 = 2.25

Estimate 2 = (5-6.5)2 = 2.25
```

Now for the key question: Are these two estimates independent? The answer is no because each height contributed to the calculation of M. Since the first Martian's height of 8 influenced M, it also influenced Estimate 2. If the first height had been, for example, 10, then M would have been 7.5 and Estimate 2 would have been $(5-7.5)^2 = 6.25$ instead of 2.25. The important point is that the two estimates are not independent and therefore we do not have two degrees of freedom. Another way to think about the non-independence is to consider that if you knew the mean and one of the scores, you would know the other score. For example, if one score is 5 and the mean is 6.5, you can compute that the total of the two scores is 13 and therefore that the other score must be 13-5 = 8.

In general, the degrees of freedom for an estimate is equal to the number of values minus the number of parameters estimated en route to the estimate in question. In the Martians example, there are two values (8 and 5) and we had to estimate one parameter (μ) on the way to estimating the parameter of interest (σ^2). Therefore, the estimate of variance has 2 - 1 = 1 degree of freedom. If we had sampled 12 Martians, then our estimate of variance would have had 11 degrees of freedom. Therefore, the degrees of freedom of an estimate of variance is equal to N - 1 where N is the number of observations.

Recall from the section on variability that the formula for estimating the variance in a sample is:

$$s^2 = \frac{\Sigma (X - M)^2}{N - 1}$$

The denominator of this formula is the degrees of freedom.

Characteristics of Estimators

by David M. Lane

Prerequisites
- Chapter 3: Measures of Central Tendency
- Chapter 3: Variability
- Chapter 9: Introduction to Sampling Distributions
- Chapter 9: Sampling Distribution of the Mean
- Chapter 10: Introduction to Estimation
- Chapter 10: Degrees of Freedom

Learning Objectives
1. Define bias
2. Define sampling variability
3. Define expected value
4. Define relative efficiency

This section discusses two important characteristics of statistics used as point estimates of parameters: bias and sampling variability. Bias refers to whether an estimator tends to either over or underestimate the parameter. Sampling variability refers to how much the estimate varies from sample to sample.

Have you ever noticed that some bathroom scales give you very different weights each time you weigh yourself? With this in mind, let's compare two scales. Scale 1 is a very high-tech digital scale and gives essentially the same weight each time you weigh yourself; it varies by at most 0.02 pounds from weighing to weighing. Although this scale has the potential to be very accurate, it is calibrated incorrectly and, on average, overstates your weight by one pound. Scale 2 is a cheap scale and gives very different results from weighing to weighing. However, it is just as likely to underestimate as overestimate your weight. Sometimes it vastly overestimates it and sometimes it vastly underestimates it. However, the average of a large number of measurements would be your actual weight. Scale 1 is biased since, on average, its measurements are one pound higher than your actual weight. Scale 2, by contrast, gives unbiased estimates of your weight. However, Scale 2 is highly variable and its measurements are often very far from your true weight. Scale 1, in spite of being biased, is fairly accurate. Its measurements are never more than 1.02 pounds from your actual weight.

We now turn to more formal definitions of variability and precision. However, the basic ideas are the same as in the bathroom scale example.

Bias

A statistic is biased if the long-term average value of the statistic is not the parameter it is estimating. More formally, a statistic is biased if the mean of the sampling distribution of the statistic is not equal to the parameter. The mean of the sampling distribution of a statistic is sometimes referred to as the expected value of the statistic.

As we saw in the section on the sampling distribution of the mean, the mean of the sampling distribution of the (sample) mean is the population mean (μ). Therefore the sample mean is an unbiased estimate of μ. Any given sample mean may underestimate or overestimate μ, but there is no systematic tendency for sample means to either under or overestimate μ.

In the section on variability, we saw that the formula for the variance in a population is

$$\sigma^2 = \frac{\Sigma(X - \mu)^2}{N}$$

whereas the formula to estimate the variance from a sample is

$$s^2 = \frac{\Sigma(X - M)^2}{N - 1}$$

Notice that the denominators of the formulas are different: N for the population and N-1 for the sample. If N is used in the formula for s^2, then the estimates tend to be too low and therefore biased. The formula with N-1 in the denominator gives an unbiased estimate of the population variance. Note that N-1 is the degrees of freedom.

Sampling Variability

The sampling variability of a statistic refers to how much the statistic varies from sample to sample and is usually measured by its standard error ; the smaller the standard error, the less the sampling variability. For example, the standard error of the mean is a measure of the sampling variability of the mean. Recall that the formula for the standard error of the mean is

$$\sigma_M^2 = \frac{\sigma^2}{N}$$

The larger the sample size (N), the smaller the standard error of the mean and therefore the lower the sampling variability.

Statistics differ in their sampling variability even with the same sample size. For example, for normal distributions, the standard error of the median is larger than the standard error of the mean. The smaller the standard error of a statistic, the more efficient the statistic. The relative efficiency of two statistics is typically defined as the ratio of their standard errors. However, it is sometimes defined as the ratio of their squared standard errors.

Confidence Intervals

by David M. Lane

These sections show how to compute confidence intervals for a variety of parameters.

Introduction to Confidence Intervals

by David M. Lane

Prerequisites
• Chapter 5: Introduction to Probability
• Chapter 10: Introduction to Estimation
• Chapter 10: Characteristics of Estimators

Learning Objectives
1. Define confidence interval
2. State why a confidence interval is not the probability the interval contains the parameter

Say you were interested in the mean weight of 10-year-old girls living in the United States. Since it would have been impractical to weigh all the 10-year-old girls in the United States, you took a sample of 16 and found that the mean weight was 90 pounds. This sample mean of 90 is a point estimate of the population mean. A point estimate by itself is of limited usefulness because it does not reveal the uncertainty associated with the estimate; you do not have a good sense of how far this sample mean may be from the population mean. For example, can you be confident that the population mean is within 5 pounds of 90? You simply do not know.

Confidence intervals provide more information than point estimates. Confidence intervals for means are intervals constructed using a procedure (presented in the next section) that will contain the population mean a specified proportion of the time, typically either 95% or 99% of the time. These intervals are referred to as 95% and 99% confidence intervals respectively. An example of a 95% confidence interval is shown below:

$$72.85 < \mu < 107.15$$

There is good reason to believe that the population mean lies between these two bounds of 72.85 and 107.15 since 95% of the time confidence intervals contain the true mean.

If repeated samples were taken and the 95% confidence interval computed for each sample, 95% of the intervals would contain the population mean. Naturally, 5% of the intervals would not contain the population mean.

It is natural to interpret a 95% confidence interval as an interval with a 0.95 probability of containing the population mean. However, the proper interpretation is not that simple. One problem is that the computation of a confidence interval does not take into account any other information you might have about the value of the population mean. For example, if numerous prior studies had all found sample means above 110, it would not make sense to conclude that there is a 0.95 probability that the population mean is between 72.85 and 107.15. What about situations in which there is no prior information about the value of the population mean? Even here the interpretation is complex. The problem is that there can be more than one procedure that produces intervals that contain the population parameter 95% of the time. Which procedure produces the "true" 95% confidence interval? Although the various methods are equal from a purely mathematical point of view, the standard method of computing confidence intervals has two desirable properties: each interval is symmetric about the point estimate and each interval is contiguous. Recall from the introductory section in the chapter on probability that, for some purposes, probability is best thought of as subjective. It is reasonable, although not required by the laws of probability, that one adopt a subjective probability of 0.95 that a 95% confidence interval, as typically computed, contains the parameter in question.

Confidence intervals can be computed for various parameters, not just the mean. For example, later in this chapter you will see how to compute a confidence interval for ϱ, the population value of Pearson's r, based on sample data.

t Distribution

by David M. Lane

Prerequisites
• Chapter 7: Normal Distribution,
• Chapter 7: Areas Under Normal Distributions
• Chapter 10: Degrees of Freedom

Learning Objectives
1. State the difference between the shape of the t distribution and the normal distribution
2. State how the difference between the shape of the t distribution and normal distribution is affected by the degrees of freedom
3. Use a t table to find the value of t to use in a confidence interval
4. Use the t calculator to find the value of t to use in a confidence interval

In the introduction to normal distributions it was shown that 95% of the area of a normal distribution is within 1.96 standard deviations of the mean. Therefore, if you randomly sampled a value from a normal distribution with a mean of 100, the probability it would be within 1.96σ of 100 is 0.95. Similarly, if you sample N values from the population, the probability that the sample mean (M) will be within 1.96 σ_M of 100 is 0.95.

Now consider the case in which you have a normal distribution but you do not know the standard deviation. You sample N values and compute the sample mean (M) and estimate the standard error of the mean (σ_M) with s_M. What is the probability that M will be within 1.96 s_M of the population mean (μ)? This is a difficult problem because there are two ways in which M could be more than 1.96 s_M from μ: (1) M could, by chance, be either very high or very low and (2) s_M could, by chance, be very low. Intuitively, it makes sense that the probability of being within 1.96 standard errors of the mean should be smaller than in the case when the standard deviation is known (and cannot be underestimated). But exactly how much smaller? Fortunately, the way to work out this type of problem was solved in the early 20th century by W. S. Gosset who determined the distribution of a mean divided by its estimate of the standard error. This distribution is called the Student's t distribution or sometimes just the t distribution. Gosset worked out the t distribution and associated statistical tests while working for a brewery in Ireland. Because of a contractual agreement with the brewery, he published the article under the pseudonym "Student." That is why the t test is called the "Student's t test."

The t distribution is very similar to the normal distribution when the estimate of variance is based on many degrees of freedom, but has relatively more scores in its tails when there are fewer degrees of freedom. Figure 1 shows t distributions with 2, 4, and 10 degrees of freedom and the standard normal distribution. Notice that the normal distribution has relatively more scores in the center of the distribution and the t distribution has relatively more in the tails. The t distribution is therefore leptokurtic. The t distribution approaches the normal distribution as the degrees of freedom increase.

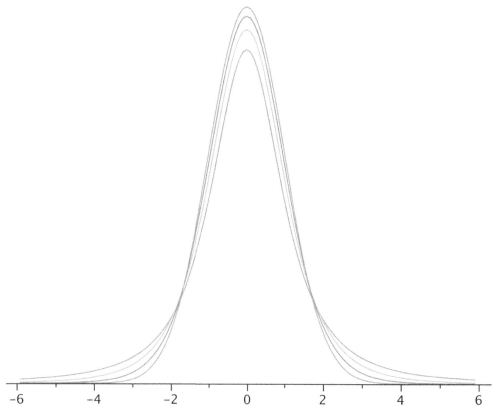

Figure 1. A comparison of t distributions with 2, 4, and 10 df and the standard normal distribution. The distribution with the highest peak is the 2 df distribution, the next highest is 4 df, the highest after that is 10 df, and the lowest is the standard normal distribution.

Since the t distribution is leptokurtic, the percentage of the distribution within 1.96 standard deviations of the mean is less than the 95% for the normal distribution. Table 1 shows the number of standard deviations from the mean required to contain 95% and 99% of the area of the t distribution for various degrees of freedom. These are the values of t that you use in a confidence interval. The corresponding values for the normal distribution are 1.96 and 2.58 respectively. Notice that with few degrees of freedom, the values of t are much higher than the corresponding values for a normal distribution and that the difference decreases as the degrees of freedom increase. The values in Table 1 can be obtained from the "Find t for a confidence interval" calculator.

Table 1. Abbreviated t table.

df	0.95	0.99
2	4.303	9.925
3	3.182	5.841
4	2.776	4.604
5	2.571	4.032
8	2.306	3.355
10	2.228	3.169
20	2.086	2.845
50	2.009	2.678
100	1.984	2.626

Returning to the problem posed at the beginning of this section, suppose you sampled 9 values from a normal population and estimated the standard error of the mean (σ_M) with s_M. What is the probability that M would be within $1.96s_M$ of μ? Since the sample size is 9, there are $N - 1 = 8$ df. From Table 1 you can see that with 8 df the probability is 0.95 that the mean will be within $2.306\ s_M$ of μ. The probability that it will be within 1.96 sM of μ is therefore lower than 0.95.

A "t distribution" calculator can be used to find that 0.086 of the area of a t distribution is more than 1.96 standard deviations from the mean, so the probability that M would be less than $1.96s_M$ from μ is $1 - 0.086 = 0.914$.

As expected, this probability is less than 0.95 that would have been obtained if σ_M had been known instead of estimated.

Confidence Interval for the Mean

by David M. Lane

Prerequisites
- Chapter 7: Areas Under Normal Distributions
- Chapter 9: Sampling Distribution of the Mean
- Chapter 10: Introduction to Estimation
- Chapter 10: Introduction to Confidence Intervals
- Chapter 10: t distribution

Learning Objectives
1. Use the inverse normal distribution calculator to find the value of z to use for a confidence interval
2. Compute a confidence interval on the mean when σ is known
3. Determine whether to use a t distribution or a normal distribution
4. Compute a confidence interval on the mean when σ is estimated

When you compute a confidence interval on the mean, you compute the mean of a sample in order to estimate the mean of the population. Clearly, if you already knew the population mean, there would be no need for a confidence interval. However, to explain how confidence intervals are constructed, we are going to work backwards and begin by assuming characteristics of the population. Then we will show how sample data can be used to construct a confidence interval.

Assume that the weights of 10-year-old children are normally distributed with a mean of 90 and a standard deviation of 36. What is the sampling distribution of the mean for a sample size of 9? Recall from the section on the sampling distribution of the mean that the mean of the sampling distribution is μ and the standard error of the mean is

$$\sigma_M = \frac{\sigma}{\sqrt{N}}$$

For the present example, the sampling distribution of the mean has a mean of 90 and a standard deviation of 36/3 = 12. Note that the standard deviation of a sampling distribution is its standard error. Figure 1 shows this distribution. The shaded area represents the middle 95% of the distribution and stretches from 66.48

to 113.52. These limits were computed by adding and subtracting 1.96 standard deviations to/from the mean of 90 as follows:

```
90 - (1.96)(12) = 66.48
90 + (1.96)(12) = 113.52
```

The value of 1.96 is based on the fact that 95% of the area of a normal distribution is within 1.96 standard deviations of the mean; 12 is the standard error of the mean.

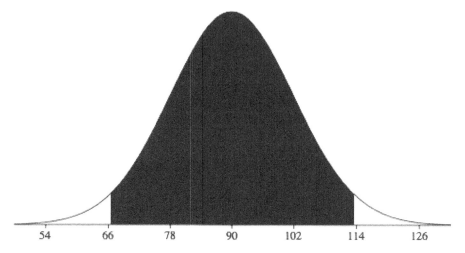

Figure 1. The sampling distribution of the mean for N=9. The middle 95% of the distribution is shaded.

Figure 1 shows that 95% of the means are no more than 23.52 units (1.96 standard deviations) from the mean of 90. Now consider the probability that a sample mean computed in a random sample is within 23.52 units of the population mean of 90. Since 95% of the distribution is within 23.52 of 90, the probability that the mean from any given sample will be within 23.52 of 90 is 0.95. This means that if we repeatedly compute the mean (M) from a sample, and create an interval ranging from M - 23.52 to M + 23.52, this interval will contain the population mean 95% of the time. In general, you compute the 95% confidence interval for the mean with the following formula:

```
Lower limit = M - Z.95σm
Upper limit = M + Z.95σm
```

where $Z_{.95}$ is the number of standard deviations extending from the mean of a normal distribution required to contain 0.95 of the area and σ_M is the standard error of the mean.

If you look closely at this formula for a confidence interval, you will notice that you need to know the standard deviation (σ) in order to estimate the mean. This may sound unrealistic, and it is. However, computing a confidence interval when σ is known is easier than when σ has to be estimated, and serves a pedagogical purpose. Later in this section we will show how to compute a confidence interval for the mean when σ has to be estimated.

Suppose the following five numbers were sampled from a normal distribution with a standard deviation of 2.5: 2, 3, 5, 6, and 9. To compute the 95% confidence interval, start by computing the mean and standard error:

```
M = (2 + 3 + 5 + 6 + 9)/5 = 5.
```

$$\sigma_M = \frac{\sigma}{\sqrt{N}} = \frac{2.5}{\sqrt{5}} = 1.118$$

$Z_{.95}$ can be found using the normal distribution calculator and specifying that the area is 0.95 and indicating that you want the area to be between the cutoff points. The value is 1.96. If you had wanted to compute the 99% confidence interval, you would have set the shaded area to 0.99 and the result would have been 2.58.

The confidence interval can then be computed as follows:

```
Lower limit = 5 - (1.96)(1.118)= 2.81
Upper limit = 5 + (1.96)(1.118)= 7.19
```

You should use the t distribution rather than the normal distribution when the variance is not known and has to be estimated from sample data. When the sample size is large, say 100 or above, the t distribution is very similar to the standard normal distribution. However, with smaller sample sizes, the t distribution is leptokurtic, which means it has relatively more scores in its tails than does the normal distribution. As a result, you have to extend farther from the mean to contain a given proportion of the area. Recall that with a normal distribution, 95% of the distribution is within 1.96 standard deviations of the mean. Using the t distribution, if you have a sample size of only 5, 95% of the area is within 2.78

standard deviations of the mean. Therefore, the standard error of the mean would be multiplied by 2.78 rather than 1.96.

The values of t to be used in a confidence interval can be looked up in a table of the t distribution. A small version of such a table is shown in Table 1. The first column, df, stands for degrees of freedom, and for confidence intervals on the mean, df is equal to N - 1, where N is the sample size.

Table 1. Abbreviated t table.

df	0.95	0.99
2	4.303	9.925
3	3.182	5.841
4	2.776	4.604
5	2.571	4.032
8	2.306	3.355
10	2.228	3.169
20	2.086	2.845
50	2.009	2.678
100	1.984	2.626

You can also use the "inverse t distribution" calculator to find the t values to use in confidence intervals.

Assume that the following five numbers are sampled from a normal distribution: 2, 3, 5, 6, and 9 and that the standard deviation is not known. The first steps are to compute the sample mean and variance:

$$M = 5$$
$$s^2 = 7.5$$

The next step is to estimate the standard error of the mean. If we knew the population variance, we could use the following formula:

$$\sigma_M = \frac{\sigma}{\sqrt{N}}$$

Instead we compute an estimate of the standard error (s_M):

$$s_m = \frac{s}{\sqrt{N}} = 1.225$$

The next step is to find the value of t. As you can see from Table 1, the value for the 95% confidence interval for df = N - 1 = 4 is 2.776. The confidence interval is then computed just as it is with σ_M. The only differences are that s_M and t rather than σ_M and Z are used.

```
Lower limit = 5 - (2.776)(1.225) = 1.60
Upper limit = 5 + (2.776)(1.225) = 8.40
```

More generally, the formula for the 95% confidence interval on the mean is:

```
Lower limit = M - (tCL)(sM)
Upper limit = M + (tCL)(sM)
```

where M is the sample mean, t_{CL} is the t for the confidence level desired (0.95 in the above example), and s_M is the estimated standard error of the mean.

We will finish with an analysis of the Stroop Data. Specifically, we will compute a confidence interval on the mean difference score. Recall that 47 subjects named the color of ink that words were written in. The names conflicted so that, for example, they would name the ink color of the word "blue" written in red ink. The correct response is to say "red" and ignore the fact that the word is "blue." In a second condition, subjects named the ink color of colored rectangles.

Table 2. Response times in seconds for 10 subjects.

Naming Colored Rectangle	Interference	Difference
17	38	21
15	58	43
18	35	17
20	39	19
18	33	15
20	32	12
20	45	25
19	52	33
17	31	14
21	29	8

Table 2 shows the time difference between the interference and color-naming conditions for 10 of the 47 subjects. The mean time difference for all 47 subjects is 16.362 seconds and the standard deviation is 7.470 seconds. The standard error of the mean is 1.090. A t table shows the critical value of t for 47 - 1 = 46 degrees of freedom is 2.013 (for a 95% confidence interval). Therefore the confidence interval is computed as follows:

```
Lower limit = 16.362 - (2.013)(1.090) = 14.17
Upper limit = 16.362 + (2.013)(1.090) = 18.56
```

Therefore, the interference effect (difference) for the whole population is likely to be between 14.17 and 18.56 seconds.

Difference between Means

by David M. Lane

Prerequisites
- Chapter 9: Sampling Distribution of Difference between Means
- Chapter 10: Confidence Intervals
- Chapter 10: Confidence Interval on the Mean

Learning Objectives
1. State the assumptions for computing a confidence interval on the difference between means
2. Compute a confidence interval on the difference between means
3. Format data for computer analysis

It is much more common for a researcher to be interested in the difference between means than in the specific values of the means themselves. We take as an example the data from the "Animal Research" case study. In this experiment, students rated (on a 7-point scale) whether they thought animal research is wrong. The sample sizes, means, and variances are shown separately for males and females in Table 1.

Table 1. Means and Variances in Animal Research study.

Condition	n	Mean	Variance
Females	17	5.353	2.743
Males	17	3.882	2.985

As you can see, the females rated animal research as more wrong than did the males. This sample difference between the female mean of 5.35 and the male mean of 3.88 is 1.47. However, the gender difference in this particular sample is not very important. What is important is the difference in the population. The difference in sample means is used to estimate the difference in population means. The accuracy of the estimate is revealed by a confidence interval.

In order to construct a confidence interval, we are going to make three assumptions:
1. The two populations have the same variance. This assumption is called the assumption of homogeneity of variance.
2. The populations are normally distributed.

3. Each value is sampled independently from each other value.

The consequences of violating these assumptions are discussed in Chapter 12. For now, suffice it to say that small-to-moderate violations of assumptions 1 and 2 do not make much difference.

A confidence interval on the difference between means is computed using the following formula:

$$Lower\ Limit = M_1 - M_2 - (t_{CL})(S_{M_1-M_2})$$

$$Upper\ Limit = M_1 - M_2 + (t_{CL})(S_{M_1-M_2})$$

where $M_1 - M_2$ is the difference between sample means, t_{CL} is the t for the desired level of confidence, and $(S_{M_1-M_2})$ is the estimated standard error of the difference between sample means. The meanings of these terms will be made clearer as the calculations are demonstrated.

We continue to use the data from the "Animal Research" case study and will compute a confidence interval on the difference between the mean score of the females and the mean score of the males. For this calculation, we will assume that the variances in each of the two populations are equal.

The first step is to compute the estimate of the standard error of the difference between means $(S_{M_1-M_2})$. Recall from the relevant section in the chapter on sampling distributions that the formula for the standard error of the difference in means in the population is:

$$\sigma_{M_1-M_2} = \sqrt{\frac{\sigma_1^2}{n_1} + \frac{\sigma_2^2}{n_2}} = \sqrt{\frac{\sigma^2}{n} + \frac{\sigma^2}{n}} = \sqrt{\frac{2\sigma^2}{n}}$$

In order to estimate this quantity, we estimate σ^2 and use that estimate in place of σ^2. Since we are assuming the population variances are the same, we estimate this variance by averaging our two sample variances. Thus, our estimate of variance is computed using the following formula:

$$MSE = \frac{s_1^2 + s_2^2}{2}$$

where MSE is our estimate of σ^2. In this example,

MSE = (2.743 + 2.985)/2 = 2.864.

Note that MSE stands for "mean square error" and is the mean squared deviation of each score from its group's mean.

Since n (the number of scores in each condition) is 17,

$$s_{M_1-M_2} = \sqrt{\frac{2MSE}{n}} = \sqrt{\frac{(2)(2.864)}{17}} = 0.5805.$$

The next step is to find the t to use for the confidence interval (t_{CL}). To calculate t_{CL}, we need to know the degrees of freedom. The degrees of freedom is the number of independent estimates of variance on which MSE is based. This is equal to $(n_1 - 1) + (n_2 - 1)$ where n_1 is the sample size of the first group and n_2 is the sample size of the second group. For this example, $n_1 = n_2 = 17$. When $n_1 = n_2$, it is conventional to use "n" to refer to the sample size of each group. Therefore, the degrees of freedom is 16 + 16 = 32.

From either the above calculator or a t table, you can find that the t for a 95% confidence interval for 32 df is 2.037.

We now have all the components needed to compute the confidence interval. First, we know the difference between means:

```
M₁ - M₂ = 5.353 - 3.882 = 1.471
```

We know the standard error of the difference between means is

$$s_{M_1-M_2} = 0.5805$$

and that the t for the 95% confidence interval with 32 df is

```
t_CL = 2.037
```

Therefore, the 95% confidence interval is

```
Lower Limit = 1.471 - (2.037)(0.5805) = 0.29

Upper Limit = 1.471 + (2.037)(0.5805) = 2.65
```

We can write the confidence interval as:

$$0.29 \leq \mu_f - \mu_m \leq 2.65$$

where μ_f is the population mean for females and μ_m is the population mean for males. This analysis provides evidence that the mean for females is higher than the mean for males, and that the difference between means in the population is likely to be between 0.29 and 2.65.

Formatting Data for Computer Analysis

Most computer programs that compute t tests require your data to be in a specific form. Consider the data in Table 2.

Table 2. Example Data

Group 1	Group 2
3	5
4	6
5	7

Here there are two groups, each with three observations. To format these data for a computer program, you normally have to use two variables: the first specifies the group the subject is in and the second is the score itself. For the data in Table 2, the reformatted data look as follows:

Table 3. Reformatted Data

G	Y
1	3
1	4
1	5
2	5
2	6
2	7

Computations for Unequal Sample Sizes (optional)

The calculations are somewhat more complicated when the sample sizes are not equal. One consideration is that MSE, the estimate of variance, counts the sample with the larger sample size more than the sample with the smaller sample size. Computationally this is done by computing the sum of squares error (SSE) as follows:

$$SSE = \sum(X - M_1)^2 + \sum(X - M_2)^2$$

where M_1 is the mean for group 1 and M_2 is the mean for group 2. Consider the following small example:

Table 4. Example Data

Group 1	Group 2
3	2
4	4
5	

$M_1 = 4$ and $M_2 = 3$.

$SSE = (3-4)^2 + (4-4)^2 + (5-4)^2 + (2-3)^2 + (4-3)^2 = 4$

Then, MSE is computed by:

```
MSE = SSE/df
```

where the degrees of freedom (df) is computed as before:

```
df = (n1 -1) + (n2 -1) = (3-1) + (2-1) = 3.
MSE = SSE/df = 4/3 = 1.333.
```

The formula

$$s_{M_1-M_2} = \sqrt{\frac{2MSE}{n}}$$

is replaced by

$$s_{M_1-M_2} = \sqrt{\frac{2MSE}{n_h}}$$

where n_h is the harmonic mean of the sample sizes and is computed as follows:

$$n_h = \frac{2}{\frac{1}{n_1}+\frac{1}{n_1}} = \frac{2}{\frac{1}{3}+\frac{1}{2}} = 2.4$$

and

$$s_{M_1-M_2} = \sqrt{\frac{(2)(1.333)}{2.4}} = 1.054.$$

t_{CL} for 3 df and the 0.05 level = 3.182.

Therefore the 95% confidence interval is

```
Lower Limit = 1 - (3.182)(1.054) = -2.35
```

```
Upper Limit = 1 + (3.182)(1.054) = 4.35
```

We can write the confidence interval as:

$$-2.35 \leq \mu_1 - \mu_2 \leq 4.35$$

Correlation

by David M. Lane

Prerequisites
- Chapter 4: Values of the Pearson Correlation
- Chapter 9: Sampling Distribution of Pearson's r
- Chapter 10: Confidence Intervals

Learning Objectives
1. State why the z' transformation is necessary
2. Compute the standard error of z'
3. Compute a confidence interval on ϱ

The computation of a confidence interval on the population value of Pearson's correlation (ϱ) is complicated by the fact that the sampling distribution of r is not normally distributed. The solution lies with Fisher's z' transformation described in the section on the sampling distribution of Pearson's r. The steps in computing a confidence interval for p are:
1. Convert r to z'
2. Compute a confidence interval in terms of z'
3. Convert the confidence interval back to r.

Let's take the data from the case study Animal Research as an example. In this study, students were asked to rate the degree to which they thought animal research is wrong and the degree to which they thought it is necessary. As you might have expected, there was a negative relationship between these two variables: the more that students thought animal research is wrong, the less they thought it is necessary. The correlation based on 34 observations is -0.654. The problem is to compute a 95% confidence interval on ϱ based on this r of -0.654.

The conversion of r to z' can be done using a calculator. This calculator shows that the z' associated with an r of -0.654 is -0.78.

The sampling distribution of z' is approximately normally distributed and has a standard error of

$$\frac{1}{\sqrt{N-3}}$$

For this example, N = 34 and therefore the standard error is 0.180. The Z for a 95% confidence interval (Z.95) is 1.96, as can be found using the normal distribution calculator (setting the shaded area to .95 and clicking on the "Between" button). The confidence interval is therefore computed as:

```
Lower limit = -0.78 - (1.96)(0.18)= -1.13
Upper limit = -0.78 + (1.96)(0.18)= -0.43
```

The final step is to convert the endpoints of the interval back to r using a table or the calculator. The r associated with a z' of -1.13 is -0.81 and the r associated with a z' of -0.43 is -0.40. Therefore, the population correlation (p) is likely to be between -0.81 and -0.40. The 95% confidence interval is:

```
-0.81 ≤ ρ ≤ -0.40
```

To calculate the 99% confidence interval, you use the Z for a 99% confidence interval of 2.58 as follows:

```
Lower limit = -0.775 - (2.58)(0.18) = -1.24
Upper limit = -0.775 + (2.58)(0.18) = -0.32
```

Converting back to r, the confidence interval is:

```
-0.84 ≤ ρ ≤ -0.31
```

Naturally, the 99% confidence interval is wider than the 95% confidence interval.

Proportion

by David M. Lane

Prerequisites
- Chapter 7: Introduction to the Normal Distribution
- Chapter 7: Normal Approximation to the Binomial
- Chapter 9: Sampling Distribution of the Mean
- Chapter 9: Sampling Distribution of a Proportion
- Chapter 10: Confidence Intervals
- Chapter 10: Confidence Interval on the Mean

Learning Objectives
1. Estimate the population proportion from sample proportions
2. Apply the correction for continuity
3. Compute a confidence interval

A candidate in a two-person election commissions a poll to determine who is ahead. The pollster randomly chooses 500 registered voters and determines that 260 out of the 500 favor the candidate. In other words, 0.52 of the sample favors the candidate. Although this point estimate of the proportion is informative, it is important to also compute a confidence interval. The confidence interval is computed based on the mean and standard deviation of the sampling distribution of a proportion. The formulas for these two parameters are shown below:

$$\mu_p = \pi$$

$$\sigma_p = \sqrt{\frac{\pi(1-\pi)}{N}}$$

Since we do not know the population parameter π, we use the sample proportion p as an estimate. The estimated standard error of p is therefore

$$s_p = \sqrt{\frac{p(1-p)}{N}}$$

We start by taking our statistic (p) and creating an interval that ranges $(Z_{.95})(s_p)$ in both directions where $Z_{.95}$ is the number of standard deviations extending from the mean of a normal distribution required to contain 0.95 of the area. (See the section on the confidence interval for the mean). The value of $Z_{.95}$ is computed with the normal calculator and is equal to 1.96. We then make a slight adjustment to correct for the fact that the distribution is discrete rather than continuous.

s_p is calculated as shown below:

$$s_p = \sqrt{\frac{.52(1 - .52)}{500}} = 0.0223$$

To correct for the fact that we are approximating a discrete distribution with a continuous distribution (the normal distribution), we subtract 0.5/N from the lower limit and add 0.5/N to the upper limit of the interval. Therefore the confidence interval is

$$p \pm Z_{.95}\sqrt{\frac{p(1-p)}{N}} \pm \frac{0.5}{N}$$

```
Lower: 0.52 - (1.96)(0.0223) - 0.001 = 0.475
Upper: 0.52 + (1.96)(0.0223) + 0.001 = 0.565
```

$$.475 \leq \pi \leq .565$$

Since the interval extends 0.045 in both directions, the margin of error is 0.045. In terms of percent, between 47.5% and 56.5% of the voters favor the candidate and the margin of error is 4.5%. Keep in mind that the margin of error of 4.5% is the margin of error for the percent favoring the candidate and not the margin of error for the difference between the percent favoring the candidate and the percent favoring the opponent. The margin of error for the difference is 9%, twice the margin of error for the individual percent. Keep this in mind when you hear reports in the media; the media often get this wrong.

Statistical Literacy

by David M. Lane

Prerequisites
- Chapter 10: Proportions

In July of 2011, Gene Munster of Piper Jaffray reported the results of a survey in a note to clients. This research was reported throughout the media. Perhaps the fullest description was presented on the CNNMoney website (A service of CNN, Fortune, and Money) in an article entitled "Survey: iPhone retention 94% vs. Android 47%." The data were collected by asking people in food courts and baseball stadiums what their current phone was and what phone they planned to buy next. The data were collected in the summer of 2011. Below is a portion of the data:

Phone	Keep	Change	Proportion
iPhone	58	4	0.94
Android	17	19	0.47

What do you think?

The article contains the strong caution: "It's only a tiny sample, so large conclusions must not be drawn." This caution appears to be a welcome change from the overstating of findings typically found in the media. But has this report understated the importance of the study? Perhaps it is valid to draw some "large conclusions."?

> The confidence interval on the proportion extends from 0.87 to 1.0 (some methods give the interval from 0.85 to 0.97). Even the lower bound indicates the vast majority of iPhone owners plan to buy another iPhone. A strong conclusion can be made even with this sample size.

Exercises

• All material presented in the Estimation Chapter

1. When would the mean grade in a class on a final exam be considered a statistic? When would it be considered a parameter?

2. Define bias in terms of expected value.

3. Is it possible for a statistic to be unbiased yet very imprecise? How about being very accurate but biased?

4. Why is a 99% confidence interval wider than a 95% confidence interval?

5. When you construct a 95% confidence interval, what are you 95% confident about?

6. What is the difference in the computation of a confidence interval between cases in which you know the population standard deviation and cases in which you have to estimate it?

7. Assume a researcher found that the correlation between a test he or she developed and job performance was 0.55 in a study of 28 employees. If correlations under .35 are considered unacceptable, would you have any reservations about using this test to screen job applicants?

8. What is the effect of sample size on the width of a confidence interval?

9. How does the t distribution compare with the normal distribution? How does this difference affect the size of confidence intervals constructed using z relative to those constructed using t? Does sample size make a difference?

10. The effectiveness of a blood-pressure drug is being investigated. How might an experimenter demonstrate that, on average, the reduction in systolic blood pressure is 20 or more?

11. A population is known to be normally distributed with a standard deviation of 2.8. (a) Compute the 95% confidence interval on the mean based on the following sample of nine: 8, 9, 10, 13, 14, 16, 17, 20, 21. (b) Now compute the 99% confidence interval using the same data.

12. A person claims to be able to predict the outcome of flipping a coin. This person is correct 16/25 times. Compute the 95% confidence interval on the proportion of times this person can predict coin flips correctly. What conclusion can you draw about this test of his ability to predict the future?

13. What does it mean that the variance (computed by dividing by N) is a biased statistic?

14. A confidence interval for the population mean computed from an N of 16 ranges from 12 to 28. A new sample of 36 observations is going to be taken. You can't know in advance exactly what the confidence interval will be because it depends on the random sample. Even so, you should have some idea of what it will be. Give your best estimation.

15. You take a sample of 22 from a population of test scores, and the mean of your sample is 60. (a) You know the standard deviation of the population is 10. What is the 99% confidence interval on the population mean. (b) Now assume that you do not know the population standard deviation, but the standard deviation in your sample is 10. What is the 99% confidence interval on the mean now?

16. You read about a survey in a newspaper and find that 70% of the 250 people sampled prefer Candidate A. You are surprised by this survey because you thought that more like 50% of the population preferred this candidate. Based on this sample, is 50% a possible population proportion? Compute the 95% confidence interval to be sure.

17. Heights for teenage boys and girls were calculated. The mean height for the sample of 12 boys was 174 cm and the variance was 62. For the sample of 12 girls, the mean was 166 cm and the variance was 65. Assuming equal variances and normal distributions in the population, (a) What is the 95% confidence interval on the difference between population means? (b) What is the 99%

confidence interval on the difference between population means? (c) Do you think it is very unlikely that the mean difference in the population is about 5? Why or why not?

18. You were interested in how long the average psychology major at your college studies per night, so you asked 10 psychology majors to tell you the amount they study. They told you the following times: 2, 1.5, 3, 2, 3.5, 1, 0.5, 3, 2, 4. (a) Find the 95% confidence interval on the population mean. (b) Find the 90% confidence interval on the population mean.

19. True/false: As the sample size gets larger, the probability that the confidence interval will contain the population mean gets higher.

20. True/false: You have a sample of 9 men and a sample of 8 women. The degrees of freedom for the t value in your confidence interval on the difference between means is 16.

21. True/false: Greek letters are used for statistics as opposed to parameters.

22. True/false: In order to construct a confidence interval on the difference between means, you need to assume that the populations have the same variance and are both normally distributed.

23. True/false: The red distribution represents the t distribution and the blue distribution represents the normal distribution.

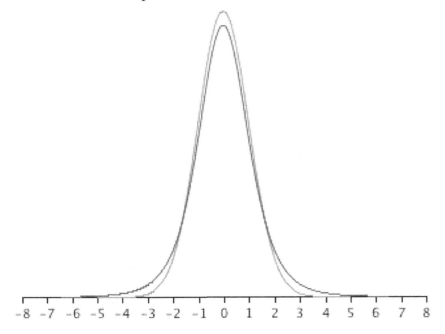

Questions from Case Studies

Angry Moods (AM) case study

24. (AM) Is there a difference in how much males and females use aggressive behavior to improve an angry mood? For the "Anger-Out" scores, compute a 99% confidence interval on the difference between gender means.

25. (AM) Calculate the 95% confidence interval for the difference between the mean Anger-In score for the athletes and non-athletes. What can you conclude?

26. (AM) Find the 95% confidence interval on the population correlation between the Anger- Out and Control-Out scores.

Flatulence (F) case study

27. (F) Compare men and women on the variable "perday." Compute the 95% confidence interval on the difference between means.

28. (F) What is the 95% confidence interval of the mean time people wait before farting in front of a romantic partner.

Animal Research (AR) case study

29. (AR) What percentage of the women studied in this sample strongly agreed (gave a rating of 7) that using animals for research is wrong?

30. (AR) Use the proportion you computed in #29. Compute the 95% confidence interval on the population proportion of women who strongly agree that animal research is wrong.

31. (AR) Compute a 95% confidence interval on the difference between the gender means with respect to their beliefs that animal research is wrong.

ADHD Treatment (AT) case study

32. (AT) What is the correlation between the participants' correct number of responses after taking the placebo and their correct number of responses after taking 0.60 mg/kg of MPH? Compute the 95% confidence interval on the population correlation.

Weapons and Aggression (WA) case study

33. (WA) Recall that the hypothesis is that a person can name an aggressive word more quickly if it is preceded by a weapon word prime than if it is preceded by a neutral word prime. The first step in testing this hypothesis is to compute the difference between (a) the naming time of aggressive words when preceded by a neutral word prime and (b) the naming time of aggressive words when preceded by a weapon word prime separately for each of the 32 participants. That is, compute an - aw for each participant.

a. (WA) Would the hypothesis of this study be supported if the difference were positive or if it were negative?

b. What is the mean of this difference score?

c. What is the standard deviation of this difference score?

d. What is the 95% confidence interval of the mean difference score?

e. What does the confidence interval computed in (d) say about the hypothesis.

Diet and Health (DH) case study

34. (DH) Compute a 95% confidence interval on the proportion of people who are healthy on the AHA diet.

	Cancers	Deaths	Nonfatal illness	Healthy	Total
AHA	15	24	25	239	303
Mediterranean	7	14	8	273	302
Total	22	38	33	512	605

The following questions are from ARTIST (reproduced with permission)

Assessment
Resource
Tools for
Improving
Statistical
Thinking

35. Suppose that you take a random sample of 10,000 Americans and find that 1,111 are left- handed. You perform a test of significance to assess whether the sample data provide evidence that more than 10% of all Americans are left-handed, and you calculate a test statistic of 3.70 and a p-value of .0001. Furthermore, you calculate a 99% confidence interval for the proportion of left-handers in America to be (.103,.119). Consider the following statements: The sample provides strong evidence that more than 10% of all Americans are left-handed. The sample provides evidence that the proportion of left-handers in America is much larger than 10%. Which of these two statements is the more appropriate conclusion to draw? Explain your answer based on the results of the significance test and confidence interval.

36. A student wanted to study the ages of couples applying for marriage licenses in his county. He studied a sample of 94 marriage licenses and found that in 67 cases the husband was older than the wife. Do the sample data provide strong evidence that the husband is usually older than the wife among couples

applying for marriage licenses in that county? Explain briefly and justify your answer.

37. Imagine that there are 100 different researchers each studying the sleeping habits of college freshmen. Each researcher takes a random sample of size 50 from the same population of freshmen. Each researcher is trying to estimate the mean hours of sleep that freshmen get at night, and each one constructs a 95% confidence interval for the mean. Approximately how many of these 100 confidence intervals will NOT capture the true mean?

a. None

b. 1 or 2

c. 3 to 7

d. about half

e. 95 to 100

f. other

20. Case Studies

The case studies give examples of practical applications of statistical analyses. Many of the case studies contain the actual raw data. Some contain discussions of how the the data were analyzed.

All links below are external links.

1. Angry Moods
2. Flatulence
3. Physicians Reactions to Patient Size
4. Teacher Ratings
5. Mediterranean Diet and Health
6. Smiles and Leniency
7. Animal Research
8. ADHD Treatment
9. Weapons and Aggression
10. SAT and College GPA
11. Stereograms
12. Driving
13. Stroop Interference
14. TV Violence
15. Bias Against Associates of the Obese
16. Shaking and Stirring Martinis
17. Adolescent Lifestyle Choices
18. Chocolate and Body Weight
19. Bedroom TV and Hispanic Children
20. Weight and Sleep Apnea
21. Misusing SEM
22. School Gardens and Vegetable Consumption
23. TV and Hypertension
24. Dietary Supplements
25. Young People and Binge Drinking

21. Glossary

***a priori* Comparison**
A comparison that is planned before (a priori) conducting the experiment or at least before the data are examined.

Absolute Deviation
The absolute value of the difference between two numbers. The absolute deviation between 5 and 3 is 2; between 3 and 5 is 2; and between -4 and 2 it is 6.

Alternative Hypothesis
In hypothesis testing, the null hypothesis and an alternative hypothesis are put forward. If the data are sufficiently strong to reject the null hypothesis, then the null hypothesis is rejected in favor of an alternative hypothesis. For instance, if the null hypothesis were that $\mu_1 = \mu_2$ then the alternative hypothesis (for a two-tailed test) would be $\mu_1 \neq \mu_2$.

Analysis of Variance
Analysis of variance is a method for testing hypotheses about means. It is the most widely-used method of statistical inference for the analysis of experimental data.

Antilog
Taking the anti-log of a number undoes the operation of taking the log. Therefore, since $Log_{10}(1000) = 3$, the antilog$_{10}$ of 3 is 1,000. Taking the antilog of X raises the base of the logarithm in question to X.

Average
(i) The (arithmetic) mean

(ii) Any measure of central tendency

Bar Chart
A graphical method of presenting data. A bar is drawn for each level of a variable. The height of each bar contains the value of the variable. Bar charts are useful for displaying things such as frequency counts and percent increases. They are not recommended for displaying means (despite the widespread practice) since box plots present more information in the same amount of space.

Base Rate
The true proportion of a population having some condition, attribute or disease. For example, the proportion of people with schizophrenia is about 0.01. It is very important to consider the base rate when classifying people. As the saying goes, "if you hear hoofs, think horse not zebra" since you are more likely to encounter a horse than a zebra (at least in most places.)

Bayes' Theorem

Bayes' theorem considers both the prior probability of an event and the diagnostic value of a test to determine the posterior probability of the event. The theorem is shown below:

$$P(D \mid T) = \frac{P(T \mid D)P(D)}{P(T \mid D)P(D) + P(T \mid D')P(D')}$$

where P(D|T) is the posterior probability of condition D given test result T, P(T|D) is the conditional probability of T given D, P(D) is the prior probability of D, P(T|D') is the conditional probability of T given not D, and P(D') is the probability of not D'.

Beta weight

A standardized regression coefficient.

Between-Subjects Factor/Variable

Between-subject variables are independent variables or factors in which a different group of subjects is used for each level of the variable. If an experiment is conducted comparing four methods of teaching vocabulary and if a different group of subjects is used for each of the four teaching methods, then teaching method is a between-subjects variable.

Bias

1. A sampling method is biased if each element does not have an equal chance of being selected. A sample of internet users found reading an online statistics book would be a biased sample of all internet users. A random sample is unbiased. Note that possible bias refers to the sampling method, not the result. An unbiased method could, by chance, lead to a very non-representative sample.

2. An estimator is biased if it systematically overestimates or underestimates the parameter it is estimating. In other words, it is biased if the mean of the sampling distribution of the statistic is not the parameter it is estimating, The sample mean is an unbiased estimate of the population mean. The mean squared deviation of sample scores from their mean is a biased estimate of the variance since it tends to underestimate the population variance.

Bimodal Distribution

A distribution with two distinct peaks.

Binomial Distribution

A probability distribution for independent events for which there are only two possible outcomes such as a coin flip. If one of the two outcomes is defined as a success, then the probability of exactly x successes out of N trials (events) is given by:

$$P(x) = \frac{N!}{x!(N-x)!} \pi^{x} (1-\pi)^{N-x}$$

Bin Width

Also known as the class interval, the bin width is a division of data for use in a histogram. For instance, it is possible to partition scores on a 100 point test into class intervals of 1-25, 26-49, 50-74 and 75-100.

Bivariate

Bivariate data is data for which there are two variables for each observation. That is, two scores per subject.

Bonferroni Correction

In general, to keep the familywise error rate (FER) at or below .05, the per-comparison error rate (PCER) should be: PCER = .05/c where c is the number of comparisons. More generally, to insure that the FER is less than or equal to alpha, use PCER = alpha/c.

Box Plot

One of the more effective graphical summaries of a data set, the box plot generally shows mean, median, 25th and 75th percentiles, and outliers. A standard box plot is composed of the median, upper hinge, lower hinge, higher adjacent value, lower adjacent value, outside values, and far out values. An example is shown below. Parallel box plots are very useful for comparing distributions.

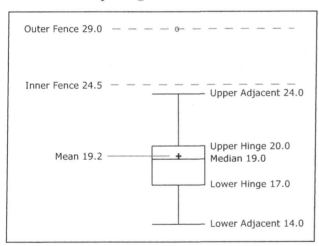

Central Tendency

There are many measures of the center of a distribution. These are called measures of central tendency. The most common are the mean, median, and, mode. Others include the trimean, trimmed mean, and geometric mean.)

Class Frequency

One of the components of a histogram, the class frequency is the number of observations in each class interval. See also: relative frequency.

Class Interval
Also known as bin width, the class interval is a division of data for use in a histogram. For instance, it is possible to partition scores on a 100 point test into class intervals of 1-25, 26-49, 50-74 and 75-100.

Conditional Probability
The probability that event A occurs given that event B has already occurred is called the conditional probability of A given B. Symbolically, this is written as P(A|B). The probability it rains on Monday given that it rained on Sunday would be written as P(Rain on Monday | Rain on Sunday).

Confidence Interval
A confidence interval is a range of scores likely to contain the parameter being estimated. Intervals can be constructed to be more or less likely to contain the parameter: 95% of 95% confidence intervals contain the estimated parameter whereas 99% of 99% confidence intervals contain the estimated parameter. The wider the confidence interval, the more uncertainty there is about the value of the parameter.

Confounding
Two or more variables are confounded if their effects cannot be separated because they vary together. For example, if a study on the effect of light inadvertently manipulated heat along with light, then light and heat would be confounded.

Cook's D
Cook's D is a measure of the influence of an observation in regression and is proportional to the sum of the squared differences between predictions made with all observations in the analysis and predictions made leaving out the observation in question.

Constant
A value that does not change. Values such as π, or the mass of the Earth are constants.

Continuous Variables
Variables that can take on any value in a certain range. Time and distance are continuous; gender, SAT score and "time rounded to the nearest second" are not. Variables that are not continuous are known as discrete variables. No measured variable is truly continuous; however, discrete variables measured with enough precision can often be considered continuous for practical purposes.

Counterbalance
Counterbalancing is a method of avoiding confounding among variables. Consider an experiment in which subjects are tested on both an auditory reaction time task (in which subjects respond to an auditory stimulus) and a visual reaction time task (in which subjects respond to a visual stimulus). Half of the subjects are given the visual task first and the

other half of the subjects are given the auditory task first. That way, there is no confounding of order of presentation and task.

Criterion Variable

In regression analysis (such as linear regression) the criterion variable is the variable being predicted. In general, the criterion variable is the dependent variable.

Cumulative Frequency Distribution

A distribution showing the number of observations less than or equal to values on the X-axis. The following graph shows a cumulative distribution for scores on a test.

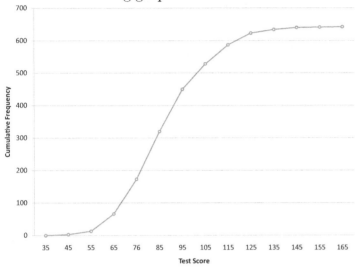

Dependent Variable

A variable that measures the experimental outcome. In most experiments, the effects of the independent variable on the dependent variables are observed. For example, if a study investigated the effectiveness of an experimental treatment for depression, then the measure of depression would be the dependent variable.

Descriptive Statistics

1. The branch of statistics concerned with describing and summarizing data.

2. A set of statistics such as the mean, standard deviation, and skew that describe a distribution.

Deviation Scores

Scores that are expressed as differences (deviations) from some value, usually the mean. To convert data to deviation scores typically means to subtract the mean score from each other score. Thus, the values 1, 2, and 3 in deviation-score form would be computed by subtracting the mean of 2 from each value and would be -1, 0, 1.

Degrees of Freedom

The degrees of freedom of an estimate is the number of independent pieces of information that go into the estimate. In general, the degrees of freedom for an estimate is equal to the number of values minus the number of parameters estimated en route to the estimate in question. For example, to estimate the population variance, one must first estimate the population mean. Therefore, if the estimate of variance is based on N observations, there are N-1 degrees of freedom.

Discrete Variables

Variables that can only take on a finite number of values are called "discrete variables." All qualitative variables are discrete. Some quantitative variables are discrete, such as performance rated as 1,2,3,4, or 5, or temperature rounded to the nearest degree. Sometimes, a variable that takes on enough discrete values can be considered to be continuous for practical purposes. One example is time to the nearest millisecond.

Distribution

The distribution of empirical data is called a frequency distribution and consists of a count of the number of occurrences of each value. If the data are continuous, then a grouped frequency distribution is used. Typically, a distribution is portrayed using a frequency polygon or a histogram.

Mathematical equations are often used to define distributions. The normal distribution is, perhaps, the best known example. Many empirical distributions are approximated well by mathematical distributions such as the normal distribution.

Expected Value

The expected value of a statistic is the mean of the sampling distribution of the statistic. It can be loosely thought of as the long-run average value of the statistic.

Factor (Independent Variable)

Variables that are manipulated by the experimenter, as opposed to dependent variables. Most experiments consist of observing the effect of the independent variable(s) on the dependent variable(s).

Factorial Design

In a factorial design, each level of each independent variable is paired with each level of each other independent variable. Thus, a 2 x 3 factorial design consists of the 6 possible combinations of the levels of the independent variables.

False Positive

A false positive occurs when a diagnostic procedure returns a positive result while the true state of the subject is negative. For example, if a test for strep says the patient has strep when in fact he or she does not, then the error in diagnosis would be called a false positive. In some contexts, a false positive is called a false alarm. The concept is similar to a Type I error in significance testing.

Familywise Error Rate

When a series of significance tests is conducted, the familywise error rate (FER) is the probability that one or more of the significance tests results in a Type I error.

Far Out Value

One of the components of a box plot, far out values are those that are more than 2 steps beyond the nearest hinge. They are beyond an outer fence.

Favorable Outcome

A favorable outcome is the outcome of interest. For example one could define a favorable outcome in the flip of a coin as a head. The term "favorable outcome" does not necessarily mean that the outcome is desirable – in some experiments, the favorable outcome could be the failure of a test, or the occurrence of an undesirable event.

Frequency Distribution

For a discrete variable, a frequency distribution consists of the distribution of the number of occurrences for each value of the variable. For a continuous variable, it is the number of occurrences for a variety of ranges of variables.

Frequency Polygon

A frequency polygon is a graphical representation of a distribution. It partitions the variable on the x-axis into various contiguous class intervals of (usually) equal widths. The heights of the polygon's points represent the class frequencies.

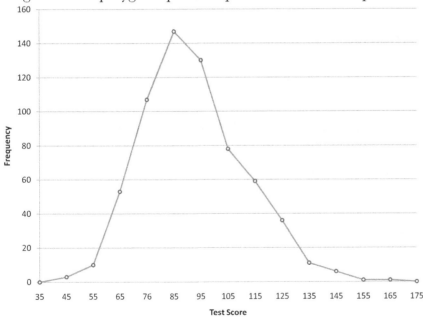

Frequency Table

A table containing the number of occurrences in each class of data; for example, the number of each color of M&Ms in a bag. Frequency tables often used to create histograms and frequency polygons. When a frequency table is created for a quantitative variable, a grouped frequency table is generally used.

Grouped Frequency Table

A grouped frequency table shows the number of values for various ranges of scores. Below is shown a grouped frequency table for response times (in milliseconds) for a simple motor task.

Range	Frequency
500-600	3
600-700	6
700-800	5
800-900	5
900-1000	0
1000-1100	1

Geometric Mean

The geometric mean is a measure of central tendency. The geometric mean of n numbers is obtained by multiplying all of them together, and then taking the nth root of them. For example, for the numbers 1, 10, and 100, the product of all the numbers is: 1 x 10 x 100 = 1,000. Since there are three numbers, we take the cubed root of the product (1,000) which is equal to 10.

Grouped Frequency Distribution

A grouped frequency distribution is a frequency distribution in which frequencies are displayed for ranges of data rather than for individual values. For example, the distribution of heights might be calculated by defining one-inch ranges. The frequency of individuals with various heights rounded off to the nearest inch would then be tabulated.

Harmonic Mean

The harmonic mean of n numbers $(x_1$ to $x_n)$ is computed using the formula

$$n_h = \frac{\frac{1}{x_1} + \frac{1}{x_2} + ... + \frac{1}{x_n}}{n}$$

where n_h is the harmonic mean. Often the harmonic mean of sample sizes is computed.

Histogram

A histogram is a graphical representation of a distribution . It partitions the variable on the x-axis into various contiguous class intervals of (usually) equal widths. The heights of the bars represent the class frequencies.

History Effect

A problem of confounding where the passage of time, and not the variable of interest, is responsible for observed effects. See also: third variable problem.

Homogeneity of Variance

The assumption that the variances of all the populations are equal.

Homoscedasticity

In linear regression, the assumption that the varance around the regression line is the same for all values of the predictor variable.

H-Spread

One of the components of a box plot, the H-spread is the difference between the upper hinge and the lower hinge.

Independence

Two variables are said to be independent if the value of one variable provides no information about the value of the other variable. These two variables would be uncorrelated so that Pearson's r would be 0.

Two events are independent if the probability the second event occurring is the same regardless of whether or not the first event occurred.

Independent Events

Events A and B are independent events if the probability of Event B occurring is the same whether or not Event A occurs. For example, if you throw two dice, the probability that the second die comes up 1 is independent of whether the first die came up 1. Formally, this can be stated in terms of conditional probabilities: $P(A|B) = P(A)$ and $P(B|A) = P(B)$.

Independent Variable (Factor)

Variables that are manipulated by the experimenter, as opposed to dependent variables. Most experiments consist of observing the effect of the independent variable(s) on the dependent variable(s).

Inferential Statistics

The branch of statistics concerned with drawing conclusions about a population from a sample. This is generally done through random sampling, followed by inferences made about central tendency, or any of a number of other aspects of a distribution.

Influence

Influence refers to the degree to which a single observation in regression influences the estimation of the regression parameters. It is often measured in terms how much the predicted scores for other observations would differ if the observation in question were not included.

Inner Fence

In a box plot, the lower inner fence is one step below the lower hinge while the upper inner fence is one step above the upper hinge.

Interaction

Two independent variables interact if the effect of one of the variables differs depending on the level of the other variable.

Interaction Plot

An interaction plot displays the levels of one variable on the X axis and has a separate line for the means of each level of the other variable. The Y axis is the dependent variable. A look at this graph shows that the effect of dosage is different for males than it is for females.

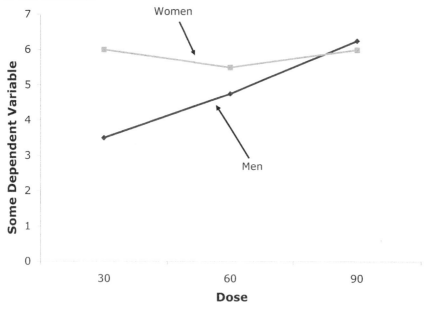

Interquartile Range

The Interquartile Range (IQR) is the 75th percentile minus the 25th percentile. It is a robust measure of variability.

Interval Estimate

An interval estimate is a range of scores likely to contain the estimated parameter. It can be used synonymously with "confidence interval."

Interval Scale

One of four commonly used levels of measurement, an interval scales is a numerical scales in which intervals have the same meaning throughout. As an example, consider the Fahrenheit scale of temperature. The difference between 30 degrees and 40 degrees represents the same temperature difference as the difference between 80 degrees and 90 degrees. This is because each 10 degree interval has the same physical meaning (in terms of the kinetic energy. Unlike ratio scales, interval scales do not have a true zero point.

Jitter

When points in a graph are jittered, the are moved horizontally so that all the points can be seen and none are hidden due to overlapping values. An example is shown below:

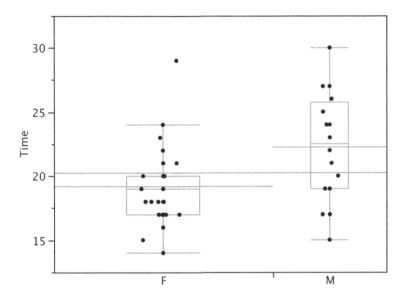

Kurtosis

Kurtosis measures how fat or thin the tails of a distribution are relative to a normal distribution. It is commonly defined as:

$$\sum \frac{(X-\mu)^4}{N\sigma^4} - 3$$

Distributions with long tails are called leptokurtic; distributions with short tails are called platykurtic. Normal distributions have zero kurtosis.

Leptokurtic

A distribution with long tails relative to a normal distribution is leptokurtic.

Level

When a factor consists of various treatment conditions, each treatment condition is considered a level of that factor. For example, if the factor were drug dosage, and three doses were tested, then each dosage would be one level of the factor and the factor would have three levels.

Levels of Measurement
Measurement scales differ in their level of measurement. There are four common levels of measurement:

1. Nominal scales are only labels.

2. Ordinal Scales are ordered but are not truly quantitative. Equal intervals on the ordinal scale do not imply equal intervals on the underlying trait.

3. Interval scales are are ordered and equal intervals equal intervals on the underlying trait. However, interval scales do not have a true zero point.

4. Ratio scales are interval scales that do have a true zero point. With ratio scales, it is sensible to talk about one value being twice as large as another, for example.

Leverage
Leverage is a factor affecting the influence of an observation in regression. Leverage is based on how much the observation's value on the predictor variable differs from the mean of the predictor variable. The greater an observation's leverage, the more potential it has to be an influential observation.

Lie Factor
Many problems can arise when fancy graphs are used over plain ones. Distortions can occur when the heights of objects are used to indicate the value because most people will pay attention to the areas of the objects rather than their height. The lie factor is the ratio of the effect apparent in the graph to actual effect in the data; if it deviates by more than 0.05 from 1, the graph is generally unacceptable. The lie factor in the following graph is almost 6.

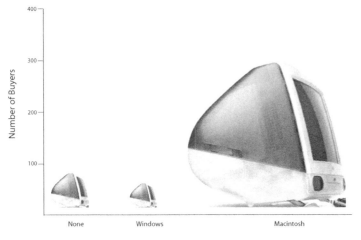

Lies
There are three types of lies:

1. regular lies

2. damned lies

3. statistics

This is according to Benjamin Disraeli as quoted by Mark Twain.

Line Graph

Essentially a bar graph in which the height of each par is represented by a single point, with each of these points connected by a line. Line graphs are best used to show change over time, and should not be used if your X-axis is not an ordered variable. An example is shown below.

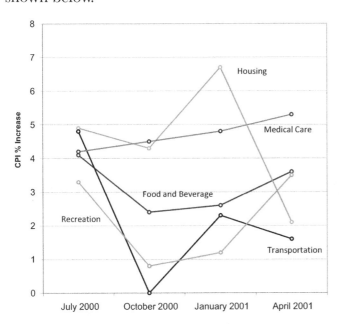

Linear Combination

A linear combination of variables is a way of creating a new variable by combining other variables. A linear combination is one in which each variable is multiplied by a coefficient and the are products summed. For example, if

$$Y = 3X_1 + 2X_2 + .5X_3$$

then Y is a linear combination of the variables X_1, X_2, and X_3.

Linear Regression

Linear regression is a method for predicting a criterion variable from one or more predictor variable. In simple regression, the criterion is predicted from a single predictor variable and the best-fitting straight line is of the form

$$Y' = bX + A$$

where Y' is the predicted score, X is the predictor variable, b is the slope, and A is the Y intercept. Typically, the criterion for the "best fitting" line is the line for which the sum of the squared errors of prediction is minimized. In multiple regression, the criterion is predicted from two or more predictor variables.

Linear Relationship

There is a perfect linear relationship between two variables if a scatterplot of the points falls on a straight line. The relationship is linear even if the points diverge from the line as long as the divergence is random rather than being systematic.

Linear Transformation

A linear transformation is any transformation of a variable that can be achieved by multiplying it by a constant, and then adding a second constant. If Y is the transformed value of X, then $Y = aX + b$. The transformation from degrees Fahrenheit to degrees Centigrade is linear and is done using the formula:

$$C = 0.55556F - 17.7778.$$

Logarithm

The logarithm of a number is the power the base of the logarithm has to be raised to in order to equal the number. If the base of the logarithm is 10 and the number is 1,000, then the log is 3 since 10 has to be raised to the 3rd power to equal 1,000.

Lower Adjacent Value

A component of a box plot, the lower adjacent value is smallest value in the data above the inner lower fence.

Lower Hinge

A component of a box plot, the lower hinge is the 25th percentile. The upper hinge is the 75th percentile.

Main Effect

A main effect of an independent variable is the effect of the variable averaging over all levels of the other variable(s). For example, in a design with age and gender as factors, the main effect of gender would be the difference between the genders averaging across all ages used in the experiment.

Margin of Error

When a statistic is used to estimate a parameter, it is common to compute a confidence interval. The margin of error is the difference between the statistic and the endpoints of the interval. For example, if the statistic were 0.6 and the confidence interval ranged from 0.4 to 0.8, then the margin of error would be 0.20. Unless otherwise specified, the 95% confidence interval is used.

Marginal Mean

In a design with two factors, the marginal means for one factor are the means for that factor averaged across all levels of the other factor. In the table shown below, the two factors are "Relationship" and "Companion Weight." The marginal means for each of the two levels of Relationship (Girl Friend and Acquaintance) are computed by averaging across the two levels of Companion Weight. Thus, the marginal mean for Acquaintance of 6.37 is the mean of 6.15 and 6.59.

		Companion Weight		
		Obese	Typical	Marginal Mean
Relationship	Girl Friend	5.65	6.19	**5.92**
	Acquaintance	6.15	6.59	**6.37**
	Marginal Mean	**5.9**	**6.39**	

Mean

Also known as the arithmetic mean, the mean is typically what is meant by the word "average." The mean is perhaps the most common measure of central tendency. The mean of a variable is given by (the sum of all its values)/(the number of values). For example, the mean of 4, 8, and 9 is 7. The sample mean is written as M, and the population mean as the Greek letter mu (μ). Despite its popularity, the mean may not be an appropriate measure of central tendency for skewed distributions, or in situations with outliers. Other than the arithmetic mean, there is the geometric mean and the harmonic mean.

Median

The median is a popular measure of central tendency. It is the 50th percentile of a distribution. To find the median of a number of values, first order them, then find the observation in the middle: the median of 5, 2, 7, 9, and 4 is 5. (Note that if there is an even number of values, one takes the average of the middle two: the median of 4, 6, 8, and 10 is 7.) The median is often more appropriate than the mean in skewed distributions and in situations with outliers.

Misses

Misses occur when a diagnostic test returns a negative result, but the true state of the subject is positive. For example, if a person has strep throat and the diagnostic test fails to indicate it, then a miss has occurred. The concept is similar to a Type II error in significance testing.

Mode

The mode is a measure of central tendency. It is the most frequent value in a distribution: the mode of 3, 4, 4, 5, 5, 5, 8 is 5. Note that the mode may be very different from the mean and the median.

Multiple Regression

Multiple regression is linear regression in which two or more predictor variables are used to predict the criterion.

Negative Association

There is a negative association between variables X and Y if smaller values of X are associated with larger values of Y and larger values of X are associated with smaller values of Y.

Nominal Scales

A nominal scale is one of four commonly-used levels of measurement. No ordering is implied, and addition/subtraction and multiplication/division would be inappropriate for a variable on a nominal scale. {Female, Male} and {Buddhist, Christian, Hindu, Muslim} have no natural ordering (except alphabetic). Occasionally, numeric values are nominal: for instance, if a variable were coded as Female = 1, Male =2, the set {1,2} is still nominal.

Non-representative

A non-representative sample is a sample that does not accurately reflect the population.

Normal Distribution

One of the most common continuous distributions, a normal distribution is sometimes referred to as a "bell-shaped distribution." If μ is the distribution mean, and σ the standard deviation, then the height (ordinate) of the normal distribution is given by

$$\frac{1}{\sqrt{2\pi\sigma^2}} e^{\frac{-(x-\mu)^2}{2\sigma^2}}$$

A graph of a normal distribution with a mean of 50 and a standard deviation of 10 is shown below.

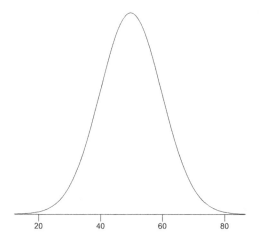

If the mean is 0 and the standard deviation is 1, the distribution is referred to as the "standard normal distribution."

Null Hypothesis

A null hypothesis is a hypothesis tested in significance testing. It is typically the hypothesis that a parameter is zero or that a difference between parameters is zero. For example, the null hypothesis might be that the difference between population means is zero. Experimenters typically design experiments to allow the null hypothesis to be rejected.

Omnibus Null Hypothesis

The null hypothesis that all population means are equal.

One Tailed

The last step in significance testing involves calculating the probability that a statistic would differ as much or more from the parameter specified in the null hypothesis as does the statistics obtained in the experiment.

A probability computed considering differences in only one direction, such as the statistic is larger than the parameter, is called a one-tailed probability. For example, if a parameter is 0 and the statistic is 12, a one-tailed probability (the positive tail) would be the probability of a statistic being $\geq$ to 12. Compare with the two-tailed probability which would be the probability of being either $\leq$ -12 or $\geq$ 12.

Ordinal Scales

One of four commonly-used levels of measurement, an ordinal scale is a set of ordered values. However, there is no set distance between scale values. For instance, for the scale: (Very Poor, Poor, Average, Good, Very Good) is an ordinal scale. You can assign numerical values to an ordinal scale: rating performance such as 1 for "Very Poor," 2 for "Poor," etc, but there is no assurance that the difference between a score of 1 and 2 means the same thing as the difference between a score of and 2 and 3.

Orthogonal Comparisons

When comparisons among means provide completely independent information, the comparisons are called "orthogonal." If an experiment with four groups were conducted, then a comparison of Groups 1 and 2 would be orthogonal to a comparison of Groups 3 and 4 since there is nothing in the comparison of Groups 1 and 2 that provides information about the comparison of Groups 3 and 4.

Outer Fence

In a box plot, the lower outer fence is two steps below the lower hinge whereas the upper inner fence is two steps above the upper hinge.

Outlier

Outliers are atypical, infrequent observations; values that have an extreme deviation from the center of the distribution. There is no universally-agreed on criterion for defining an outlier, and outliers should only be discarded with extreme caution. However, one should always assess the effects of outliers on the statistical conclusions.

Outside Values

A component of a box plot, outside values are more than one step beyond the nearest hinge but not more than two steps. They are beyond an inner fence but not beyond an outer fence.

Pairwise Comparisons

Two or more box plots drawn on the same Y-axis. These are often useful in comparing features of distributions. An example portraying the times it took samples of women and men to do a task is shown below.

Parallel Box Plots

Two or more box plots drawn on the same Y-axis. These are often useful in comparing features of distributions. An example portraying the times it took samples of women and men to do a task is shown below.

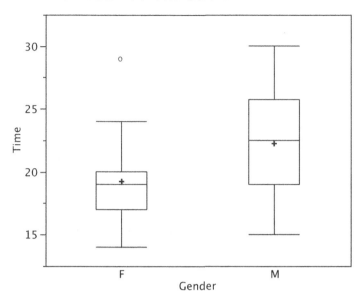

Parameter

A value calculated in a population. For example, the mean of the numbers in a population is a parameter. Compare with a statistic, which is a value computed in a sample to estimate a parameter.

Partial slope

The partial slope in multiple regression is the slope of the relationship between the part of the predictor variable that is independent of the other predictor variables and criterion. It is also the regression coefficient for the predictor variable in question.

Pearson's r

Pearson's correlation is a measure of the strength of the linear relationship between two variables. It ranges from -1 for a perfect negative relationship to +1 for a perfect positive relationship. A correlation of 0 means that there is no linear relationship.

Percentiles

There is no universally accepted definition of a percentile. Using the 65th percentile as an example, some statisticians define the 65th percentile as the lowest score that is *greater* than 65% of the scores. Others have defined the 65th percentile as the lowest score that is *greater than or equal* to 65% of the scores. A more sophisticated definition is given below.

The first step is to compute the rank (R) of the percentile in question. This is done using the following formula:

$$R = P/100 \times (N + 1)$$

where P is the desired percentile and N is the number of numbers. If R is an integer, then the Pth percentile is the number with rank R. When R is not an integer, we compute the Pth percentile by interpolation as follows:

1. Define IR as the integer portion of R (the number to the left of the decimal point).

2. Define FR as the fractional portion or R.

3. Find the scores with Rank IR and with Rank IR + 1.

4. Interpolate by multiplying the difference between the scores by FR and add the result to the lower score.

Per-Comparison Error Rate
The per-comparison error rate refers to the Type I error rate of any one significance test conducted as part of a series of significance tests. Thus, if 10 significance tests were each conducted at 0.05 significance level, then the per-comparison error rate would be 0.05. Compare with the familywise error rate.

Pie Chart
A graphical representation of data, the pie chart shows relative frequencies of classes of data. It is a circle cut into a number of wedges, one for each class, with the area of each wedge proportional to its relative frequency. Pie charts are only effective for a small number of classes, and are one of the less effective graphical representations.

Placebo
A device used in clinical trials, the placebo is visually indistinguishable from the study medication, but in reality has no medical effect (often, a sugar pill). A group of subjects chosen randomly takes the placebo, the others take one or another type of medication. This is done to prevent confounding the medical and psychological effects of the drug. Even a sugar pill can lead some patients to report improvement and side effects.

Planned Comparison
A comparison that is planned before conducting the experiment or at least before the data are examined. Also called an *a priori* comparison.

Platykurtic
A distribution with short tails relative to a normal distribution is platykurtic. See also "kurtosis."

Point Estimate
When a parameter is being estimated, the estimate can be either a single number or it can be a range of numbers such as in a confidence interval. When the estimate is a single number, the estimate is called a "point estimate."

Polynomial Regression

Polynomial regression is a form of multiple regression in which powers of a predictor variable instead of other predictor variables are used. In the following example, the criterion (Y) is predicted by X, X^2 and, X^3.

$$Y = b_1X + b_2X^2 + b_3X^3 + A$$

Population

A population is the complete set of observations a researcher is interested in. Contrast this with a sample which is a subset of a population. A population can be defined in a manner convenient for a researcher. For example, one could define a population as all girls in fourth grade in Houston, Texas. Or, a different population is the set of all girls in fourth grade in the United States. Inferential statistics are computed from sample data in order to make inferences about the population.

Positive Association

There is a positive association between variables X and Y if smaller values of X are associated with smaller values of Y and larger values of X are associated with larger values of Y.

Posterior Probability

The posterior probability of an event is the probability of the event computed following the collection of new data. One begins with a prior probability of an event and revises it in the light of new data. For example, if 0.01 of a population has schizophrenia then the probability that a person drawn at random would have schizophrenia is 0.01. This is the prior probability. If you then learn that that their score on a personality test suggests the person is schizophrenic, you would adjust your probability accordingly. The adjusted probability is the posterior probability.

Power

In significance testing, power is the probability of rejecting a false null hypothesis.

Precision

A statistic's precision concerns to how close it is expected to be to the parameter it is estimating. Precise statistics are vary less from sample to sample. The precision of a statistic is usually defined in terms of it standard error.

Predictor

A predictor variable is a variable used in regression to predict another variable. It is sometimes referred to as an independent variable if it is manipulated rather than just measured.

Prior Probability

The prior probability of an event is the probability of the event computed before the collection of new data. One begins with a prior probability of an event and revises it in the light of new data. For example, if 0.01 of a population has schizophrenia then the probability that a person drawn at random would have schizophrenia is 0.01. This is the prior probability. If you then learn that that there score on a personality test suggests the person is schizophrenic, you would adjust your probability accordingly. The adjusted probability is the posterior probability.

Probability Density

For a discrete random variable, a probability distribution contains the probability of each possible outcome. However, for a continuous random variable, the probability of any one outcome is zero (if you specify it to enough decimal places). A probability density function is a formula that can be used to compute probabilities of a range of outcomes for a continuous random variable. The sum of all densities is always 1.0 and the value of the function is always greater or equal to zero.

Probability Distribution

For a discrete random variable, a probability distribution contains the probability of each possible outcome. The sum of all probabilities is always 1.0. See binomial distribution for an example.

Probability Value

In significance testing, the probability value (sometimes called the p value) is the probability of obtaining a statistic as different or more different from the parameter specified in the null hypothesis as the statistic obtained in the experiment. The probability value is computed assuming the null hypothesis is true. The lower the probability value, the stronger the evidence that the null hypothesis is false. Traditionally, the null hypothesis is rejected if the probability value is below 0.05.

Qualitative Variable

Also known as categorical variables, qualitative variables are variables with no natural sense of ordering. They are therefore measured on a nominal scale. For instance, hair color (Black, Brown, Gray, Red, Yellow) is a qualitative variable, as is name (Adam, Becky, Christina, Dave . . .). Qualitative variables can be coded to appear numeric but their numbers are meaningless, as in male=1, female=2. Variables that are not qualitative are known as quantitative variables.

Quantitative Variable

Variables that are measured on a numeric or quantitative scale. Ordinal, interval and ratio scales are quantitative. A country's population, a person's shoe size, or a car's speed are all quantitative variables. Variables that are not quantitative are known as qualitative variables.

Quantile-Quantile Plot

A quantile-quantile or q-q plot is an exploratory graphical device used to check the validity of a distributional assumption for a data set. In general, the basic idea is to compute the theoretically expected value for each data point based on the distribution in question. If the data indeed follow the assumed distribution, then the points on the q-q plot will fall approximately on a straight line.

Random Assignment

Random assignment occurs when the subjects in an experiment are randomly assigned to conditions. Random assignment prevents systematic confounding of treatment effects with other variables.

Random Sampling

The process of selecting a subset of a population for the purposes of statistical inference. Random sampling means that every member of the population is equally likely to be chosen.

Range

The difference between the maximum and minimum values of a variable or distribution. The range is the simplest measure of variability.

Ratio Scale

One of the four basic levels of measurement, a ratio scale is a numerical scale with a true zero point and in which a given size interval has the same interpretation for the entire scale. Weight is a ratio scale, Therefore, it is meaningful to say that a 200 pound person weighs twice as much as a 100 pound person.

Regression

Regression means "prediction." The regression of Y on X means the prediction of Y by X.

Regression Coefficient

A regression coefficient is the slope of the regression line in simple regression or the partial slope in multiple regression.

Regression Line

In linear regression, the line of best fit is called the regression line.

Relative Frequency

The proportion of observations falling into a given class. For example, if a bag of 55 M & M's has 11 green M&M's, then the frequency of green M&M's is 11 and the relative frequency is $11/55 = 0.20$. Relative frequencies are often used in histograms, pie charts, and bar graphs.

Relative Frequency Distribution

A relative frequency distribution is just like a frequency distribution except that it consists of the proportions of occurrences instead of the numbers of occurrences for each value (or range of values) of a variable.

Reliability

Although there are many ways to conceive of the reliability of a test, the classical way is to define the reliability as the correlation between two parallel forms of the test. When defined this way, the reliability is the ratio of true score variance to test score variance. Chronbach's α is a common measure of reliability.

Repeated Measures Factor

A within-subjects variable is an independent variable that is manipulated by testing each subject at each level of the variable. Compare with a between-subjects variable in which different groups of subjects are used for each level of the variable. Also called a "repeated measures variable."

Repeated Measures Variable

A within-subjects variable is an independent variable that is manipulated by testing each subject at each level of the variable. Compare with a between-subjects variable in which different groups of subjects are used for each level of the variable. Also called a "repeated measures factor."

Representative Sample

A representative sample is a sample chosen to match the qualities of the population from which it is drawn. With a large sample size, random sampling will approximate a representative sample; stratified random sampling can be used to make a small sample more representative.

Robust

Something is robust if it holds up well in the face of adversity. A measure of central tendency or variability is considered robust if it is not greatly affected by a few extreme scores. A statistical test is considered robust if it works well in spite of moderate violations of the assumptions on which it is based.

Sample

A sample is a subset of a population, often taken for the purpose of statistical inference. Generally, one uses a random sample.

Sampling Distribution

A sampling distribution can be thought of as a relative frequency distribution with a very large number of samples. More precisely, a relative frequency distribution approaches the sampling distribution as the number of samples approaches infinity. When a variable is discrete, the heights of the distribution are probabilities. When a variable is continuous, the class intervals have no width and and the heights of the distribution are probability densities.

Scatter Plot

A scatter plot of two variables shows the values of one variable on the Y axis and the values of the other variable on the X axis. Scatter plots are well suited for revealing the relationship between two variables. The scatter plot shown below illustrates the relationship between grip strength and arm strength in a sample of workers.

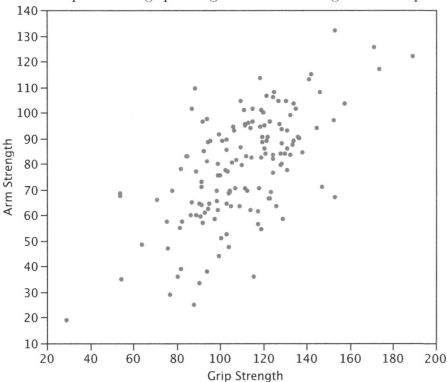

Semi-Interquartile Range

The semi interquartile range is the interquartile range divided by 2. It is a robust measure of variability. The Interquartile Range is the (75th percentile – 25th percentile).

Significance Level

In significance testing, the significance level is the highest value of a probability value for which the null hypothesis is rejected. Common significance levels are 0.05 and 0.01. If the 0.05 level is used, then the null hypothesis is rejected if the probability value is less than or equal to 0.05.

Significance Testing

A statistical procedure that tests the viability of the null hypothesis. If data (or more extreme data) are very unlikely given that the null hypothesis is true, then the null hypothesis is rejected. If the data or more extreme data are not unlikely, then the null hypothesis is not rejected. If the null hypothesis is rejected, then the result of the test is said to be significant. A statistically significant effect does not mean the effect is important.

Simple effect

The simple effect of a factor is the effect of that factor at a single level of another factor. For example, in a design with age and gender as factors, the effect of age for females would be one of the simple effects of age.

Simple Regression

Simple regression is linear regression in which one more predictor variable is used to predict the criterion.

Skew

A distribution is skewed if one tail extends out further than the other. A distribution has a positive skew (is skewed to the right) if the tail to the right is longer. It has a negative skew (skewed to the left) if the tail to the left is longer.

Slope

The slope of a line is the change in Y for each change of one unit of X. It is sometimes defined as "rise over run" which is the same thing. The slope of the black line in the graph is 0.675 because the line increases by 0.675 each time X increases by 1.0.

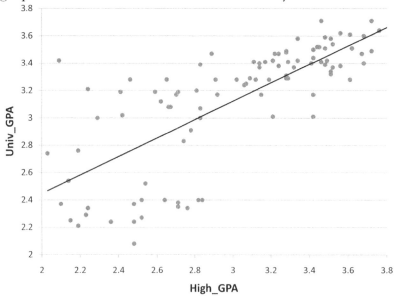

Squared Deviation

A squared deviation is the difference between two values, squared. The number that minimizes the sum of squared deviations for a variable is its mean.

Standard Deviation

The standard deviation is a widely used measure of variability. It is computed by taking the square root of the variance. An important attribute of the standard deviation as a measure of variability is that if the mean and standard deviation of a normal distribution are known, it is possible to compute the percentile rank associated with any given score.

Standard Error

The standard error of a statistic is the standard deviation of the sampling distribution of that statistic. For example, the standard error of the mean is the standard deviation of the sampling distribution of the mean. Standard errors play a critical role in constructing confidence intervals and in significance testing.

Standard Error of Measurement

In test theory, the standard error of measurement is the standard deviation of observed test scores for a given true score. It is usually estimated with the following formula in which s_{test} is the standard deviation of the test scores and $r_{test,test}$ is the reliability of the test.

$$S_{measurement} = S_{test}\sqrt{1 - r_{test,test}}$$

Standard Error of the Estimate

The standard error of the estimate is the standard deviation of the error of prediction in linear regression. It is a measure of the accuracy of prediction.

In the population is is calculated with the following formula:

$$\sigma_{est} = \sqrt{\frac{\sum(Y - Y')^2}{N}}$$

In a sample, it is estimated with:

$$s_{est} = \sqrt{\frac{\sum(Y - Y')^2}{N - 2}}$$

Standard Error of the Mean

he standard error of the mean is the standard deviation of the sampling distribution of the mean. The formula for the standard error of the mean in a population is:

$$\sigma_m = \frac{\sigma}{\sqrt{N}}$$

where σ is the standard deviation and N is the sample size. When computed in a sample, the estimate of the standard error of the mean is:

$$s_M = \frac{s}{\sqrt{N}}$$

Standard Normal Distribution
The standard normal distribution is a normal distribution with a mean of 0 and a standard deviation of 1.

Standard Normal Deviate
The number of standard deviations a score is from the mean of its population. The term "normal deviate" should only be used in reference to normal distributions. The transformation from a raw score X to a z score can be done using the following formula:

$$z = (X - \mu)/\sigma$$

Transforming a variable in this way is called "standardizing" the variable. It should be kept in mind that if X is not normally distributed then the transformed variable will not be normally distributed either.

Standardize
A variable is standardized if it has a mean of 0 and a standard deviation of 1. The transformation from a raw score X to a standard score can be done using the following formula:

$$X_{standardized} = (X - \mu)/\sigma$$

where μ is the mean and σ is the standard deviation. Transforming a variable in this way is called "standardizing" the variable. It should be kept in mind that if X is not normally distributed then the transformed variable will not be normally distributed either.

Statistics
1. What you are studying right now, also known as statistical analysis, or statistical inference. It is a field of study concerned with summarizing data, interpreting data, and making decisions based on data.

2. A quantity calculated in a sample to estimate a value in a population is called a "statistic."

Stem and Leaf Display
A quasi-graphical representation of numerical data. Generally, all but the final digit of each value is a stem, the final digit is the leaf. The stems are placed in a vertical list, with each matched leaf on one side. Stem and leaf displays can be very useful for visualizing small data sets with no more than two significant digits. An example is shown below. In

this example, you multiply the stems by 10 and add the value of the leaf to obtain the numeric value. Thus the maximum number of touchdown passes is $3 \times 10 + 7 = 37$.

```
3|2337
2|001112223889
1|2244456888899
0|69
```

Step
One of the components of a box plot, the step is 1.5 times the difference between the upper hinge and the lower hinge. See also: H-spread.

Stratified Random Sampling
In stratified random sampling, the population is divided into a number of subgroups (or strata). Random samples are then taken from each subgroup with sample sizes proportional to the size of the subgroup in the population. For instance, if a population contained equal numbers of men and women, and the variable of interest is suspected to vary by gender, one might conduct stratified random sampling to insure a representative sample.

Studentized Range Distribution
The studentized range distribution is used to test the difference between the largest and smallest means. It is similar to the t distribution which is used when there are only two means.

Sturgis' Rule
One method of determining the number of classes for a histogram, Sturgis' rule is to take $1 + Log_2(N)$ classes, rounded to the nearest integer.

Sum of Squares Error
In linear regression, the sum of squares error is the sum of squared errors of prediction. In analysis of variance, it is the sum of squared deviations from cell means for between-subjects factors and the Subjects x Treatment interaction for within-subject factors.

Symmetric Distribution
In a symmetric distribution, the upper and lower halves of the distribution are mirror images of each other. In a symmetric distribution, the mean is equal to the median.

t distribution
The t distribution is the distribution of a value sampled from a normal distribution divided by an estimate of the distribution's standard deviation. In practice, the value is typically a statistic such as the mean or the difference between means and the standard

deviation is an estimate of the standard error of the statistic. The t distribution in leptokurtic.

t test
Most commonly, a significance test of the difference between means based on the t distribution. Other applications include (a) testing the significance of the difference between a sample mean and a hypothesized value of the mean and (b) testing a specific contrast among means.

Third Variable Problem
A type of confounding in which a third variable leads to a mistaken causal relationship between two others. For instance, cities with a greater number of churches have a higher crime rate. However, more churches do not lead to more crime, but instead the third variable, population, leads to both more churches and more crime.

Touchdown Pass
In American football, a touchdown pass occurs when a completed pass results in a touchdown. The pass may be to a player in the end zone or to a player who subsequently runs into the end zone. A touchdown is worth 6 points and allows for a chance at one (and by some rules two) additional point(s).

Trimean
The trimean is a robust measure of central tendency; it is a weighted average of the 25th, 50th, and 75th percentiles. Specifically it is computed as follows:

Trimean = 0.25 x 25th + 0.5 x 50th + 0.25 x 75th.

Trimmed Mean
The trimmed mean is a robust measure of central tendency generally falling between the mean and the median. As in the computation of the median, all observations are ordered. Next, the highest and lowest alpha percent of the data are removed, where alpha ranges from 0 to 50. Finally, the mean of the remaining observations is taken. The trimmed mean has advantages over both the mean and median, but is analytically more intractable.

True Score
A person's true score on a test is the mean score they would get if they took the test over and over again assuming no practice effects. In practice, the true score is not known but it is important theoretical concept.

Tukey HSD Test
The "Honestly Significantly Different" (HSD) test developed by the statistician John Tukey to test all pairwise comparisons among means. The test is based on the "studentized range distribution."

Two Tailed

The last step in significance testing involves calculating the probability that a statistic would differ as much or more from the parameter specified in the null hypothesis as does the statistics obtained in the experiment.

A probability computed considering differences in both direction (statistic either larger or smaller than the parameter) is called two-tailed probability. For example, if a parameter is 0 and the statistic is 12, a two-tailed probability would be the he probability of being either $\leq$ -12 or $\geq$ 12. Compare with the one-tailed probability which would be the probability of a statistic being $\geq$ to 12 if that were the direction specified in advance.

Type I Error

In significance testing, the error of rejecting a true null hypothesis.

Type II Error

In significance testing, the failure to reject a false null hypothesis.

Unbiased

A sample is said to be unbiased when every individual has an equal chance of being chosen from the population.

An estimator is unbiased if it does not systematically overestimate or underestimate the parameter it is estimating. In other words, it is unbiased if the mean of the sampling distribution of the statistic is the parameter it is estimating, The sample mean is an unbiased estimate of the population mean.

Unplanned Comparison

When the comparison among means is decided on after viewing the data, the comparison is called an "unplanned comparison" or a *post-hoc* comparison. Different statistical tests are required for unplanned comparisons than for planned comparisons.

Upper Hinge

The upper hinge is one of the components of a box plot; it is the 75th percentile.

Upper Adjacent Value

One of the components of a box plot, the higher adjacent value is the largest value in the data below the 75th percentile.

Variability

Variability refers to the extent to which values differ from one another. That is, how much they vary. Variability can also be thought of as how spread out a distribution is. The standard deviation and the semi-interquartile range are measures of variability.

Variable

Something that can take on different values. For example, different subjects in an experiment weigh different amounts. Therefore "weight" is a variable in the experiment.

Or, subjects may be given different doses of a drug. This would make "dosage" a variable. Variables can be dependent or independent, qualitative or quantitative, and continuous or discrete.

Variance

The variance is a widely used measure of variability. It is defined as the mean squared deviation of scores from the mean. The formula for variance computed in an entire population is:

$$\sigma^2 = \frac{\Sigma(X - \mu)^2}{N}$$

where σ^2 represents the variance, μ is the mean, and N is the number of scores.

When computed in a sample in order to estimate the variance in the population, the formula is:

$$s^2 = \frac{\Sigma(X - M)^2}{N - 1}$$

where s^2 is the estimate of variance, M is the sample mean, and N is the number of scores in the sample.

Variance Sum Law

The variance sum law is an expression for the variance of the sum of two variables. If the variables are independent and therefore Pearson's r = 0, the following formula represents the variance of the sum and difference of the variables X and Y:

$$\sigma^2_{X \pm Y} = \sigma^2_X + \sigma^2_Y$$

Note that you add the variances for both X + Y and X - Y.

If X and Y are correlated, then the following formula (which the former is a special case) should be used:

$$\sigma^2_{X \pm Y} = \sigma^2_X + \sigma^2_Y - 2\rho\sigma_X\sigma_Y$$

where ρ is the population value of the correlation. In a sample r is used as an estimate of ρ.

Within-Subjects Design
An experimental design in which the independent variable is a within-subjects variable.

Within-Subjects Factor
A within-subjects factor is an independent variable that is manipulated by testing each subject at each level of the variable. Compare with a between-subjects factor in which different groups of subjects are used for each level of the variable.

Within-Subjects Variable
A within-subjects variable is an independent variable that is manipulated by testing each subject at each level of the variable. Compare with a between-subjects variable in which different groups of subjects are used for each level of the variable.

Y Intercept
The Y-intercept of a line is the value of Y at the point that the line intercepts the Y axis. It is the value of Y when X equals 0. The Y intercept of the black line shown in the graph is 0.785.

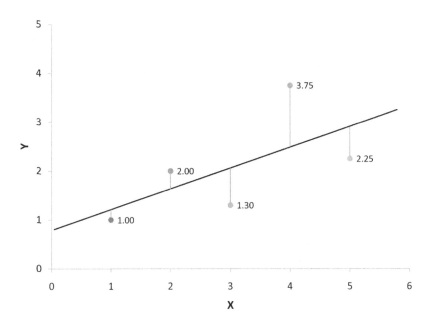

z score
The number of standard deviations a score is from the mean of its population. The term "standard score" is usually used for normal populations; the terms "z score" and "normal deviate" should only be used in reference to normal distributions. The transformation from a raw score X to a z score can be done using the following formula:

$$z = (X - \mu)/\sigma$$

Transforming a variable in this way is called "standardizing" the variable. It should be kept in mind that if X is not normally distributed then the transformed variable will not be normally distributed either.

Made in the USA
Las Vegas, NV
26 January 2024

84911049R00223